# Shamans of the 20th Century

The paper used in this publication meets the minimum requirements of
American National Standard for Information Sciences—
Permanence of Paper for Printed Library Materials,
ANSI Z39.48-1984.

# Ruth-Inge Heinze

# Shamans Of The 20th Century

**With contributions by
Charlotte Berney, Etzel Cardeña,
Chungmoo Choi, Sarah Dubin-Vaughn,
Stanley Krippner, and Alok Saklani**

*A volume in the Frontiers of Consciousness series
Series editor, Stanley Krippner*

## IRVINGTON PUBLISHERS, INC.
## NEW YORK

**Irvington Publishers, Inc.**
**Executive offices: 522 E. 82nd St., Suite 1, NY, NY 10028**
**Customer service and warehouse in care of: Integrated Distribution Services**
**195 McGregor St., Manchester, NH 03102, (603) 669-5933**


**Library of Congress Cataloging-in-Publication Data**
Heinze, Ruth-Inge.
Shamans of the 20th century / Ruth-Inge Heinze ; with
contributions by Charlotte Berney ... [et al.].
p.    cm.
Includes bibliographical references and index.
ISBN 0-8290-2456-5 (Cloth)
ISBN 0-8290-2459-X (Paper)
1. Shamanism—History—20th century.  2. Shamans—Case studies.
I. Title.
BL2370.S5H418   1991
291.6'2—dc20                    90-44703
                                  CIP

First Printing 1991
3 5 7 9 10 8 6 4 2


Title page illustration by Bird Brother
Cover photo: Elizabeth Cogburn, Shaman

Design and production by

THE
BRAMBLE
COMPANY
Falls Village, Connecticut


**Printed in the United States of America**

# Table of Contents

# List of Photos

Photos 1-6 and 13-20 have been taken by Dr. Ruth-Inge Heinze, photos 7 and 12 by Dr. Etzel Cardeña, photo 8 by Dr. Stanley Krippner, photo 9 by Charlotte Berney, photo 10 by Chungmoo Choi, photo 11 by Elizabeth Cogburn.

# Acknowledgements

I am deeply indebted to all shamans who worked with me during the last five decades. They did not only permit me to observe and participate in their activities but also invited me into their homes and treated me like a member of their family. The insights I gained through these close relationships brought a better understanding of their role in rapidly modernizing societies. The knowledge shared by shamans, coming from different ethnic groups, operating on different socio-economic levels, and within different belief systems, also increased my awareness of the wide range of shamanic personalities.

On the academic side, I wish to thank the Council for International Exchange of Scholars for providing me with Fulbright-Hays Research Grant #1069-83079 which allowed me to stay, from June 1978 to June 1979, for another full year in Southeast Asia to conduct follow-up fieldwork. I also want to express my gratitude for the hospitality and intellectual companionship so generously offered by Dr. Sandhu and his staff at the Institute for Southeast Asian Studies during my stay in Singapore. My thanks are extended to the colleagues from the Departments of Sociology, Philosophy, and Malay Studies at Singapore University, now National University of Singapore, as well as to the colleagues from the Department of English at Prince Songkhla University, Pattani, the Department of Religious Studies at Mahidol University, Bangkok, and the Department of Anthropology, Chiang Mai University, Thailand.

On suggestion of the Institute of Oriental and Orissan Studies, Cuttack, I have been guest of state in Orissa, India. I worked also with colleagues in Calcutta, Benares, Bombay, and Madras. In Nepal, I collaborated with colleagues at Tribhuvan University, Kathmandu, and lamas at the Tibetan monasteries at Bodha. In Indonesia I remember in-depth dicussions with colleagues at the University in Jakarta and Jodgjakarta; in the People's Republic of China I exchanged notes with scholars at the Institute for Nationalities and the Institute of Southeast Asian Studies, Kunming, Yunnan; as well as at Hong Kong University and Kyoto University, Japan.

In the United States, I was stimulated by discussions with Stanley Krippner who has conducted extensive cross-cultural studies of shamanism himself. William S. Lyon introduced me to the Lakota shaman Wallace Black Elk and I witnessed one of Wallace Black Elk's sun dances in Oregon. Royal Alsup allowed me to witness the White Deer Dance of the Indians of the Northwest, and last, not least, Felicitas Goodman opened for me the world of the Indians in the Southwest of the United States in taking me, for example, to the powerful Corn Dance of the Santo Domingo Indians.

This book is a token of my gratitude for what I have been taught: how to access and how to reconnect with the "source."

*Ruth-Inge Heinze*
*Berkeley, California*

# Foreword

## by Stanley Krippner

Shamanic traditions have not been taken seriously by Western, industrialized nations despite the fact that many shamans, over the centuries, have developed sophisticated models of human behavior and experience. Furthermore, many of the shamans have been flexible enough to survive the contact with Western medicine and technology and have even incorporated some Western practices.

Nevertheless, the ignorance about shamanic traditions, coupled with the general prejudice against tribal people, has resulted in shamanism being ignored or scorned by most members of the Western medical, scientific, and academic establishments. They do not recall that shamans were the world's first physicians, first diagnosticians, first psychotherapists, first religious functionaries, first magicians, first performing artists, and first story-tellers. Shamans can be defined as community-assigned magico-religious professionals who deliberately alter their consciousness in order to obtain information from the "spirit world." They use this knowledge and power to help and to heal members of their community, as well as the community as a whole. Shamans were originally active in hunting and gathering tribes and in fishing societies where they still exist in their most unadulterated form. However, shamans and shamanically-oriented healers can also be found in agricultural settings and even in urban centers today.

In an academic milieu where shamanism is ignored or, at best, viewed condescendingly, Ruth-Inge Heinze stands as an exception. For several decades, Dr. Heinze has taken the shamanic tradition seriously, realizing that it provides a rich heritage for the study of mythology, psychotherapy, medicine, and the arts. Her fieldwork in Southeast Asia and in other parts of the world uncovered contemporary shamans whose services are a vital part of their community. To the question,

"Are there practicing twentieth century shamans?" Dr. Heinze's answer is strongly in the affirmative.

Dr. Heinze's scholarship is exemplary in several areas of shamanism. For example, she has found that shamans enter their profession in a variety of ways, depending on their tribal or community tradition. Some inherit their status; others may earn it, buy it, or have it thrust upon them. They may display a body sign upon birth (such as an extra finger or toe) or behavior (such as epileptic-like seizures) which culturally determines their social role. Shamans may be "called" by spirits or power animals in dreams or in daytime reveries. They may survive a serious disease and interpret their recovery as a "call to heal." Sometimes, several of these factors come together when shamans are called to their profession.

Among the Inuit Eskimos, it is necessary to dream of spirits in order to be called to shamanize. Once the spirit appears in a dream, the dreamer spits blood, becomes ill, and withdraws from society. While alone, he sees a *tunerak* which looks like a human being but it is actually a spirit. At first, this *tunerak* takes possession of the individual, compelling him to wander about naked. Gradually, the shaman-elect gains control of the spirit. He makes a drum and begins to assume his shamanic role.

A person may be called at any age, depending on the tradition of the shaman's tribe. However, only individuals who have passed the age of puberty are allowed to shamanize. The summons may come in childhood as the result of a dream, a fever, or a visitation from a purported spirit entity. It may come in adolescence during a vision quest. In some cases, the call may come late in life, giving shamans the opportunity to continue their services to the group in ways that utilize their life experiences. A Navajo man usually is not admitted into training until he can be called *hastiin* or elder. This term is applied when he is in his middle years and has established himself as a reliable worker, a dedicated parent, and capable community member.

The strange and erratic behaviors of a tribal member may be interpreted by the community as a "call," thereby channeling potentially disruptive actions into behavior patterns that are perceived to be beneficial.

For at least a decade, the apprentice shamans of the Ammassalik Eskimos in Greenland perform a series of rituals in the summertime until they see an emaciated bear rise from the sea. The bear devours the apprentice alive, the initiate loses consciousness, then is vomited up. When the apprentice regains consciousness, he performs additional rituals to acquire his helping spirits. Finally, he notifies his family that he is ready to perform his first public ceremony.

In some societies there is no specific training period, while in others the process may continue for several years. The teachers may be older shamans or even purported spirit guides (e.g., one's ancestors, power animals, souls of the dead, nature spirits). The spirit guides frequently are reported to give instructions in the neophyte's dreams. Among the skills to be learned are contacting souls of the dead, diagnosing and treating illness, interpreting dreams, practicing herbology, hexing tribal enemies, mastering techniques to alter one's consciousness, prophesying, story-telling, supervising of shamanic rituals, and predicting weather patterns. Not all tribes assign all of these functions to shamans, but there are remarkable similarities among shamanic societies.

Dr. Heinze's research demonstrates that it would be erroneous to claim that shamans represent a single constellation of traits or that there is a typical shamanic personality. Some shamans, perhaps, have bordered on psychosis, living in a fantasy world that is honored by their tribe as long as their role is effectively filled and their duties are conscientiously performed. Others undoubtedly have been men and women of great talent, mastering a complex vocabulary and an extensive storehouse of knowledge about herbs, rituals, and the purported spirit world.

Some social scientists have observed the links between shamanism and changed states of consciousness, concluding that these represent schizophrenic conditions. Julian Silverman has postulated that shamanism is a form of socially sanctioned schizophrenia, noting that the two conditions share "grossly non-reality-oriented ideation, abnormal perceptual experience, profound emotional upheavals, and bizarre mannerisms" (1969:22). Silverman, a psychiatrist, has claimed that the only difference between shamanic schizophrenia and schizophrenic conditions in industrialized countries is the degree of cultural acceptance of the individual's psychological resolution of a life crisis. Silverman claims that the social supports available to the shaman are usually unavailable to the schizophrenic in Western culture.

George Devereux, a psychoanalyst, took the position that shamans are neurotics. For Devereux, the shaman's reliance on dreams and fantasy could be seen as defense mechanisms to protect a fragile personality structure (1961:1008-1090).

L.B. Boyer and his associates attempted to gather data regarding this controversy. They administered the Rorschach inkblots to twelve male Apache shamans, fifty-two non-shamans, and several Apache men who claimed to possess shamanic powers but who had not been accorded that position by members of their tribe. (Psychologists have collected a great deal of information about underlying personality structure through studying and comparing people's descriptions of these inkblots.)

An examination of the responses to the inkblots demonstrated that the shamans showed as high a degree of reality-testing potential as did the Apaches who were not shamans. If the shamans had been schizophrenic, they would not have been able to describe the inkblots in the same way as other tribal members. However, the "pseudo-shamans" did not do as well on this dimension and demonstrated impoverished and stunted personality development.

When an ambiguous, unclear inkblot was described, shamans and non-shamans gave similar descriptions with a few exceptions. The shamans demonstrated a keener awareness of peculiarities, a greater sense of childlike humor, more responses of a philosophical nature, and a greater proportion of responses involving sex, color, and the human body.

The conclusions reached by Boyer and his co-workers were that

> *shamans are healthier than their societal co-members....This finding argues against [the] stand*

*that the shaman is severely neurotic or psychotic, at*
*least insofar as the Apaches are concerned*
*(1964:179).*

The "pseudo-shamans," on the other hand, did show more
signs of mental illness than did members of the other two
groups.

A similar study was conducted by Richard Shweder with
Zinacanteco shamans of Chiapas, Mexico. Shweder presented shamans and other tribal members with a set of
Rorschach-type blurry photos and told them that they could
label them with pre-set categories (such as "shoe," "flower,"
and "man") or respond "I don't know." The shamans, unlike
members of the control group, made up their own answers and
denied there were any photos unfamiliar to them. Shweder
concluded that shamans seem to have their own categories,
and appear to be "inner-directed," able to control a situation
through their own resources (1979:327-331).

Richard Noll, a psychologist, took another approach to the
controversy, in collecting shamans' reports of their experiences in altered states of consciousness. He compared these
reports to symptoms of mental illness listed in the third edition
of the American Psychiatric Association's Diagnostic and
Statistical Manual. Noll reported that the shamans' experiences did not match the criteria for schizophrenia or other
serious disorders from the psychiatric manual. Instead, he
proposed that shamans may be especially adept at fantasy
production (1985:443-452).

Two specialists in psychological hypnosis, S.C. Wilson
and T.X. Barber, have found that a small percentage of the
American subjects they tested often confused memories of
real-life events with memories of fantasies. While about 24
per cent of ordinary people sometimes suffer from this type of
confusion, 85 per cent of "fantasy-prone" individuals do so.
Although members of this fantasy-prone group are easier to
hypnotize, they are neither more nor less neurotic or psychotic
than other people.

Some unique blend of genetic inheritance and early experience makes these individuals extremely prone to "see"

visions, "hear" voices, and "touch" imaginary companions. They claim to have an excellent recall of their early life episodes. Wilson and Barber found that these abilities characterize about 4 per cent of the general American population, although it might differ from culture to culture (Wilson and Barber, 1983:340-387). Their work has been repeated with larger samples of subjects by other psychologists who have obtained similar results (Lynn and Rhue, 1986:404-408).

As children, fantasy-prone individuals live in a make-believe world much of the time. They pretend or believe that their dolls and toy animals are alive, have feelings, and demonstrate unique personalities. One woman stated, in an interview, that she took a different toy to bed with her every night so that she would not hurt the feelings of the other toys. While children, they believe in elves, guardian angels, and fairies, sometimes thinking that they have played with them. They often have imaginary companions (people or animals), become one of the characters in books they are reading, or imagine they are someone else. One subject told the interviewer that she imagined she was a princess living in a castle; she told her friends about this experience and they ridiculed her. Most fantasy-prone individuals, therefore, soon learn how to conceal this information from their peers.

As an adult, the fantasy-prone individual often ""smells" or "sees" what is being described in a conversation, takes the time to engage in fantasy (often having a special place where he or she engages in this pastime), and frequently has sexual fantasies so vivid that they lead to orgasm. Nine of ten individuals asked reported anomalous experiences, such as clairvoyance, telepathy, and precognition. Many reported out-of-body experiences or automatic writing. More than two-third told the examiners that they believe they possess the ability to heal sick people; three out of four claimed to have encountered apparitions, ghosts, or spirits.

While engaging in fantasy, a person sets a theme; then an imaginative scenario unfolds that has some of the characteristics of a story or a dream. If fantasy-prone individuals were raised in a tribal group, it is likely that many of them would become shamans. Fantasy-prone individuals often claim to see "auras," talk to dead people, receive guidance in their dreams; however, they spend considerable amounts of time in a private world that is not shared by their peers. Life experiences that led to fantasy-prone behavior include isolation and restriction, seldom to encouragement by others to engage in make-believe games.

When the characteristics of Wilson and Barber's fantasy-prone group are similar to those of shamans, it can also be said that

> *subjects with a propensity for...fantasy are as well adjusted as...the average person. It appears that the life experiences and skill developments that underlie the ability for...fantasy are more or less independent of the kinds of life experience that lead to psychopathology (Wilson and Barber, 1983:379).*

In other words, there are individual cases that suggest a link between mental illness and shamanism, but the bulk of anthropological and psychological research data do not support this claim.

Each year, Dr. Heinze convenes a conference in which investigators from all over the world share their research in shamanism. The relations of shamanism to altered states of consciousness serves as a focal point of many of the discussions during which "consciousness" has been defined as an organism's total pattern of thinking and feeling at any given time. An "ordinary" state of consciousness is characterized by an individual's day-by-day behavior and experience; it serves as the baseline by which "altered" states can be determined. Altered states are experienced as being different from this individual's baseline or are noted to differ also from an outside observer's baseline.

Some anthropologists claim that the first Siberian shamans were nature healers; during a later "feudal" phrase of social evolution, spirits were invented that necessitated the development of altered states of consciousness to deal with them (Hultkrantz, 1978:27-58). Most other scholars, however, favor the idea that altered consciousness states are basic to shamanism. Erika Bourguignon studied 488 societies (57 per cent of those represented in an ethnographic atlas). She found that 89 per cent were reported to have one or more institutionalized, culturally patterned altered state of consciousness. She concluded that the capacity to experience altered states is a basic psychobiological human potential (Bourguignon, 1968:3-34).

L.B. Peters and David Price-Williams compared 42 societies from four different cultural areas to determine commonalities among shamanic altered conscious states. They identified three different states: voluntary control of entrance and duration of the altered state; ability to communicate with others during the altered state; memory of the experience at the conclusion of the altered state. Shamans in 18 of the cultures they studied engaged in spirit "incorporation," 10 in out-of-body experience, 11 in both, and 3 in some other altered state. Peters and Price-Williams compared these altered states to rites of passage in which an episode characterized by panic or anxiety gives way to an experience yielding insights that produce a new level of personality integration (1980:397-418).

Shamans use a variety of procedures to induce altered states. These include ingesting mind-altering plants, chanting, concentration, dancing, drumming, jumping, fasting, running, visualizing, engaging in sexual activity, and going without sleep. Rarely is only one procedure used. For example, mind-altering plants are sometimes ingested before a chanting or drumming ceremony begins.

Dr. Heinze's conferences also discuss alternative modes of healing and the medicinal and psychotherapeutic practices used by shamans in various parts of the world. There are shamanic healing methods that closely parallel contemporary behavior therapy, chemotherapy, dream interpretation, family therapy, hypnotherapy, milieu therapy, and psychodrama. It is clear that shamans, psychotherapists, and physicians have more in common than is generally suspected. After studying Otami shamans in Mexico, James Dow concluded that the similarities between shamanic healing and Western psychotherapy outweigh the differences (1986). However, for shamans the spiritual dimension of healing is extremely important while contemporary physicians and psychotherapists typically ignore it. Shamans often retrieve lost souls, communicate with spirits, emphasize the interconnectedness of their patients with the community and the earth, facilitate spiritual purification for those who have violated social taboos, explain dreams and visions, and stress the importance of spiritual growth, life purpose, and being of service to humanity and to nature.

In this book, the reader will have the opportunity to partake of Dr. Heinze's studies of shamans, their models of reality, their inner journeys, and the services they perform for their communities. Western, industrialized societies have made great advances in technology but have paid a heavy price in losing their contact with the sacred dimensions of life and their concern for their environment. Shamans have always been technicians of the sacred and have been advocates of humankind's responsibility to protect and enhance the earth, the oceans, the atmosphere, and the creatures that live there.

*Shamans of the Twentieth Century* makes a splendid contribution to the literature in human science. But it also offers its readers an opportunity to begin an initiation and enter into a shamanistic journey with Dr. Heinze to rediscover a legacy that contemporary society needs to remember if it is to resurrect its spirit and save its natural environment.

# Author and Contributors

## Author, Compiler, and Editor

**Ruth-Inge Heinze**, Ph.D., has been active in the field of comparative religion and psychological anthropology for more than 30 years. She has conducted fieldwork in Asia, Europe and the United States where she lived and worked with shamans of a wide range of different ethnic groups in the framework of different religions. Since 1974, she has been Research Associate at the Center for Southeast Asia Studies, University, of California, Berkeley.

## Contributors

**Charlotte Berney** is a writer and editor in San Jose, California. She has conducted research on Hawaiian shamanism for over 10 years and has studied with Jack and Josephine Gray in San Francisco and Marian Charlton in Hawaii who all base their work on that of David K. Bray.

**Chungmoo Choi**, Ph.D., has conducted extensive research among shamans in her native country, Korea, where she discovered that Korean shamans had no difficulties in continuing their traditional practices in a modern setting, e.g., in front of television cameras. She is presently Professor of Anthropology at the University of California, Santa Barbara.

**Etzel Cardeña**, Ph.D., has conducted research in the fields of psychology and theatre which included fieldwork with shamans in Haiti and collaboration with Grotowski in Mexico. Cardeña is currently visiting scholar at Stanford University, Palo Alto, and is part of the core faculty of the California Institute of Integral Studies, San Francisco. In his publications, he discusses, e.g., the phenomenology of altered states of consciousness, dissociation, hypnosis, and the psychology of performance.

**Sarah Dubin-Vaughn**, Ph.D., is a transpersonal psychologist in private practice in Del Mar, California. She has studied ceremonial rituals and other shamanic art around the world, during the past fourteen years especially with Elizabeth Cogburn, New Mexico. Viewing ritual celebration of life transitions as a significant art, she creates and provides ceremonies for individuals and groups as an integral part of her professional work.

**Stanley Krippner**, Ph.D., is professor of psychology and director of the Center of Consciousness Studies at Saybrook Institute, San Francisco. He investigated developments in consciousness and conducted research on shamanism and healing on three continents. His work is reflected in more than 700 essays and numerous books (e.g., *Personal Mythology* with David Feinstein, *Healing States* with Alberto Villoldo). Krippner has served as president of the Association for Humanistic Psychology, the Parapsychology Association, and the Humanistic Psychology Division of the American Psychological Association. He was also director of the Dream Laboratory at Maimonides Medical Center in Brooklyn.

**Alok Saklani**, Ph.D., Reader in Commerce at Garhwal University, Srinagar, U.P., India, has conducted extensive research among tribal people in the Himalayas.

# Part I

# Introduction

## Why Did I Write This Book?

We are told that the main task of shamans is to mediate between the sacred and the profane. Everybody who sets out to observe practicing shamans will find that they, indeed, provide direct access to the "Divine."

This book has been written for all who want to know what shamanism is. It has been written not only to record research and life experience of over sixty years but to demonstrate how shamans work and how the shamanic view of reality can contribute to the modern world. The book discusses the importance, even the necessity, of that contribution which offers insights into how an individual can acquire access to the realities of a shaman, even if the reader does not expect to become a shaman him- or herself. Some suggestions are also made about directions into which the study of shamans and shamanism can and should continue.

In using a multi-dimensional approach, the book attempts to fulfill not only the expectations of academicians and other professionals but also the curiosity of "unprepared" readers who are seeking more in-depth information.

To prove that shamans are not relics of the past, the book introduces you to tribal shamans whose work is still embed-

1

ded in more or less intact traditions but you will also meet urban shamans who emerged without direct connection to any specific tradition. Shamans continue to play a vital role and fulfill specific needs of their community which otherwise are not met.

I have to add here that, in the twentieth century, "community" does not necessarily mean people living together in the same geographic area. Clients approach those shamans who best fulfill their personal needs. For example, shamans living in Thailand's capital, Bangkok, are called to satisfy needs of communities hundreds of miles away in the north or people from all over Thailand come to consult a certain shaman outside their own province. The same situation has been reported by other anthropologists, e.g., Laurel Kendall for South Korea (1988b:4-5). In the United States, we find also that clients of one shaman do not always live in the same geographic area. Shamans may travel to those in need or clients cover large distances to meet the shaman of their choice.

As soon as the success of a shaman becomes known, loosely-structured communities begin to form around individual shamans. The reason for such "communities" is that social contact reinforces the belief and legitimizes the practice.

Becoming more closely involved with one shaman, however, does not necessarily lead to the formation of a new cult. In fact, in the cases I studied, shamanic communities congregate only for specific purposes. Such open-ended relationships escape the effects of rigidifying codification world religions are suffering from. The needs of clients and the solutions shamans offer do change with time and location. These changes will be discussed in Part III.

## Why Do We Need Shamans?

There are not many tribal shamans left and hardly anybody in the twentieth century lives in hunting and gathering societies anymore. The question, therefore, arises whether it is nostalgia for the so-called "golden age" which draws urbanites, and especially many Westerners, to shamanism. There was once a state where man and nature lived in perfect harmony. Do we nourish a silent wish to return to that state of complete harmony? Do we expect "magical" intervention? Many of us do.

To understand why people look for shamans, it is necessary to go out into the field, i.e., to live and work with shamans and talk to the people who consult them. I found that basic needs cluster around three main areas:

1. *health problems (from a common cold to exorcism or, for example, the blessing of medicine prescribed by "modern" physicians),*

2. *problems in the family (between spouses, parents and children, in-laws) or*

3. *professional concerns (career issues, passing an exam, getting a promotion, when to buy or sell a house. etc.).*

There are also three minor areas which may require the assistance of shamans:

1. *fertility,*

2. *longevity (especially among Chinese), and*

3. *wealth in general.*

These needs appear to be rather worldly. They speak of pragmatic concerns, however, the clients coming to shamans expect solutions which go beyond ordinary needs. Their main reason to consult shamans is based on the belief that shamans have access to other dimensions and can enlist supernatural support.

More detailed information about the above and other physical as well as emotional, social, intellectual, and spiritual needs can be found in Part IV.

## *Manifestations of the Sacred*

Eliade speaks of "the manifestation of something of a wholly different order, a reality that does not belong to our world, in objects that are an integral part of our natural 'profane' world" (1957:11)

Christians believe that, during the Holy Communion, Christ manifests in the host. Hindus know that, during rituals, their priests call the gods and these gods will manifest in the temple's statues. Other ethnic groups have rituals to evoke nature spirits (residing in stones, trees, mountains), they may also evoke deified ancestors or the "nameless" Divine, the life force per se.

Evocative rituals are most effective when participants share the belief system on which the rituals have been built. The second prerequisite is that the ritual space has to be marked and consecrated. These precautions are necessary to protect the ritual during which ordinary time and space are suspended. When shamans facilitate transcendence, the doors to different dimensions open and transformation, i.e., change, becomes possible.

During each shamanic ritual, "something sacred shows itself." To convey this glimpse of "ultimate" knowledge, shamans have then to translate the ineffable message into ordinary language and apply it to specific situations (see Part IV and V). Most importantly, each shamanic performance is by nature unique.

In the twentieth century, we cannot revive the heritage of the paleolithic. Nobody can bring back the past. Our environment, the society we live in, even the climate, kept changing and so have forms of shamanism. Like a snake shedding its skin, shamanism has kept renewing itself, from the inside out. Imitators of ancient traditions, therefore, deceive themselves when they "religiously" repeat old patterns. Not familiar with the belief system on which "old" rituals have been built, their "blind" imitation obstructs the process of ritual development. In other words, different times give birth to different rituals (see, Part II, Elizabeth Cogburn on her New Sun Dance Song

Ritual or Grotowski about his work; see also, Part III, the discussion on rituals, esp. the genesis of the Sun Dance ritual).

In addition to changing conditions in time and space, we have also to keep in mind that the variations among shamans of one ethnic group are often greater than the variations between different ethnic groups (see, Part II and Part III). This relates not only to the fact that shamans reached different stages in their own spiritual development but to idiosyncratic differences in the respective shaman's temperament and character. Shamans treat personal problems individually and, on account of their own character structure and life experience, some shamans are therefore more effective with certain problems than others.

## Previous Studies of Shamanism

It was not before the second half of the nineteenth century that shamanism became a legitimate topic in academia and scholars could openly talk about their research. (The results of my literary and historical survey can be found in Part III of this book.) In the past, we had to resort to the accounts of travelers and missionaries who introduced their own biases to their descriptions of shamanic performances. During the past one hundred years, professional ethnographers have collected data, but their findings still reflect personal biases.

Studies which attempt to interpret native customs, sacred experiences, and "anomalous" phenomena have, similarly, been unsatisfactory. (The controversy about the pathology of shamans, for example, is discussed in Part III.)

We suffer, in fact, from a lack of first-hand data. The ideal case would be to invite shamans to speak about themselves. However, not all shamans may be willing to do so because they don't feel moved to reflect on themselves or they want to protect their knowledge from being abused by less responsible individuals. To draw reliable correlations, we need systematically collected, cross-culturally comparable data, i.e., cooperation between scholars and shamans (e.g., Wallace Black Elk and William S. Lyon, 1990) on a large scale.

Part II presents profiles of contemporary shamans (see, e.g., Kendall, 1988:11-17, about the value of life stories) as well as data collected during participant observation by six colleagues and myself. Comparisons, pointing to communalities and differences and the different developments toward greater individualization, are drawn in Part III.

One of the main reasons for writing this book is to show that the services of shamans are needed when the relationship between man and the universe has weakened or has been interrupted. Shamans stay closer to the "source." They are called to be the mediators between the sacred and the secular.

To understand the nature of shamanism, we have to add other dimensions to the three-dimensional space-time model of the past. We should no longer deceive ourselves by limiting our range of perception and knowledge. Our present Cartesian model of thinking is not equipped to accept and to explain "supernatural" phenomena. The model refuses, for example, to admit the existence of anything "supernatural" because it does not fit into the materialistic definition of "nature." Only fairly recently science and religion have begun to compare notes and discovered that shamanic phenomena are not "supernatural" at all. They only appeared to be so when material sciences tried to put them on an Procrustean bed. Now the sciences are more willing to work with more open-ended structures. That means, being the mediators between the sacred and the profane, shamans have worked within more than three dimensions already for several thousand years, physicists today finally begin to admit that there are more than three dimensions.

We have to keep an open mind. We should not project preconceived ideas and judgment on everything connected with shamanism. To understand shamanism and to broaden our knowledge about ourselves and the world, we have to test ideas and activities ourselves.

Most of all, we should apply caution when individuals claim to be shamans. "Professional" shamans never make such claims. They need not advertise, because they become known through their work. Their "miraculous" healing of sick minds and bodies, their retrieval of otherwise not accessible information, their beneficial effects on their community become known fast through word of mouth.

The rules of shamanic ethics are the same as for any other professionals, esp. in the religious realm. It would be unethical for "enlightened" individuals, for example, to publicly announce their enlightenment. The degree of spiritual development is reflected in an individual's demeanor, actions, and success. The most successful shamans I met were also the most humble. They would stress that they are only the servants of the sacred and the mediators who continue to learn throughout their life. They would never put themselves into a position where they have to defend their "claims." Shamans even refuse cases when they feel they cannot offer a solution. In a case of a severely ill Singaporean man, for example, I heard a shaman say that he would attempt to plead with the deities to save this man, but when the patient's time was up he could not change his fate.

The recent interest in shamanism seems to be connected with the insight that the limited Western world views need to be expanded. Limitations are felt especially in the fields of medicine, psychotherapy, and science; but there is hope, some scientists have broken through these limitations. For example, Werner Heisenberg's "uncertainty principle" demonstrates that when one feature of an object becomes measurable other features cannot be measured at the same time. Consequently, discussions of multi-disciplinary and multi-dimensional approaches are appearing in professional journals.

Bohm is offering new paradigms in quantum mechanics. His thoughts about the implicate and explicate order of things and Bell's theorem will, therefore, be discussed in Part V and an attempt will be made to develop models for a better understanding of shamanism.

## Origin of the Word "Shaman"

The origin of the term "shaman" is unknown because it was coined in an oral tradition. Therefore, we won't find any written record which documents when the word was used first.

Laufer did not think that the Pali word *samana* and the Sanskrit word *sramana*, "one who performs acts of mortification or austerity, an ascetic, monk, devotee, religious mendicant" (Sanskrit-English Dictionary, ed. Monier Williams, 1964:1096) as well as the Chinese word *sha-men* diffused and finally reached, among others, the Evenki in northern Siberia. He suggests that "the Evenk *saman*..., Mongol *saman*, Turkish *kam* and *xam*, are close and inseparable allies grown and nourished on the soil of northern Asia" (Laufer, 1917:371). Vilmos Diószegi (1947:211) talks about the possibility that the Evenk word *saman* may come from the Tunguso-Manchurian verb *sa* meaning "to know" and Hultkrantz (1973:34) sees a connection with a Tungus word which stands for "a social functionary who, with the help of guardian spirits, attains ecstasy in order to create a rapport with the supernatural world on behalf of his group members."

Over time, however, the term "shaman" has become one of the most abused words, especially in Western countries. It is used either with positive or negative implications for too many practitioners and not all of them qualify to be called shamans. (Castaneda's Don Juan, for example, is a sorcerer; see also, the discussion of "Who is the Shaman" below.)

Furthermore, ethnic groups are using different terms for shamans. The Yoruba of West Africa call their shamans *babalawo*, the Eskimo *angakok*, the Mongols *kami*; in Part II, the Haitian shaman is called a *houngan*, the Zulu shaman a *sangoma*, the Hawaiian shaman a *kahuna*, the Korean shaman a *mudang*, the Garhwali shaman a *bakia*, the Singaporean shaman a *tang-ki* (divining youth), the Malay shaman a *bomoh*, and the Thai shaman a *ma khi* (horse of the spirit).

## Who is a Shaman?

During the last decades, we have increasingly become familiar with a wide range of specialists who deal with the "supernatural" but not all of the following practitioners are shamans.

There are channels who claim they are in direct contact

with, and speak on behalf of, beings who "inhabit a higher dimension of reality than our own." In his book on *Channeling,* Jon Klimo explored the "nature of the messages received, the scientific theories that explain it, and the techniques we can use to unfold our own latent capacities for channeling" (1987, book jacket). These are methods to get in contact with the "source" but channels go seldom beyond relating messages, they do not actively implement these messages. They also do not claim to be on the same level as mystics who keep cultivating closer relationships to the "Divine."

Christian and Jewish readers are reminded of Moses "speaking" to God and other prophets mentioned in the Old Testament. They were, indeed, "divinely inspired" and conveyed divine messages. For Muslim, Muhammed "received" the holy Qur'an by "listening" to the Archangel Gabriel, and the Shi'ites as well as the Sufi continue to experience revelations coming directly from the Divine Source. In Chinese Folk Taoism, revelations never ceased despite periods of severe prosecution. Such revelations were, in fact, used to legitimize political uprisings.

The major difference between channels, mystics, prophets and shamans is that the former may be able to convey the encounter with the "Divine" while shamans facilitate its manifestations in the Here and Now and actively participate in the dynamic relationships between the explicate and the implicate order.

Especially in Asia, I found that it is important for people to come into the presence of deities and spirits. Clients of shamans expect to see and to experience a manifestation of divine power. They recognize the presence of divine powers, for example, in the "possession" trances of shamans. In other cases, shamans become the actors and retrieve otherwise inaccessible information during their "magical flights" (see, Part III, Trances).

In the framework of world religions, beliefs become increasingly petrified and the resultant dogma less flexible. This development leads to the establishment of priestly hierarchies whose task is to uphold and defend the dogma as well as the priests' own position. World religions require, therefore, individuals who are trained and ordained to dispense the "holy communion," to confer blessings, and to perform religious rituals according to elaborate manuals. Shamans who, at times, assume priestly functions too, remain open to change. Despite some rituals which have to be performed in a certain way to appease the spirits, shamans continue to create new rituals. Shamans are less predictable because they adapt to the specific conditions at the time of consultation. The shamanic concept of the universe is also non-linear and the "instructions," how to access and how to interpret universal knowledge, are constantly rewritten.

It is important to mention that, esp. in Asia, shamans also act as spirit mediums. Among the folk religions I studied, the tradition of spirit mediums remained unbroken. It is believed that mediums can call spiritual entities into their body. The spirit of the individual is then considered to be displaced and may visit the spirit world while the individual's body is used by a spirit who wants to assist earthly beings. It is said in Thailand, for example, that a spirit may have difficulties to be reborn in this world and has to use the body of a living being to improve his/her own karma (Heinze, 1988:50, 284-285; Zühlsdorf 1972:85). That means spirits can improve the quality of their karma only by performing good deeds on this earth, either by reincarnating or by using the body of another living being.

Furthermore, the need to communicate with deceased family members or deified heroes has continued since prehistoric times. People all over the world have felt the urge to contact the dead. A last will could not be located or some wishes of ancestors have not yet been fulfilled. When spirits are properly pacified and propitiated, they are believed to assist their descendants in whatever problems require a solution. Such office of a necromancer may no longer be known in the West, however, psychics have been asked to contact the spirits of the dead for the above or similar reasons. Individuals are also using a ouija board or are participating in spiritist sessions to contact beings from "another world." Another form of receiving messages from the beyond is "automatic writing" which is practiced in many forms all over the world. It is believed that the spirits guide the hands of the individuals who are holding the writing implements (see, photo 1.). The human hands are, therefore, only the vehicle and not the actors in the writing process.

Scientific literature is discussing other "unusual" faculties like clairvoyance for some time already and individuals with ESP (extrasensory perception) have been employed by law-enforcing agencies to locate missing persons and objects or to provide clues for solving crimes. Clairvoyants are able to perceive objects and events through yet unrecognized sensory processes and some of them are even adept in precognition. However, such faculties alone do not suffice to call these practitioners shamans.

There are also oneirocritics who interpret dreams. There are astrologers who cast horoscopes and interpret the movements of the stars. There are diviners who foretell the future by various means, e.g., casting bones (Africa), casting coins or counting yarrow stalks (China), looking at the intestines of animals (South America), etc., or fortune tellers, reading Tarot or other cards or the lines of their client's hands (palmistry, chiromancy) but individuals who use the reading of Tarot cards or cast the I-Ching for self-exploration should not call themselves shamans for the simple reason that they may not be willing and are not necessarily performing any service for the community.

Aside from the conventional tools to diagnose the condition of an individual, new interpretative methods have been developed. It is, for example, possible to observe biorhythms which indicate the changing interrelationships between the physical, emotional, and intellectual curves of an individual. These curves start at the moment of birth and are of different length. Reading them can be used to understand the dynamics of an individual's life. Though the work on biorhythms requires more research, it seems to have potentials for recognizing patterns of action, i.e., when there is the right time to act, when there is the right time for rest, and when there is the time to be especially cautious. Biofeedback instruments, which monitor heart beat and brain wave patterns, are already used in holistic health clinics, but the use of these techniques themselves can not yet be called shamanic. Shamans have an intuitive knowledge of physical, emotional, and intellectual processes. They operate also on the social and the spiritual levels which are not reflected in the biorhythm charts.

To balance the interactions of individuals with their environment, Chinese, for example, developed the art of geomancy and practiced it already for several thousand years. Geomancers divine by looking at the contours of mountains. They observe a location's relationships to nearby trees and water courses to determine, for example, the auspicious site for a house, and especially a grave because it is important to put the dead at a place where their remains are protected and not attacked by natural forces. To protect the intimate connection of individuals with nature, indeed, with any environment, and to balance any shift in "energies," is one of the major tasks of shamans all over the world. Shamans are true geomancers although not all geomancers are shamans.

The belief that "supernatural" powers can be manipulated has led people, furthermore, to seek conjurers who use magic spells and, among others, magical tatoos (see, photo 2.). Spells may also be used by magicians who are mainly performers employing illusions and sleight of hand. Some of them, however, claim to command also the services of spiritual entities. Spells may be used in cases of love magic too, but most conjurers are sorcerers whose magic aims at harming, even killing people. In popular belief, there are also warlocks and witches who use "supernatural" powers acquired through a pact with entities from the spiritual world. And there are exorcists who expel intruding, i.e., "possessing," spirits. The Catholic Church, for example, has codified rites for exorcism in the *Rituale Romanum* (1614). Such exorcisms are by no means rituals of the past. Felicitas Goodman (1981), analyzing a well-documented possession case of a young female student in Germany, describes an exorcism conducted by Catholic priests in the 1970s. All practitioners mentioned in this paragraph are, however, more involved in manipulating powers than in restoring harmony between the sacred and the profane which is the main task of shamans.

Finally, there are healers and medicine men as well as women who use natural means such as massage, bathing, and herbs. They utilize a knowledge accumulated by trial and error over millennia and do not necessarily access different states of consciousness.

Practitioners may master any combination of the above skills but only those individuals can be called shamans who

1.  *can access alternate states of consciousness at will (this is an important feature because medicine men and women, for example, do not enter trances),*

2.  *fulfill needs of their community which otherwise are not met (e.g., using holistic approaches in contrast to physicians and psychiatrists who are constrained by the rules of their discipline), and*

3.  *are, in fact, the mediators between the sacred and the profane (i.e., use symbols and rituals to encode the ineffable messages from the spiritual world).*

The first of these three criteria is compatible with Eliade's classical definition of shamans as masters of the "archaic technique of ecstasy" (1964). However, the following three of Eliade's characteristics that shamans,

1.  *are masters of fire,*

2.  *go through a phase of dismemberment and resurrection during initiation, and*

3.  *have animal guardians,*

do not apply to all shamans. For some shamans the mastery of fire (e.g., walking on fire, putting their arms into boiling oil, etc.) is very important, other shamans smile about such obvious demonstrations of unusual faculties. In some Chinese as well Indian communities, even ordinary people will walk on fire to fulfill a vow or to prove that they are protected by the deity. These are acts of faith but none of the firewalkers will maintain to be a shaman. I saw eight hundred people walking on fire in Singapore and less than five per cent got burned.

Similar events are reported from Sri Lanka and southern India among Tamils.

There is another aspect to this "power over fire" which is connected with the magic of metals. Eliade talks about a symbiosis between smiths and shamans or medicine men. The presence of smiths in the initiatory societies (Männerbünde) is documented among the ancient Germans and the Japanese. Similar relations between metallurgy, magic, and the founders of dynasties have been found in Chinese mythological tradition (1974:473).

"Mystical heat" is known also in belief systems other than shamanism. We read about Tibetan monks who dry out wet sheets wrapped around them in the icy climate of their country solely with the concentration of their meditation. We read about the *tapas* (inner heat) of Indian ascetics (Eliade, 1974:475-476) and the "boiling energy" of the Kung (Katz, 1982). But most shamans do not talk about their physical experience of energy and, as I mentioned before, consider it blasphemous to put their unusual faculties on display.

Some shamans go through a period of dismemberment and resurrection during "initiatory illnesses," others either inherit their faculties or follow the instructions of their dreams and visions. Some go on vision quests (e.g., North American Indians) or simply apprentice themselves to accomplished shamans (see paragraphs on call, initiation, and training in Part III).

Most of all, especially among Buddhists, Taoists, and Hindus, spirit mediums are expected to be possessed (i.e., temporarily inhabited) by spirits of a higher order. These may be benevolent ancestor spirits, deified heroes, bodhisattvas, even deities of the Hindu pantheon. Westerners don't have elaborate maps about the different realms of existence which have been used by Hindus, Buddhists, and Taoists for thousands of years. In Southeast Asia, for example, it is believed that spirits belonging to so-called "lower realms" are closer to earth and have the tendency to be more playful and less reliable. If their presence is disturbing peace and harmony in the community, these spirits have to be exorcised or, and this is important, the possessed individuals are trained so that they can utilize their faculty and become spirit mediums. Spirits per se are neither good nor evil, that means, spirits closer to earth can be propitiated to assist in human affairs and spirits of a higher order may punish when individuals have displayed disrespectful or unethical behavior. In sum, one should be on guard and on good terms with spirits of all realms at all times.

In many Asian belief systems, animal spirits belong to a realm far below that inhabited by humans. Animal spirits are, therefore, not in such high regard as they are with North American Indians. I found, however, animal spirits evoked by Malay (Muslim) shamans. They claim that shamans become "white tigers" (i.e., spirit tigers) when they die. These "white tigers" then look for candidates whom they can teach their knowledge. One of the Malay shamans I worked with in Pattani (southern Thailand) offered to transform himself into a tiger (see, photo 3). After forty minutes of evocative chanting during which he called several animal spirits but also Muslim sages, he indeed "became a tiger." Although he did not physically change his shape, his facial expressions became tigerlike and he moved and jumped like a tiger in a way no human being would have been able to do during a normal waking state. Weretigers are well known throughout Southeast Asia. Frequently evoked are also elephant, horse (see, photo 4), monkey, snake, and shark spirits; see, among others, Heinze, 1988:252-254.

My three main criteria differ from other explanations of shamanism because I include trance mediums. (I have to stress here that I am excluding American trance mediums who recently developed a style of their own.) I am compelled to include trance mediums, since I discovered in Asia that both shamans as well as mediums go on "magical flights" to the world of spirits where they talk directly with whomever they encounter. For example, they meet souls of the deceased and bring their messages back to the world of the living. Or they call spiritual entities into their body and these spiritual energies then become the actors. That means, shamans often become also mediums who call spirits into their body and mediums are capable of going on magical flights too. Both can do what the other is doing. Most of them enter a wide range of alternating states of consciousness during a single session (see, Trances, Part III; also, Heinze, 1988; Lewis, 1975; Peters and Price-Williams, 1980; Winkelman, 1986). Therefore, it is more accurate to use one generic term, shaman, rather than having to refer to the same individual at one time as a shaman and at another time (perhaps only a few minutes later) as a medium. (The mind-expanding or dissociative trances of shamans will be discussed in Part III.)

As mediators between the sacred and the profane, shamans may also become "image makers." This does not necessarily mean that they create images of spirits and deities. Images themselves, if not activated during a ritual, are ineffective. Because sacred messages are formless and ineffable, shamans have to provide symbolic representations of the sacred in the material world, and they achieve this, for example, non-verbally during their rituals and through their paraphernalia and the objects they use during their sessions.

A shaman, combining a wide range of faculties, is indeed

> *the original artist, dancer, musician, singer, drama-*
> *tist, intellectual, poet, bard, ambassador, advisor of*
> *chiefs and kings, entertainer, actor and clown, curer,*
> *stage magician, juggler, jongleur, folksinger, weath-*
> *erman, artisan, culture hero and trickster-trans-*
> *former (La Barre, 1979:7-11).*

## Topics To Be Discussed

I selected, for this book, not only shamans who moved to cities and adapted to urban life but also individuals who were born in big cities and began to shamanize without any overt or covert connection to previous traditions. I witnessed the development of new shamanic traditions, for example, in urban centers such as Singapore and Bangkok but we have to investigate how "new" these forms of shamanism actually are.

Twelve profiles of twentieth century shamans can be found in Part II. These profiles document the shamans' call, training, initiation and their practice. The reader will be introduced to the work of a Caucasian shaman and a Polish director/shaman working in the United States, a Haitian shaman who holds a degree in biochemistry from Cornell University, a Hawaiian kahuna who also taught "in the West," Korean shamans who became TV stars without losing the main characteristics of a traditional shaman, a "traditional" Garhwali shaman working in the Himalayas; and an African shaman who is caught in the political unrest of his own and neighboring countries. Presented are also three cases of urban shamanism in Southeast Asia (Singapore, and Bangkok, Thailand). The reader will, furthermore, learn more about the background of the oracle who is still consulted by the Dalai Lama at his residence at Daramsala, Northern India, and the shamanistic work of a "Western" lawyer in the United States.

In Part III, *Diversity and Individualization,* a brief historical overview will look at the available reports on the development of shamanism from hunting and gathering societies in prehistoric times to horticulturist (Shintoist in Japan and the Huicholes in Mexico), nomadic pastoralist (Evenki in North Siberia and the Hungarian horsemen) and agriculturist societies. Each ethnic community cultivated its specific forms of shamanism and this development did not cease when shamans moved to cities or forms of shamanism emerged in cities on their own.

Drawing from the profiles in Part II and my own fieldwork, differences and similarities in call, initiation, training, trances, paraphernalia, rituals, and symbolism of shamans practicing in Europe, Asia, the Americas, and Africa will be discussed in Part III. In multi-ethnic and multi-religious societies, we can expect greater diversity and individualism. In other words, whenever an environment develops needs, we can expect the emergence of a new shaman and it is the individual shaman who translates the sacred into the secular in a language s/he creates along the way.

Part IV looks at the specific needs which are fulfilled by contemporary shamans. Some needs obviously changed over time. Existential needs, however, come from deep-seated fears common to all mankind and it is the urgency to respond to these needs which leads to the emergence of new shamans. It becomes important to find mediators between the sacred and the profane because people want to come into the presence of the sacred. Not having the training to do so, they seek specialists who mediate and guarantee a safe return to the everyday situation. This safe return includes the assurance that any psychic opening has been closed.

Part IV discusses, furthermore, the nature of shamanic methods to solve problems on the physical, emotional, social, mental, and spiritual levels. Shamanic techniques are success-ful, for example, in treating dissociative disorders. Shamans reconnect individuals with their families, their social and ecological environment and counteract the alienation felt by large sections of the population. When shamans cause a shift of attention in their clients and literally "break the old mold," transformational processes can take place and self-healing powers are triggered. These are, however, the words of a Western observer and not so much the vocabulary shamans would use.

Part V, *New Paradigms,* attempts to bridge the gap be-tween science and religion, using the language of quantum mechanics and Bell's theorem. Shamanic thoughts need to be translated into modern language. We have, indeed, to develop a new vocabulary which will ease the phobia about so far unexplained phenomena.

The other five volumes in this series intend to continue the discussion why shamans play an important role in the twenti-eth century.

## *Personal Involvement*

This book has been on my mind for a long time. Over sixty-five years ago, when I was of pre-school age, I con-nected with everything around me, the sun, the wind, the sea, the earth. This experience at the shores of the Baltic Sea was truly ineffable. I kept it to myself and, in times of despair, I would recall the infinite love and energy I had felt pulsing through me at that time.

Twelve years later, as a teenager, I visited a village in West Prussia (now Poland) where my mother had lived before she moved to Berlin (Germany). A woman whom I had never met before greeted me and told me that my grandfather had been a healer and had helped her in critical times. This incident puzzled me because my grandfather had died over thirty years before I was born. How could she recognize me as his granddaughter? She did not even know that I would come. It was the first time that somebody spoke about the philanthrophic work of my grandfather. My mother had only told me that her father had been an overseer of a princely estate in the East. Now I learned that he had also fulfilled needs which otherwise were not met.

I was raised Lutheran and had difficulties of accepting the Christian dogma. During Bible class, before my "confirmation," the tenet of "original sin" became intolerable, but an understanding pastor prevented me from officially leaving the Church. He told me that God and he (the pastor) knew of my doubts and I should consider my "confirmation" to be a social duty toward my parents and the community. "God loves those," he said, "who have to investigate and don't believe blindly. Continue your search, there is nothing wrong with it." I am still not drawn to Christian churches, except to "high masses" in Catholic cathedrals or, e.g., when Trappist monks are chanting at New Clairvaux Monastery in northern California (where I am invited once in a while to lecture on Buddhism and Buddhist practices).

Since my teens, I have been studying the beliefs and customs of different religions. It was easy in the Berlin of the thirties because Berlin was the capital of Germany, situated in the middle of Europe, at the crossroads from east to west and north to south. Different Christian sects and schools (not as prolific as in the United States but still differing considerably in practice and worldview), Judaic traditions (orthodox as well as Hascidic movements), Islam in its various forms (Sunn'ite, Shi'ite, Sufi, etc.), Buddhism (Theravada, Mahayana, Vajrayana), and Taoism (the philosophical school of Laotse as well as the manifold forms of Folk Taoism) could not only to be read about in books at the university library but also be observed by participating in their practice.

I survived the dark years (1933-1945) in Germany (which

included two-and-half years of starvation and bombing in Berlin during World War II) by drawing from inner resources which connected me to what I have termed "divine" or "cosmic energy." I lost the fear of death. Remembering my childhood experience during which I had met the infinite source, I learned to access this source every time I needed nourishment. I learned to shift from "ordinary" to "ultimate" reality and back with ease, until I could distinguish the qualities of each state. A greater awareness for the Here and Now was the result. It made ascent or descent easier with each "encounter."

From 1971-1972, I conducted fieldwork in Thailand where Buddhism has been state religion for over seven hundred years and where over 90 per cent of all Thai citizens are Buddhists. I wrote my dissertation on *The Role of Buddhism in Modern Thailand*. In 1960 already, and during my one-year stay in the seventies, I travelled to all provinces of Thailand where I met also rich forms of folk religions which were practiced literally "at the feet of the Buddha." The laity, monks, and the royal family participated in animist as well as brahmin customs, too. Errant souls, for example, had to be called back into the body of the sick. Deities and other spirits had to be evoked to bless private houses as well as public buildings, bridges, and roads (see, Heinze, 1982:48-55, 1988:48-49).

Consequently, I wrote a grant proposal to study shamans and mediums in Southeast Asia and received Fulbright-Hays Research grant #1069-83079 to live and work with shamans and mediums in Singapore, Malaysia, and Thailand for another year (1978/79).

For three decades, I have been visiting and working in other Asian countries, e.g., India (Himacha Pradesh, Bihar, Orissa, Tamilnad), Indonesia (Sumatra, Nias, Java, Bali), Burma, Cambodia, Malaysia, Philippines, Taiwan, China, Hong Kong, Japan. I stayed, among others, with tribal shamans in Orissa (India), in northern Thailand, and Kunming (Yunnan, China). I spoke to Tibetan lamas in Indian and Nepalese monasteries. I watched brahmins call deities into the statues of their gods. I saw eight hundred Tamil walk on fire in Singapore and less than five per cent of them got burned. I was present when a Thai-Malay shaman transformed himself into a spirit tiger (see, photo 3) and another Malay shaman called the spirits to heal the *"angin"* (wind) of his patients (see, photo 5). I was guest at several "spirit dances" in Chiang Mai Valley (Thailand). These dances are held to propitiate the "possessing" spirits. Being permitted to participate in these dances, the mediums are recognized by their peers and by the community. I sat next to a Thai medium who calls the spirit of King Chulalongkorn into her body. (She was healing and advising hundreds of clients for three days and three nights without leaving her seat once.) I lived in the temples of spirit mediums in Singapore and became a part of their daily routine. I observed the emergence of shamans in Bangkok and located, for example, a high official in the Thai government who admitted that he is working as a shaman in his spare time (see Part II).

My research of three decades allows me to draw comparisons from a wide range of different ethnic groups, from tribal, so-called traditional shamans to Western-educated urban shamans. I was less surprised by the diversities than amazed by similarities, esp. in the ways they fulfill universal needs. In other words, shamans accomplish what Western physicians and psychiatrists have great difficulty and often not the time to do. Shamans treat the person not the symptom.

It was not difficult for me to locate twentieth century shamans. In the countries where shamanism is still more or less overtly practiced, shamans never need to advertise. Reports about their successful work spread rapidly, one satisfied client is telling another. When I asked colleagues at Singapore University whether they knew any mediums or shamans, they were first surprised that I wanted to study a topic which they connected with superstitions, however, all of them could name at least one shaman whom "a relative of theirs" had visited. When my research yielded its first results, all of them came later to me and asked me secretly which of my shamans I would recommend so that they could get in touch with their ancestors.

Elliot predicted in 1955 that spirit mediumship is on the

decline in Singapore. Twenty-three years later, in 1978, I had no problems locating shamans. A black flag with the eight trigrams of the I-Ching in front of a house announces that a spirit medium is in residence (see, photo 6). Each shaman knows of other colleagues because all shamans are very much concerned about staying on good terms with their "colleagues." They acknowledge each other, and, most of all, they don't want to draw the wrath of another shaman on themselves. On the other hand, they are not concerned about so-called "fake" shamans and leave them to their own misery. People will not consult ineffective shamans. When shamans do not produce the expected results, clients simply cease to come. "Fake" shamans, therefore, fade away without outside interference, at least in Singapore.

Wherever I went I found the need for shamanism confirmed, and so I started to document the reasons for the effectiveness of shamans.

To gain an inside view of Asian medical systems, I studied, furthermore, acupuncture and practiced it under supervision in a Singapore clinic. I am holding a Chinese herbal license from the Taoist Academy in San Francisco, and Reiki I and II licenses from a Los Angeles Reiki Center. But, mainly, I worked with shamans in Asia, Europe, and the United States whenever there was time and opportunity. Shamans kept asking me whether I was a shaman myself. When I denied that I was a practicing shaman, they encouraged me to develop my faculties and offered to "trade off" details about diagnosis and treatment.

This book reflects research and life experience of over sixty years. It does, however, not claim to cover all aspects of shamanism. Shamans continue to work in the Here and Now and invite us to stay in midstream. They remind us that we all can follow and be carried by the dynamic flow of life.

# Part II

# Profiles of Contemporary Shamans

## What These Profiles Tell Us

I have selected three profiles of shamans from my own fieldwork in Southeast Asia to prove that new shamans emerge and continue to work successfully in the twentieth century. I have also asked six colleagues to write profiles based on their fieldwork and their close relationships with shamans, and I have added a brief introduction into the role of the Dalai Lama's Oracle and the work of a Western lawyer.

The shamans, my colleagues and I worked with, belong to a wide range of ethnic groups and belief systems. They live also in very different environments, e.g., the United States, Asia, and Africa. They use rituals and paraphernalia which neither resemble nor have any connection to those used by shamans of other groups. Reading these profiles side by side should remove the stereotype that shamans have similar personality traits or that there is only one set of authentic shamanic paraphernalia. All shamans, mentioned in this book, however, have the following characteristics in common:

1. *They access different states of consciousness at will.*

2. *They perform services for their "community" which otherwise are not available, and,*

3. *they are the mediators between the sacred and the profane.*

There may be other similarities, but the way how shamans enter their profession ("call," heritage, or by their own decision), the ways they fulfill needs of their community, and the nature of such needs differ considerably. Because these differences are greater than the similarities (sometimes the differences within each group are even greater than the differences between one ethnic group and the other), I used the above three characteristics for the selection of shamans I want to introduce in this book. Their "calling," training, initiation, rituals, and symbolism will be discussed in Part III and the "needs fulfilled" in Part IV.

Etzel Cardeña introduces you to the Voodoo shaman, Max Beauvoir, who works in Haiti (see, photo 7). Max has a Master's degree in Biochemistry from Cornell University and stands "with one foot firmly implanted in the Haitian culture" and with "the other bridging the distance to the Western world." He is certainly a representative of twentieth century shamanism.

Stanley Krippner reports on the Zulu shaman, Vusamazulu Credo Mutwa, born in the Natal area in South Africa, who has been caught in the political strife of his native country (see, photo 8). His commitment to non-violence and his opposition to apartheid has made him many enemies among black militants and white reactionaries, however, his healing activities introduce an element of moderation into the heated issues of the day. He will later be compared with a Togo shaman in Part III.

Charlotte Berney speaks of David Kaonohiokala Bray who is the heir of a long tradition of *kahunas* in Hawaii (see, photo 9). Even after Daddy Bray's death in 1968, his influence is felt not only by Hawaiians but by Westerners as well.

Shamans have become television stars in Korea (see, photo 10). Chungmoo Choi tells us that there are now 140,000 mudang in South Korea of whom 60,000 are officially registered and organized in a professional association. This is a remarkable development because, in the past, shamans in Korea found themselves on the lowest rung of the social ladder, "together with prostitutes, shoe menders, soothsayers, Buddhist monks, and dancing girls." For this reason, more women than men accepted the call because, as Achterberg says, they were the only ones that dared mediate with ancestors since they had very little to lose by engaging in such a fearsome task. When economic circumstances threw them back on their own resources, they used intuitive abilities in a supernatural application to dodge the vicissitudes of a male-dominant society (Achterberg 1985:20; Kendall, 1981:17).

Korean mudang follow the universal pattern of being chosen either by birth or adoption, by apprenticeship, or a spontaneous call of vocation (Kalweit, 1988:84). That some of them have become "Human Cultural Treasures" indicates official recognition. Their advice, however, has always been sought by the people and the elite as well.

Though not many Garhwali shamans continue to practice in the Himalayas, Alok Saklani found Usha Devi Rudola who is still a traditional shaman in this region of India. For many years, she and her family resisted the "call" that she should serve as a shaman because they had difficulties tolerating public behavior generally considered to be inappropriate for a woman. Acceptance of the call returned good fortune to the family. Although Usha acts mainly as a diviner, the main criteria of accessing different states of consciousness, fulfilling certain needs for a community, and mediating between the sacred and the profane are all present.

Sarah Dubin-Vaughn shares with us her experiences with Elizabeth Cogburn who is a Caucasian shaman (see, photo 11). Elizabeth looks back to "four generations of bright, passionate, strong-minded, independent, tough and beautiful women" of the isles of Iona and Mull in England to "builders across Kentucky, Missouri, Iowa, and Nebraska." She went through a "wave of calls" until she was re-minded of something she had always known. So she began to create rituals for a community hailing from all over the United States. Through ritual celebrations, practiced around the cycle of the year, she and her community "find points of balance for themselves, and maintain the balance" living in a confused outside world.

I asked Etzel Cardeña to write also a profile on Jerzy Grotowski who is a Polish director of theatrical performances (see, photo 12). Grotowski goes far beyond the goal of public entertainment because he intentionally seeks to "alter the basic consciousness, social and cultural structures that we have inherited along with the belief that they are immutable, to create an 'active culture' where dichotomies such as process/product, actor/spectator, are overcome."

These seven profiles, written by colleagues, already discard the stereotype of "one shamanic personality."

I looked in my own field notes for urban shamans in Southeast Asia who emerged without having a direct connection to existing traditions. The three shamans discussed were born in big cities (Singapore and Bangkok), however, each of them began to follow still available traditional patterns. An altar around which a community had formed was calling for a medium who would evoke and activate the "Divine." The second shaman discovered his propensity for healing and sought training with Taoist priests and Buddhist monks but mainly followed his own guiding spirits, and the third, a high government official, decided to be trained by peers to increase his spiritual power.

The background and personal story of the oracle of the Dalai Lama, as reported by Avedon, carries all characteristics of a traditional shaman, from early illness and visions to the day where the old oracle died and he could step into the position of being the reincarnation of a historical oracle. This oracle is, to this day, still consulted by the Dalai Lama in all important issues of state.

The last report, on the shamanistic work of a Western lawyer, is the result of personal communications and observations. The profile demonstrates how new paradigms begin to evolve in Western settings.

# Max Beauvoir

# An Island in an Ocean of Spirits

## by Etzel Cardeña

*Why couldn't these gods, why couldn't God
or one of his many expressions come exactly where we are?
Because we are all part of the same thing.
This is where the heaven is, this is where hell is,
this is where our spirits are....*
*(Max Beauvoir, summer of 1987)*

I am in the presence of Max Beauvoir, a *houngan* (Voudun priest). Low budget, low quality movies have not prepared me for this encounter; neither have the sensationalistic novels that proliferated during the most recent U.S. military occupation of Haiti (1915-1934), written by service men eager to make fast money. Max is not engaged in vengefully pinning a doll (as false stereotypes of Voudun would have it) or is preparing a "primitive" ritual of uncontrollable bloodletting and sex. No, as I enter his office, after crossing the well-kept garden of a prosperous house, he is busily typing a directory of *houngans* into his personal computer.

Beauvoir, as Haiti itself, proves to be more paradoxical,

deep and vast than I had fathomed. His size and voice remind me of a younger James Earl Jones and I eagerly anticipate the journey of ideas and experiences that we will share for a number of hours. He is not a typical *houngan,* neither by his considerable affluence, his Western education (a Master's degree in Biochemistry from Cornell, he unpretentiously confesses) or the impeccable English with which he greets me. But it is precisely his vital stance (à la Papa Legba, the Haitian *loa* or spirit that bridges the world of humans and spirits),[1] with one foot firmly implanted in the Haitian culture and the other bridging the distance to the Western world, that makes him an important representative of twentieth century shamanism. One of his roles, in addition to the traditional shamanic intercession with the realm of the spirits, is to clearly translate—and explain—the Voudun world view to the West unaccustomed to a religion of direct bodily expression. It is no coincidence that occidentally educated persons eking an entry into the Voudun culture-religion, from the ethnobotanist Wade Davis investigating the zombie phenomenon through authors probing the representational aspects of Voudun ceremonies to prospective Voudun initiates from Europe, America, and other areas, seek his (and his daughters', also Voudun practitioners) assistance.

In many ways, Max Beauvoir is a transitional figure in his brand of Voudun, melding traditional Haitian rituals and ideas with an occidentally educated sensibility. A representative example of this syncretism is found in his Voudun ceremonies. They do not have the vague temporal and spatial structure of traditional rituals; but neither do they follow the crude model of the "ceremonies for tourists," where a "spontaneous" ritual may occur after providing the correct monetary incentive, and in which the most stereotypical excesses are provided for the spectators to quench their thirst for "primitivism." Beauvoir and his initiates practice their religion in a clearly defined place, a beautiful amphitheater behind their house, with a clearly defined stage and comfortable seating for some paying guests, and there is also a temporal demarcation. But however Westernized the setting might be, however ambivalent about its role as performance or traditional ceremony, Beauvoir makes a conscious effort to preserve the spiritual intent of the traditional ceremony and avoids the extremes of the typical "tourist ceremony."[2]

This modern shaman's path from biochemistry to the full embrace of life as a total, mysterious reality, may be traced to his first experience of possession. In Voudun, as in other traditions, the most important liturgical event is transcendent possession, the immediate, intimate experience of surrendering one's self to "a major force of the Universe," usually given specific, anthropomorphic characteristics by the culture. The possessed individual does not assume that s/he has been transformed into the godhead as such, but into an expression of Its pervading force, to which everyone is linked. As described by him, Beauvoir's entry into the alternate reality of Voudun occurred when he was approximately thirty-five years of age.

An ambivalent initiate into the Voudun traditions, he had resisted losing his conscious and rational control during the ceremonies. As he describes it, being a scientist and biochemist, he had sought to maintain "his foot on the ground all the time and be aware of all that happens in the conscious world." And he had indeed maintained his ordinary footing in ordinary reality up to the time when, while talking to some friends, he suddenly felt himself "turning into a baby...[as if] somebody would be holding me [by the ankles] just like you hold a newborn." He then felt as if he had been dropped from very high and cried loudly at the experience of his head touching the concrete floor. He remembered this happening around 11 a.m. The next time he was self-conscious of anything it was 5 p.m. His self had been spirited for six hours, during which he had traversed what, for him then, was an unknown reality. On his return, he felt himself to be in a very relaxed, alert state, "more aware of certain things. I [could] view certain things...people...better." He has remained, though, entirely amnesic about his experiences during those six hours.

The consensual definitions of shamanism, however, involve not only the ability to experience alternate realities or states of consciousness, but to have developed clear, strong intent and control to enter and exit such states whenever the community requires it. Instead of madness, Beauvoir found that being possessed increased his conscious awareness and gave him new capabilities. Without his previous dread, Beauvoir allowed himself to enter more fully future experiences and became a better "horse" for spiritual forces. His full adoption of a shamanic role, and recognition by the community as such, has required him to develop the ability to enter into "the second world" at a moment's notice, without a ritual setting, even though the latter "helps to clear the place (and personal purpose?) from impurities." After years of practice, his travels between realities, he adds, are now so subtle that only a person that knows him very well can detect minute voice and behavior changes, and increased sweating. He has achieved the "ultimate stage of possession," one in which there is a presumed access to other information than that obtained through ordinary sensory and intellectual processes. He explains metaphorically that possession allows the *houngan* to lift him/herself from a grounded, horizontal perspective into a place where non-immediate spatial and temporal knowledge becomes accessible.[3] With that more extensive view from above, the *houngan* returns to the immediate present to assist those seeking his succor. Possession allows him to tap into a realm in which everyone and everything is related. Beauvoir, in classical shamanic style, claims to have expanded his conscious responsibility to forms of awareness of which most people remain ignorant.

In contrast to the relatively few instances of unwelcome possession (usually associated with unresolved personal conflicts), mentioned in the literature, Beauvoir describes his ability as a privilege, "because it is beneficial not only for you, but also for everybody else." His reputation as a *houngan* is widespread. Haitians, Americans, Europeans consult him, and ask his assistance in a variety of problems: physical ailments, existential anxiety, conflicts with a different culture, a desire to change their "bad luck," etc. Beauvoir then undergoes the form of consciousness alteration he calls possession to obtain information and heals the person seeking solace. In case, where geography prevents it, he maintains contact (to diagnose and heal in occasion) through the telephone, although he considers direct contact and touching to be more effective. In agreement with shamans of many cultures, he declares to be able to perceive what is happening at a distance and to predict, although not alter, substantially the future of a person. His reputation, he maintains, is based on the empirical observation of the patients/clients to find out for themselves whether or not he can tap a healing and omniscient source. Voudun techniques, for him, represent the accumulated knowledge of Haitian (and before them West African) people throughout the centuries, after they had conducted their own form of experimental field testing.

I do not know of any independent evaluation of Beauvoir's purported paranormal abilities, but even if he could "only" be shown to assist people through suggestions, the use of expectations and the conveyance of a shared and coherent explanation of the ailment (all elements that foster the person's own recovery mechanisms) he would fare better than most psychotherapists, frequently in a chronic state of cultural and spiritual undernourishment. Beauvoir's task, in an economically and politically devastated country, is to bridge the understanding between the occidental and Haitian perspectives, to heal the children of a culturally exuberant country exposed to the constant threat of anonymity and mediocrity of growing cultural standardization, to reinvest an afflicted body with a culturally meaningful identity, to—who knows whether metaphorically or not—recover souls lost in the crack between economical, cultural and even metaphysical contradictions. The Haitian *houngan* makes sure that the people requesting his help find their ground in a sense of community since, after all, even as physical beings they are still "islands in an ocean of spirits," in undulating partnership with other islands through the rhythmic continuity of Voudun drums and their shared heart beat.

## Notes

1. A literate and erudite account of the character of Papa Legba, along with his relation to Eshu Elegba, the trickster deity of the Yoruba, and the spirits of death and sexuality in Haiti—the Ghede—can be found in Cosentino, Donald, "Who is that fellow in the many-colored cap? Transformations of Eshu in old and new world mythologies," *Journal of American Folklore,* 200 (1987):263-275.

2. A thorough analysis of Beauvoir's ceremonies is that of Anderson, Michelle, "Authentic Voodoo is Synthetic," *The Drama Review*, 26:2, (Summer 1984):89-110. In her excellent discussion of different forms of Voudun ceremonies, Anderson particularly brings to task the social composition (mostly non-Haitians and Haitian elite) of the audience chosen by Beauvoir, and the classical "dramatic" structure of his representations. Notwithstanding this, she also comments on Beauvoir's efforts to document popular ceremonies throughout the countryside and his high standing as a *houngan* among more traditional performers. Also, unsurprisingly, her admittance to the more secret, traditional and recondite ceremonies at Nansoucri was partly mediated by Beauvoir himself. Despite the differences between the rituals in the countryside and the "performance" version of Beauvoir, Anderson concludes that there is not one authentic form of Voudun, but that forms are in constant change and, ultimately, "synthetic," which is in agreement with the general tenor of this book.

3. The theater director Grotowski, described below, makes a very similar point about Beauvoir in a recent lecture. He also draws on the importance of lifting oneself from an horizontal (i.e., purely instinctual) position to achieve the vertical—and reflective consciousness—stance that expresses the full quality of being human. See Grotowski, Jerzy, "Tu es le fils de quelqu'un" [You are somebody's son], *The Drama Review*, 31:3 (Fall 1987):30-41.

# Vusamazulu Credo Mutwa

# A Zulu Sangoma

## by Stanley Krippner

In traditional Zulu society, the two principal figures were the chief and the shaman. The chief carried the higher authority, both spiritual and political, and reigned supreme because it was believed that his or her ancestral line led most directly to Unkulunkulu, the Great Spirit. The shaman was believed to be in direct communication with the spirits of the ancestors and stood as advisor to the chief and intermediary between the spiritual realm and the members of his or her community.

In Zulu society today, chiefs have become politicians and attempt to work for the benefit of their tribe. However, over the years, they have lost any claim to spiritual leadership. On the other hand, contemporary shamans (one type of which is known as a *sangoma*) still command respect and wield considerable influence in their communities (Boshier & Costello, 1975).

## Family History

The best known Zulu *sangoma* of the twentieth century is

Vusamazulu Credo Mutwa. He was born in the Natal area of South Africa. His mother, Nomabunu, was the daughter of Ziko Shezi, a veteran of the battle of Ulundi which ended the Zulu War. He was also a *sangoma* and a custodian of Zulu relics and history. Mutwa's father was a catechism instructor in the Roman Catholic church. Because Nomabunu refused to be converted to Catholicism, Mutwa's parents did not marry. They parted just after he was born and Mutwa was placed in the protection of Ziko Shezi who shared tribal secrets with his grandson and allowed the boy to carry his medicine bags.

In 1928, Mutwa's father attempted to obtain custody of his son, arguing that as an illegitimate child, he was a disgrace to Ziko Shezi's family. Despite Numabunu's protests, Mutwa's grandfather agreed and Mutwa moved to Transvaal with his father, stepmother, and their three children. The family lived there on a farm where Mutwa's father was a laborer. In 1932, Mutwa's stepbrother died after being whipped by the farmer. For the next twenty years, the family lived on several different farms, eventually settling close to a mine near Johannesburg where Mutwa's father obtained employment as a carpenter.

In 1954, Mutwa found a position in Johannesburg at a curio shop that specialized in African art. Mutwa became an amateur artist himself and an avid student of art history, travelling throughout the country between 1946 and 1948 with Roman Catholic priests interested in native culture. In 1958, Mutwa underwent a psychological crisis and felt compelled to visit his mother and grandfather. At their command, he renounced Christianity.

His "call" had been a gradual one, having been stimulated by his discovery of African art and by his exposure to Zulu tribal legends. When Nomabunu and Ziko Shezi told him that he should prepare to assume his grandfather's role, Mutwa did not resist. He underwent a purification ceremony in order to begin training both as a *sangoma* and as a custodian of the Zulu tribal relics. As such, he has written several articles and books. He is also known for his talent as a painter and sculptor.

Mutwa married, but his wife was unfaithful. He fell in love with a young Basuto woman but she was killed by South African police who fired on a crowd of blacks during the

Sharpeville protests in March, 1960 (Mutwa, 1985:xii-xiii). Later, Mutwa married again; during a subsequent uprising in Soweto, black militants held his wife at knife point, threatening to kill her unless Mutwa endorsed their cause. An advocate of nonviolence, Mutwa refused and eventually his wife was released.

## Zulu Mythology

My wife and I visited Mutwa in 1980, following my series of lectures at the University of Witwatersrand in Johannesburg. At that time, Mutwa lived in a compound in Soweto. We entered through the "Gate of Seven Truths" to find a series of structures and statues that Mutwa had designed himself. Placed between the whitewashed mud structures with thatched roofs were wooden and clay figures of Ninavanhu-Mas (the Great Mother), the Tree of Life, and various sacred animals and birds. The compound had been subsidized by the Mendelsohn Foundation in attempt to preserve some of the Zulu art and folkways.

Mutwa invited us into the largest of the structures and we were struck by the colorful scenes from a Zulu creation myth that he had painted on the earthen walls. Patiently, he told us a story about the Great Spirit and the Great Mother. They and their two sons were depicted in his painting as living in the Upper World, looking down on Middle Earth where the earth beings were tormented by fearful monsters. Their compassion led them to send down their "He-Son" in a basket that floated on a river until two humans found it and raised the boy as their own. Eventually, the He-Son grew to young manhood and killed the dragons and monsters that were terrifying humanity. Were the earth beings grateful for this gift? Not at all, they were jealous of the He-Son and expressed their envy by hanging him from a tree until he died.

The Great Spirit and the Great Mother brought back the He-Son from the Lower World where he had gone after his death. They despaired of the ingratitude of earth beings, but decided that the pitiful creatures should have one more chance. The Great Spirit and the Great Mother sent their "She-Son" to Middle Earth. This kindly, androgenous deity taught human beings how to domesticate fowl and cattle, how to till the soil and plant gardens, and how to clean and cook food. Once again, earth beings were jealous of the She-Son's skills and killed her. This time the Great Spirit and the Great Mother decided to let the She-Son stay in the Lower World until the earth beings stop their fighting and become more peaceful. With a chuckle, Mutwa indicated that the She-Son's day of deliverance does not appear to be close at hand.

In fact, the deities soon withdrew from the earth beings. Hence, the *sangomas* never talk to the Great Spirit directly as he is simply beyond their understanding. Instead, they work with the ancestral spirits who "called" them to their profession. There are other types of magico-religious practitioners among the Zulu but the *sangomas* respond to a "call" rather than inheriting the role (as does the *inyanga*). This call is often associated with an illness or *ukutwasa* after which the elected man or woman becomes an apprentice or *twasa*.

The *twasa* must learn how to prepare herbal medicines, how to interpret dreams, how to incorporate spirits, how to diagnose illness, how to exorcise *tokoloshe* or frightening ghosts, how to control the weather, and how to foretell the future. In addition, the *twasa* must learn the tribal and community history, mythology, and ceremonies. Because much of their time is spent counteracting the *tagati* or hexes placed upon tribal members by witches, *sangomas* are often called "witch doctors," a somewhat pejorative term that many of them take in stride because it does describe one of their functions.

The *inyanga* also works with sick people but is especially skilled in locating lost and stolen objects. A survey by the National Institute for Personnel Research in South Africa indicated that 85 per cent of urban Africans regularly consult their own tribal practitioners (Boshier & Costello, 1975:5). This mirrors a report of the World Health Organization that the physical and mental health problems of most of the world's populace are still handled by traditional healers (Mahler, 1977).

# The Harvest Ceremony

We were invited to return to Mutwa's compound the following week for a harvest ceremony in which the Great Spirit would be thanked for the fruits, vegetables, grains, game, and domestic animals that provided food for the community. In some circles, this ceremony also commemorates the gifts of the She-Son who still resides in the Lower World.

Upon our arrival, we heard drum music accompanied by chanting and singing. We were told that tribal customs dictates that special drums be reserved for purposes of worship. These have the symbol of the Eternal River carved on them in a continuous pattern. Special men are often elected to look after these drums; these "Drummers of High Honor" daub the instrument periodically with animal fat to preserve both the wood and the skin. When a drum deteriorates beyond repair, it is the duty of the senior woodcarver to construct a new one. The old drum is then buried with full honors usually given a chief.

I was allowed to taperecord and photograph the ceremony. Upon inspecting the brightly-colored robes of the *sangomas* and *twasas,* I noted "Made in Switzerland" labels. Mutwa told me that a Swiss manufacturer was so struck with the beauty of the Zulu ritual clothing that he asked for permission to use the designs for his fabrics. One of the conditions of the deal was that he send a dozens of bolts of cloth to Mutwa and his colleagues every year for use in their ceremonial costumes.

Suddenly half a dozen South African soldiers appeared and pulled Mutwa off to the side. The group soon disappeared into one of the structures. A soldier told me, "We will only need to question him for a few minutes." I considered the incident tantamount to the New York police yanking a bishop from the pulpit of St. Patrick's Cathedral during High Mass. One hour later, Mutwa was released and the soldiers departed. In the meantime, his associates had continued the ceremony and Mutwa brought it to a conclusion. He then confided to us that the soldiers wanted him to accompany them to Namibia to provide propaganda against the militants who were enlisting the support of tribal people for their cause. He reiterated his refusal to cooperate with any group that used violence to attain its ends, noting that the militants sometimes obtained support by killing children and not releasing the bodies to their parents for burial until the populace cooperated with them.

In the meantime, the *twasas* were pleased that they had been given an opportunity to continue the harvest ceremony during the absence of their *baba* or teacher. One apprentice told me how she had been "called" by a snake in a dream during an illness; once she began her apprenticeship, her illness disappeared. As a *twasa,* she told me that she rises at dawn and prepares an herbal tea. Once it boils, she knows that the spirits are present as they typically travel through the air. After drinking the foam, she rubs some into her skin, then vomits as part of her purification process. She spends the day carrying out domestic chores and receiving lessons from her *baba*.

## Throwing the Bones

Every time an apprentice passes a test (on herbal knowledge, diagnosis, divination, etc.), a goat or calf is killed and a feast is held. During the dinner, the *twasa* is given the animal's bladder. The *baba* inflates it and the *twasa* wears the bladder in his or her hair. The fact that they are filled with air indicates that the spirits are constantly available, even though entering an altered state of consciousness through dancing, singing, or drumming is usually necessary to contact them.

Following the festivities, the *twasa* searches the ashes for an unbroken bone, repeating the process after each successive feast. Once s/he has found and decorated four bones or *dingaka*, divination and diagnosis can proceed. The healer and client both blow upon the bones, providing the breeze that brings both sets of their ancestral spirits to assist with the task. The bones are then thrown upon the ground and examined.

As the bones are decorated on only one side, sixteen different combinations are possible, e.g., "the rise of the snake," "the river crossing," "the warning." The four *dingaka* are named *lekhwami* or *lekgolo* (the old man), *kgadi* (the old woman), *silume* or *selume* (the young man), and *kgatsane* or *lengwe* (the young woman). If the bone faces upward, it is "smiling" but if its face is down it is "sleeping." Distances between the bones also are used in determining the configuration's meaning.

Mutwa told us, "Throwing the bones among Zulus is very much like throwing the *I Ching* among Chinese or Americans." Like with the *I Ching,* an ambiguous stimulus is presented to a person who has a problem that has not yielded to rational, logical analysis. The resulting configuration allows the unconscious to project its own meaning, one which might very well provide a solution to the unsolved dilemma.

When the bones are used to diagnose and treat an illness, it is believed that they can detect witchcraft or sorcery, as well as the malevolent presence of human spirits or of nature spirits. They can also detect if the ailment has resulted from breaking a taboo, from depleting one's energy, or from "soul loss," the most serious calamity which can befall someone. In addition to purification rituals and exorcisms, the *sangoma* might use herbs, minerals, insects, bone fragments, feathers, roots, seeds, smoke, excreta, shells, or eggs in medicines or in ceremonies. Massage is commonly used as are teas, snuffs, salves, poultices, emetics, and powders. Some substances have medicinal properties (e.g., the use of *vellozia* for the relief of asthma) while others have magical properties (e.g., the use of blood to placate disruptive spirits).

When a client is ailing, the practitioner assumes that the divine power of the universe has been misused by someone or by some entity. Thus the maladaptive symptoms must be counteracted, uprooted, punished, or put back into balance. Hospitals and Western physicians are not discounted; however, it is believed that they deal with the physical, and lower, level of the disorder. The services of a *sangoma* or *inyanga* are also needed to deal with the spiritual and mystical levels of the problem (Brame, 1984:233). The traditional practitioners, with their animal-tail whisks and leg rattles, can ward of evil influences and call upon benevolent entities for assistance.

Eventually, the *twasa's* apprenticeship is complete and an

*ukukishwa* ceremony is held welcoming him or her to the ranks of traditional healers. Some *sangomas* and *inyangas* begin a fulltime practice while others work during the day and see clients in the evening and on weekends. Mutwa has trained several dozen *sangomas* over the years and told us that there are at least 1,000 *sangomas* in the Soweto area.

## Meeting the Chief

It is estimated that there are some six million Zulus in Southern Africa, only half of them still live in their homeland, great portions of which are occupied by the sprawling farms of 13,000 white residents. Zulus have a colorful history and proud heritage; the exploits of such famous kings as Shaka, Cetshwayo, Zwelithini, and Dinzulu are told and retold. Officially classified as Bantus, modern-day Zulus are now subject to South Africa's apartheid policies.

Mutwa has worked closely with Chief Mangosuthu Gathsa Buthelezi and his National Cultural Liberation Movement. Buthelezi assumed his hereditary post as chief of the Buthelezi tribe in 1957, soon becoming the leader of the Zulu resistance to governmental policy, refusing to allow the KwaZulu region to become a "semi-independent" homeland. At the same time, Buthelezi, like Mutwa, insists on a nonviolent approach to the conflict, bringing him into conflict with the more militant leaders of black Africa (Hahn, 1982).

In 1986, I met Buthelezi when he addressed the World Affairs Council of Northern California, calling for a multiracial government in his home state of Natal that, if successful, could serve as a model for the rest of the strife-torn country (Lindberg, 1987). During the reception following his talk, I asked Buthelezi about Mutwa and was informed that the celebrated *sangoma* had left Soweto for Bophuthatswana, an allegedly semi-independent homeland. In 1989, Stephen Larsen, an American psychologist and friend of Mutwa, told me that Mutwa's commitment to nonviolence and his opposition to apartheid had won him too many enemies among the black militants and the white reactionaries for him to live safely in Soweto. Larsen reported that a group of young black extremists had "necklaced" Mutwa's son—placing a rubber tire around his neck, drenching it with kerosene, and setting it on fire. Although anguished by his son's death, Mutwa vowed to carry on his healing mission, attempting to find a more congenial atmosphere, at least until sanity and moderation return to Soweto.

## References

Boshier, A. and D. Costello. *Witchdoctor.* Johannesburg, South Africa: Museum of Man and Science, 1975.

Brame, G.A. "Religious functionaries in African traditional religion," *Journal for Religion and Psychical Research,* 7 (1984):231-241.

Hahn, L. "A Zulu voice: Fighting apartheid from within," *New Leader* (1982):8-9.

Lindberg, T. "Homegrown plan offers hope," *Insight* (November 23, 1987):64.

Mahler, H. "The staff of Aesculapius," *World Health* (November 1977):2-3.

Mutwa, V.C. *Indaba my children.* London: Kahn and Averill, 1985 (1965).

# David Kaonohiokala Bray

# A Hawaiian Kahuna

## by Charlotte Berney

By 1889, the year David Bray was born, the decline of the Hawaiian nation had reached critical proportions. Introduced diseases had caused the native Hawaiian population to shrink to a quarter of its original number. For every one acre of land owned by a Hawaiian, four were owned by foreigners. Native spiritual traditions had been mostly supplanted by Christianity, and Hawaiian culture and arts were suppressed. In six more years Queen Lili'uokalani would be incarcerated in Iolani Palace, and the Hawaiian monarchy would come to an end. Indeed, since Captain James Cook's arrival in the Hawaiian Islands in 1778, Western contact had meant near devastation for this thousand year-old Polynesian culture.

Like tiny tufts of grass that appear on lava flows, renewal can occur in even the darkest scenarios. David Bray lived in a time of trials and transition for his people, yet he rose above the difficulties to practice and teach, openly using the knowledge of the Hawaiian *kahuna*. By believing in himself and his Hawaiian traditions, he gave others hope and planted seeds for future growth. Re-introducing ancient ideas for use in modern times, he kindled interest which helped to spark the renaissance in Hawaiian cultural and spiritual life which is ongoing today. In 1959, the House of Representatives of the Territory

42

of Hawai'i recognized David Bray as a "practicing *kahuna* for over fifty years" and commended him for his service to the people.

The word *kahuna* in modern Hawai'i evokes visions of sorcerers praying for the death of victims and sending spirits on errands of destruction. By all accounts, sorcerers did exist in Hawai'i, as they do in other complex cultures living close to the spirit world. However dramatically this dark side captures our fear and imagination today, sorcerers were a small part of the overall society of the past. Actually, traditional Hawaiians relied upon *kahuna* for their most important functions, i.e., to be the trained experts in all professions such as architecture, the military, medicine, and the spiritual arts. Such professionals, male or female, acquired, after a long apprenticeship, all the knowledge in the field and then served their communities. The word *kahuna* combines the concepts of *kahu* (guardian) and *huna* (secret).

The *kahuna lapa' au* or medical priest-practitioner healed using a variety of methods. First, the healer attempted to discover the psychological, spiritual and physical causes of the ailment and then rectified these using family therapy, medicinal herbs, physical treatment and prayer. Medical and spiritual practices were intertwined, and prayers to the family gods and greater gods formed an important part of the treatment. David Bray considered himself to be a *kahuna lapa' au* who healed through prayer and faith, a "human bridge" between the spiritual and material worlds. This was his training, yet in his later years, he expanded his role to teaching the ideas at the heart of *kahuna* practice.

David Bray's blend of Hawaiian and Western traditions was given at birth. His grandmother Namahana was Hawaiian and his grandfather, William Henry Bray III, was an English-Hindu seaman who had settled in Hawai'i during the time of Kamehameha III. David's full Hawaiian name Ka-onohi-wena-ula o-kalahiki-ola-a-kala means "the seeing eye of the blazing sun of life." As a child he spoke only Hawaiian. On his mother's side, David Bray descended from a line of *kahuna* priests who served the kings of the Big Island of Hawai'i for twenty-five generations. One of his ancestors, the High Priest

Holoa'e, attended Kamehameha the Great, and interpreted the omens which foretold Kamehameha's first victory in battle. Further back, David could trace his lineage to Pa'ao, the Tahitian priest who effected great changes in Hawaiian religion and society in the thirteenth century.

But, at the turn of the century, Hawaiian gods were changing. His mother having died when he was a baby, the young David was adopted and raised by his aunt, Luika Kahalaopuna, herself a *kahuna*. She was able to see the future and to heal by faith. She, however, did not want her charge to become a *kahuna* and felt he should be reared in the modern way, which meant learning English and becoming a Christian. Thus, David was sent to Kamehameha School for Boys in Honolulu where he graduated in 1909 and later to the Kawaiahao Church Bible Training School. He remained interested in *kahuna* practices and his great-aunt Ka'ilianu, also a *kahuna,* encouraged him to pursue his interest.

David Bray was influenced at an early age by Kuamo'o, a son of Kamehameha the Great and a master *kahuna*. Kuamo'o had studied the traditional way, which meant mastering long prayers to the gods which had to be recited in a correct manner. His powers of healing were intensified by a sacred stone named *Kukapihe* which he used in his practice. The stone had been brought to Hawai'i from Tahiti in the thirteenth century. He also employed a cane named *Kauwila* for healing purposes. The cane had been given him by his father and was believed to contain Kamehameha's *mana* or spiritual power. When Kuamo'o died, he passed on these two items, as well as his spiritual powers, to his son, William H. Kaniho, who became David Bray's teacher.

Kaniho's specialty was healing through faith, and though he became a Christian, he continued to believe in Hawaiian gods and combined the two teachings. He used both the Bible and the sacred stone and cane inherited from his father for healing. Kaniho died childless and, on his deathbed, he gave the stone and cane to David who had been like an adopted son to him. The two objects became David Bray's most treasured possessions.

"Daddy" Bray (to use the Hawaiian term of respect)

helped his people as shamans have done for centuries, blending the everyday world and the world of spirit. He worked in a boy's reformatory school for eighteen years and in Hawaiian prisons, helping those whose lives had gone out of balance. He had a five-year appointment as a guide at Iolani Palace, home of the Hawaiian monarchs and the historical and cultural center of Hawai'i. In 1919, together with his family, he formed a hula troupe which was the first of its kind in this century. Its members kept Hawaiian dance and music alive for over thirty years. They appeared in movies such as *Bird of Paradise* in which David Bray portrayed a priest while his wife directed the dancing.

Daddy Bray continued to perform healing, rituals and blessings in a changed Hawai'i. He was called upon on many public occasions to bless new buildings, shopping centers, ships and even a jet fighter plane. In order to transmit the wisdom of the *kahuna,* he lectured on the mainland to non-Hawaiians in the 1960s. This caused a controversy in Hawai'i among those who felt this knowledge should be kept secret and reserved for Hawaiians only. The tradition of secrecy had been observed by the ancient practitioners who handed down their knowledge only to chosen persons, usually family members. Secrecy was later reinforced by necessity after *kahuna* practices were made illegal.

Yet Daddy Bray believed the knowledge would be lost if it were not taught openly and widely. As so few new *kahuna* were being trained in Hawaiian families, he wanted to reach outside to those who could carry on the tradition. The wisdom of his decision cannot be doubted now when so much of Hawaiian knowledge has receded into the mists. In keeping *kahuna* principles alive, his contribution has been inestimable. Daddy Bray's other premise in teaching was his belief that all persons are equal in their ability to understand and apply the principles. He felt that *kahuna* teachings could benefit all the races. This independence of thought and action characterized the man throughout his life.

What were *kahuna* practices? A story goes that a Park Service employee of Hawai'i Volcano National Park received a report that a "crazy Hawaiian" was perched on the edge of

45

Kilauea crater behaving in strange ways. An investigation found that David Bray, indeed on the rim of the caldera, was emersed in Hawaiian ritual and prayer to his '*aumakua* or personal god, Pele, the fire goddess. The Park Service employee engaged the "crazy Hawaiian" in conversation, finding him not only completely sane, but a knowledgeable, practicing *kahuna*. They subsequently became friends. A student of the Hawaiian past and traditions, the ranger, who was also the well-known author L.R. McBride, had many talks with David Bray which contributed to McBride's writing on *kahuna*.

The volcano spirit Pele and her seven sisters and brothers were important to David Bray as '*aumakua* or personal gods in his lineage. He often said, "I belong to the fire," meaning that members of the volcano family were his special '*aumakua*. A major aspect of *kahuna* practice involves praying and communicating with the spirits to receive helpful information about the livingto assist in healing and counseling. At the volcano one could be in close proximity to them in their material forms.

Another part of practice was psychological; Daddy Bray taught the importance of emotions and of keeping them clear and in balance. He believed strongly that no one could do good work when under the influence of negative emotions. His list of negative emotions included the "search for self gain and glory" and excessive fear, jealousy, hatred and greediness. They should not be repressed, but rather understood and brought into harmony with the positive emotions, some of which are humbleness, patience, self-control, kindness, and seeing "the truth of reality." He also stressed the need to keep the spiritual and material sides of life in balance. He taught that to be strong, one must combine spirituality with "sensible materialism."

One of Daddy Bray's greatest gifts was his ability to heal. At the onset of illness, the Hawaiian *kahuna* searches to find the spiritual or emotional cause of the illness. When the disharmony is identified, the *kahuna* works with the patient and the family to heal the situation. Daddy Bray would look for the inner cause of illness, then use prayer, transmission of energy, and herbal medications to effect healing. He would keep vigil with the patient around the clock until s/he improved. At other times, healing could be instantaneous.

Marian Charlton of Hawai'i, a student of Daddy Bray's in the sixties and one of the few persons outside the family given permission to teach in his line, relates an incident which occurred during her training in California. A brush fire which had been started by lightning in the mountains near Los Angeles began to move dangerously close to her home. As she watched the flames approaching, she resolved to use her new knowledge. With neophyte conviction, she began to chant a recently learned prayer to Pele, asking the fire to avoid her house. Amazingly, the flames died down, but then she began to feel pain in her mouth. Red sores covered her gums and a visit to the dentist the next day did not help. Unable to eat for two days and having difficulty talking, she went to see Daddy Bray who immediately recognized that she had been, in his own words, "playing with fire."

Daddy Bray passed his hand several times over her mouth and it was instantly healed. He then asked her to find out what her mistake had been. Charlton later understood that the fire had been cleansing an ancient Indian burial ground near her house and that, by attempting to redirect the flames and chanting without awareness, her mouth had become a source of negativity. The negativity was expressed as an illness. Thus to Charlton, Daddy Bray's attitude toward natural forces (don't interfere without knowledge), the power of the chants he used and his healing ability were demonstrated in an unforgettable experience.

Daddy Bray was often called upon to heal himself. He told in a lecture of an incident which occurred while on a speaking tour in San Francisco. He emerged with a badly broken jaw. The doctor he consulted advised him to leave immediately for Hawai'i where he could receive long-term medical care and convalesce; he decided not to go. He saw this as an opportunity for his son, Michael, who had accompanied him, to learn spiritual healing first-hand. "I'm not going home, but am going to prove to the people here that the Gods will take care of me," he said and instructed his son in healing. For a whole month thereafter, Daddy Bray lectured on the mainland, visiting people constantly in the evenings for dinner and socializing. During this time, he stated that he felt no pain. No one even knew that his jaw had been broken.

In his early years he had concentrated on healing and later on teaching the concepts which enabled him to heal and help, so that students could put them into practice in their own lives.

In the way of the ancient *kahuna,* he was well versed in working with the spirit world. He once explained that Hawaiians know both, highest and lowest spirits. The highest are the ones who contact the forces to help mankind. He says, "These want to do what is good, and try to help us. The other half are destructive and mischievous ones who want to make fools of us. This is what we have to be careful of, to understand and know them." He advises not to play with spirits and earthbound forces and to protect oneself with one's own inner strength, and the use of aids such as candles, salt and water.

In his practice he had to learn also how to deal with the power of the "black" *kahuna.* To do this one must analyze one's own emotions, finding the negative emotion or idea in oneself which has attracted the negativity in the first place. As the *kahuna* became more and more misunderstood in a Christian society, Daddy Bray was sometimes accused of using sorcery. He once said, "I stand before my great power, God, with no black spot on my hands."

The great stone *Kukapihe* was given to Daddy Bray in a dark condition, but through his ministrations rehabilitated and restored to light. The stone is believed to have been brought, along with a companion stone, to Hawai'i in the thirteenth century by the priest Pa'ao. It is thought to have come originally from Egypt. The oval-shaped stone is about four inches in diameter and white with a hard glaze on it. It holds the spiritual forces of the god Ku, who in the form of Kuka'ilimoku became Kamehameha the First's god of war. The Hawaiians believe that Kamehameha's success derived from the stone. Its name, *Kukapihe* or Death Stone, refers to the lamentations of those who mourn a warrior slain in battle.

The stone came into Kuamo'o's possession while the companion female stone was held by *kahuna* priests on the island of Kaua'i. Kuamo'o bequeathed this stone to his son

Kaniho who promised it to David Bray. In 1959, Clarice B. Taylor, in a series of articles in the *Honolulu Star Bulletin*, mentions how the stone *Kukapihe* "walked" to David Bray's house.

After Kaniho's passing, David Bray had gone to Kaniho's house and asked his family for the stone-god. The widow knew it had been promised to David, but did not want to relinquish it. She said that if the stone really belonged to him, "let it walk to your house." David went away and did not return for three months. During that time, the stone began to radiate negativity and became again the stone of death. After the third death in her family, the widow relented and a nephew delivered the stone to David Bray. It had "walked to his house."

The stone was then in an extremely negative state and had to be cleansed. David Bray bathed it periodically in water and *'olena* (tumeric) and immersed it in the sea. After five days, it was restored to positive power. The great stone *Kukapihe* is now on the island of Kaua'i with the Bray family.

What kind of person was Daddy Bray? Despite his great learning, or perhaps because of it, he was a humble person, always feeling that he had something to learn from others. "Everyone you meet is a teacher," he once said. Yet he took great pride in his Hawaiian heritage, its wisdom and traditions. He had a sense of humor, laughed easily, and was warm and approachable, yet at the same time exuded a sense of personal power. There was a feeling of authority in his teaching, perhaps because he always spoke about what he personally knew and had experienced. When hearing a new idea, he had to test it himself and, only after a long period of questioning, would he claim it as a belief. He encouraged his students to do the same. As a result, his Hawaiian rituals had the power of deep conviction.

David Bray was a family man, a working man, a religious man, a healer, a teacher, an entertainer, and one who believed deeply in his own people and culture. Given his modern education in English and Christianity, he chose to return to the gods of his ancestors when the lines of force all seemed to be moving in the opposite direction. He is remembered both for his unusual strength of character and his valuable contributions on many levels to the people of Hawai'i and beyond. His legacy continues today.

> *To thee in heaven*
> *From the rising of the sun to the setting of the sun,*
> *From the highest levels above*
> *To the earth below, contact!*
> *Arise, o Ku, the architect and builder!*
> *Arise, o Hina, mother earth, contact!*
> *Blow softly the breeze of life*
> *From the four corners of heaven above*
> *and earth below so that we may live and enjoy life.*
> *Now my prayer is free to wend its way to God.*

(Portion of a Hawaiian chant taught by Daddy Bray during a mainland class in 1964)

*Note*

The information in this essay is based on David K. Bray's writings, published in *The Kahuna Religion of Hawaii,* with Douglas Low. Vista: Borderland Sciences Research Foundation, 1959; and *Lessons for a Kahuna*. Pasadena: David K. Bray, 1967; as well as transcriptions of audiotapes of lectures given during the 1960s; and the personal recollections of his student, Marian Charlton.

# Nami, Ch'ae, and Oksun

# Superstar Shamans in Korea

## by Chungmoo Choi

In 1980, I met Nami, the Korean shamaness. It was neither at the divination table at her shrine nor at a healing ritual but through television programs and on the stage of a theater for an elite audience. I later discovered that even her shrine becomes a performing stage for the media personnel and scholars whom she personally invites to study her shamanic art (*musok yesul*). Among the phalanx of folklorists, ethnomusicologists, and reporters, the spirits she was entertaining seemed demystified. The flashing lights from the cameras and the fence of microphones surrounding the stage seemed to make the deities in the paintings on the wall above the altar mere icons. The deities also seemed entrapped in the tape recorders. Years later Nami finally expressed her fear that the excessive exposure to media might provoke the gods' rage.

Nami has gradually built her reputation for the past two decades as a folksong singer. The various prize certificates on the wall of her shrine-residence tell the history of her rise to stardom as a performing artist. In 1967, she entered the National Folk Arts Contest and sang a song from a boat ritual. For the Folk Arts Contests in 1968 and 1969, she bid for media attention by adapting shamanic rituals in the form of a festival.

51

Eventually, she won the government recognition in 1972 and her boat song was adopted for a television drama, another contribution to her lasting relationship with the media. She began regularly demonstrating shamanic ritual at the Folk Village, an outdoor museum and major tourist site. Moreover, according to the Dictionary of Korean Folk Arts (1979), Nami was a musical instrumentalist for the Unyul Mask Dance Drama of her native region. The Unyul drama is Intangible Cultural Property No. 61 whose preservation is protected under the Cultural Conservation Law. Nami affirms that she aggressively sought government and media attention by performing at the government-affiliated tourist spots, museums, theater stages and for the national television network.

What brought Nami into the focus of public attention was not the prizes she won at the Folk Arts Contest but her Ph.D. apprentice. In 1981, a Korean-American graduate student of performing arts at the University of California, Los Angeles, named Ch'ae came to Seoul in the hope of becoming, in her own words, the Carlos Castaneda of Korea. She watched the film of Nami's performance at the Korean Foundation of Arts and the Humanities. Through a noted ethnomusicologist, Ch'ae met Nami who divined that Ch'ae was destined to become a shaman. Nami officiated an extravagant "authentic" initiation ritual for Ch'ae in front of an exclusive audience of foreign and domestic scholars and media personnel. The sensation-seeking weekly magazines featured the story of the "Ph.D. shaman" and awakened the otherwise passive public in the heat of the summer.

For Koreans who regard education above everything, the notion of a scholar shaman was quite shocking and provoked a lively debate on the credibility of the "disdainful superstition." The national television station, KBS, quickly reacted and arranged to have Nami, and to a lesser extent Ch'ae, undergo a week-long examination of their superhuman abilities by various specialists, including a fire-eating magician and a hypnotist. Footage from the examination was shown on television as part of a one-hour special program, "What is Shamanic Ritual?" For this program, KBS sponsored a one-day "Ritual for the Unification of the Nation" which Nami and the "scholar shaman" officiated. In 1982, on the 100th anniversary of Korean-American diplomatic relations, Nami and her performing team were selected for a tour to America where she was joined by Ch'ae.

In 1985, Nami received the highest government recognition. The boat ritual of Hwanghae Province was designated as the Intangible Cultural Property No. 82 and Nami as the official carrier who would preserve "the original form of the disappearing ritual art." With this she joined the ever-growing number of Human Cultural Treasures, an informal title to honor the official carrier of the protected folk tradition.

As an authority on the disappearing ritual art, vested with a life-long stipend to train disciples, Nami's opinion on the matter of regional folk culture has been heavily weighed by the government appointees who, as folklorists, select the carriers of Cultural Properties. In 1988, a hitherto unknown shaman was selected as an official carrier of another form of Hwanghae Province ritual. Rumor was rife that Nami's recommendations had powerful impact on this decision. Nami's name is now ubiquitous and she has become a media personality as an official "shamanic artist." She has also been given undisputed authority to determine the authenticity of the regional folk culture.

In contrast to Nami who enjoys the public spotlight and dazzles the media as an authentic performer of the lost art of a lost province, her colleague Oksun commands public and government attention by projecting herself as an elite scholarly shaman. On January 16, 1987, the Kyonghyang News featured a success story on the Korean Shamanism Research Institute, a shaman school in Seoul, open to both laity and shamans. According to the Kyonghyang News, this informal school opened in 1983 at the residence-shrine of Oksun, "the godmother of Korean shamans," and has produced over a thousand graduates. In the same article, Oksun was quoted as saying that as many as thirty-one students applied for the 1987 winter term, which made the number of graduates appear quite hyperbolic. Among the graduates of this school was a leading anti-government activist and head of a radical theater group. He later held a series of seminars on Korean shamanism with a revolutionary theme and had ritual demonstrations performed for the interested public.

Oksun also holds the chairmanship of the shamanism committee of an obscure corporation, the Research Institute of Korean Folk Arts. The activities of this corporation included the demonstration and promotion of Oksun's comprehensive ritual repertoire in Korea and Japan. Since 1980, Oksun has performed at the Korea Arts Foundation, National Performing Arts Center and at a number of university campuses. She also has made two performing trips to Japan. In 1985, she had her ritual costumes displayed at the National Folklore Museum.

The success story of Nami, Oksun, and Chae should be understood in the context of Korea's rather complicated cultural milieu in the past two decades. While the modernization program attacks the religious content of shamanism and launches the campaign to eradicate "pre-modern superstition," the culture conservation policy makes the presentational form of shamanic ritual a museum piece. In fact, while the healing rituals at the shrines of the neighborhood shamans were often interrupted by police in the 1970s and well into the 1980s, today the National Museums, theaters, and the Cultural Properties Conservation Center regularly stage the rituals of noted shamans. Furthermore, the Korean Foundation of Arts and Humanities filmed these shamans' performances which would have been considered a national embarrassment in the previous decades.

The Cultural Conservation Law was enacted in 1961. To educate the masses and promote national pride in the cultural heritage annual exhibitions and other folk festivals and contests are broadcast through national television and radio. As of 1988, ten shamans have become Human Cultural Treasures and they earned their fame through media exposure.

Meanwhile, the upsurging nationalism among Korean university students has pushed the "official" folk culture in the opposite direction. Criticizing that the government's culture policy "taxidermizes" folk tradition and desiccates the spirit of the people, students began a folk culture revitalization movement in the 1970s. In the 1980s, folk culture itself has become a powerful instrument through which students and elites voice their revolutionary vision of social reform. They made shamans symbols of the oppressed people referring to the dynastic period; and in their eyes, the transformational nature of shamanic ritual is the cultural frame for social reform. Students and activists learn the shamanic ritual and adapt the ritual and style for this end.

The press coverage put both the official and protest folk culture under the rubric of folk culture dismissing any distinction. This fuels the ramification of folk culture in the arena of culture industry. Shamanic rituals as a form of folk culture is marketed for tourism and mass consumption. Oksun's shaman school for laity and its press publicity is a way to reach out to the public for fame and prestige, a way of exploiting her spiritual power as a commodity.

## The Construction of an Authentic Shaman

Biographies say that Nami was born either in 1930 or 1935. Nami herself revealed in a recent interview that she is fifty-seven (*Chungang Ilbo*, June 14, 1988). Since Koreans consider a newborn one year until New Year's Day and thereafter add one year on every New Year's Day, she might have been born in 1932 or 1933. Oksun also gives two birth years in her official biography; 1920 for the biological birth year and 1925 for the "registered" birth year. In her own horoscope book, Oksun wrote down her birth year as the Year of the Pig which was 1923. The discrepancy between the natural birth date and the registered date is commonly accepted because many refugees from the north may have registered in the south with inaccurate birth dates during the post-war confusion. Banking on this social knowledge, the refugee shamans lower their birth year when necessary. High age gives the refugee shaman a longer training in her native region prior to the Korean War (1950-1953) and consequently supports the authenticity of her art.

Lowering the age of spirit possession is another method of adding years to experience. Nami began showing signs of spirit possession at the age of fifteen (or eleven, according to another biography). She did not have a particular illness but suffered from insomnia and nightmares. She often had visions of the troubled lives of others. She had been married one year then and was divorced at the age of sixteen due to spirit possession. She was initiated at seventeen. By the age of nineteen, she was officiating village rituals and leading at least twenty shamans. If she was born in 1932, she had had, at the most only two years to learn the Hwanghae ritual in her native province before she fled to the south in 1950.

In official interviews, Nami neglects to mention that her maternal grandmother was a "great" shaman in the region, although she did say in passing that her grandmother offici- ated her initiation. Only the silver-haired old women, who still visit Nami's shrine out of loyalty to her maternal grand- mother, divulged this guarded information and pointed at the late shaman's altar tucked away in the attic, hidden from general view. Regardless of the length of her post-initiation training, it is quite possible that Nami had been exposed to the ritual since childhood perhaps even as a minor performer. As a well-trained performer, the careful calculation of her birthdate has little significance, except for media publicity. Also by withholding information on the shaman's genealogy within her family, Nami highlights her own charismatic power, the only culturally accepted criterion Korean scholars have recognized for "true" shamans of the North.

For Nami, spirit possession is the foundation of her career because it has been recognized as the sole recruitment method among the shamans in the northern regions. Korean scholars classify shamans into two categories, which also split along regional lines: spirit possession in the regions north of Seoul and the hereditary priesthood in the south (Kim T'aegon, 1981; Ch'oe Kil-song, 1981). Aware of this theory, shamans of the northern region must be possessed; exceptions may be challenged. Several shamans from the northern provinces come from families with extensive shaman genealogies. The ritual song gives equal credit to both a charismatic shaman with no genealogical background and one from a shaman family, but gives preference to the latter. However, even among the shamans in the northern region, spirit possession is merely a cultural idiom. The candidate undergoes a lengthy period of symbolic negotiation with the society. Once accepted, one of the crucial elements to a shaman's survival is artistic skill at performing rituals.

Ch'ae, Nami's apprentice, could be accepted as a shaman without spirit possession because she was a performing artist. The cultural logic that allows interchangeability between spirit possession and artistic gift is a metaphorical one; both shaman and performing artist live in the social space of death, an outcast status in traditional Korea. By the same logic, lack of earthly means to become a full member of the society is also considered a sign of a shaman's destiny.

Ch'ae studied Korean traditional music at Seoul National University and dance at the University of California. For a Korean woman, a career in dance and traditional Korean music is often tied with that of a courtesan. Shamans share the same attributes. While a woman divined to become a shaman often eludes the fate by becoming an entertainer, an entertainer becomes a shaman because of her unusually harsh fate, which is a sign of the call. According to her own account, Ch'ae felt a call to come to Korea. In 1981, she went through a divorce and was anticipating a remarriage, which, although a modern trend, could have been a sure sign of a touch of the spirit in the eyes of shamans.

Shamans divine that misfortune such as poverty or illness are caused by malicious spirits who wish to come alive in the mortal body and release oppressed energy. A dancer is, hence, one of the favored choices of the spirits, since dancing frees emotion and can lead to ecstasy (Hanna, 1983:27-43). Realistically, dancers make good shamans since they already possess the important skills of a shaman. Often senior shamans actively recruit a little-known dancer to their ritual performing team. The question of their spirit possession is answered simply: the fact that they are interested in the ritual is the sign of the presence of spirits. An ordination by an established senior shaman, as Nami did for Ch'ae, validates the spiritual energy of the candidate.

The more concrete sign of numinosity that shamans claim are ritual objects that candidates discover as directed in their dreams during their possession illness. Oksun's bundle of brass bells or the tiny statues of Buddha that another famous male shaman Chi Paksu unearthed exemplify the tradition of material interpretation of numinosity. In Korean cities, these objects are often purchased from manufacturers or other retiring shamans.

## Professionalization of Shamanic Training

In urban Korea a quick way to become a shaman are good performing skills and close media or government connection. The star shaman Nami has set the model for success. Young shamans have begun associating themselves with local culture preservation groups to improve their performing skills and with the hopes of finding ties with the Human Cultural Treasures and the media.

Oksun, made her public debut at the 1981 national folk festival which was designed to attain national cohesion after the political turmoil and tragedy of the previous year. Oksun gives her rationale,

> *I regret and resent that I became a lowly shaman. As everyone knows, I am using a pseudonym not to tarnish the name of my family. Even when I am shaking the [shaman's] bells, I try not to be heard outside the shrine. Now I see all these shamans, who do not know [the authentic ritual] well, go out and dance in public. That is why I decided to do it (personal communication).*

This trend in which shamans are gaining fame as artists brought Oksun out of seclusion. She now struggles for public recognition by offering institutionalized training to ambitious shamans. The goal of the school, according to Oksun, is to enhance the quality of the shamans' performance and change the society's disparaging attitude toward shamans.

The shrine school offers four-week courses twice a year during the summer and winter vacations, i.e., basic courses for university students, housewives, and foreigners and an advanced class for practicing shamans. The school curriculum covers the "doctrine" and history of shamanism, and shamanic ritual music and dance. The students also observe and participate in the actual shamanic rituals. This curriculum resembles that of the shamanism course at the Folklore Institute of Kyonghi University in Seoul. Oksun attended and received a certificate upon the completion of the course. The framed certificate with a tiny photograph of Oksun glued to one corner is hung by the entrance of her shrine. This verifies her tie with a major university and her professional status to those who visit her shrine; whether they are a chicken shop owner from the nearby market, university students, or newspaper reporters.

The concept of a shaman school is not totally new to shamans. Murayama reports in 1932 that shaman schools existed in the southern provinces of Korea for hereditary priests to learn ritual performing skills (1932:157-164). Such schools seem to be extinct now. Ordinarily, a well-established Korean shaman leads a performing team which forms a guild. When a novice is initiated, she chooses a senior shaman to learn the necessary skills; often the shaman who officiated the novice's initiation ritual becomes her teacher or "spiritual mother." Living the life of a shaman seems to be the major part of training. As kitchen helper preparing food for different deities, the novice learns the cosmology and different functions of the deities. By watching the master's divination and participating in the rituals, an apprentice acquires not only ritual knowledge and performing skills but also social skills. In fact, often it is at the master shaman's residence that an apprentice establishes her own clientele.

Now shamanism scholarship demands a shaman's perfection of the ritual text and thorough knowledge of the ritual procedure. Young shamans are aware of the importance of the text and attempt to reproduce the noted master shaman's skill to attract media attention. Shamans attempt to obtain copies of audio tapes made of major rituals. They want to learn the lengthy text by replaying the tape on the tape recorder. With the increasing demand for professionalism and availability of advanced technology, I imagine that young shamans may soon use video tapes to hone their performing skills.

## Shamans' Place in Urban Life

What Lévi-Strauss learned from the Kwakiutl shaman, Quesalid, seems relevant in urban Korea. A shaman does not become a great shaman because he cures patients; he cures patients because he has become a great shaman (Lévi-Strauss, 1967). Nami's fame and publicity attract wealthy and exclusive clients who seek a successful shaman's service to help fulfill higher material aspirations or achieve upward social mobility. Nami's frequent appearances in colorful costume on television and in weekly magazines and daily newspapers have been translated into terms of spiritual power, which means more business with higher service fees. In fact, Oksun, Nami's colleague, believes that a successful appearance is crucial to her business because the clients consider a shaman's personal success a measure of her charisma.

Regardless of the shaman's fame, most rituals I observed in the Korean cities were performed for the purpose of bringing the clients material prosperity. On the healing power of shamans Oksun, for example, makes clear-cut remarks.

*When a sick person comes to a shaman, she should send the patient to a doctor. How can a shaman cure appendicitis or cancer? Doctors should cut it off. If a shaman performs a ritual to cure such an obvious illness, she is an unscrupulous quack. A smart shaman does not take such a dumb risk. Only the unexperienced ones do...The only patient a shaman can cure is an insane person. This even doctors cannot cure, because that is a trick of the spirits. These days shamans do not cure the bodily illness. Shamans divine and perform rituals to bring fortune. Shamans are not affected by [economic] recession. The deeper the recession, the more money we make. See how I rake in money in Seoul these days. Look at Jujube-tree*

*[a shaman]. She can hardly stand up in the ritual hall
[i.e., she has poor ritual skills]. Yet clients wear out
the threshold of her door (personal communication).*

The problems that send clients to shamans are generated from the social and economic issues which influence people's everyday lives. The Korean government has emphasized and fostered the value of capitalism as the founding notion of modernization, but not without paying the price. The abrupt shift from traditional ethics which emphasized the immaterial and metaphysical, to a purely capitalistic orientation has created social confusion and uneasiness. The mass urban immigration has caused a sense of uprootedness and insecurity. The exaggerated media commercialism fans the commodity fetishism. But the uneven distribution of wealth, especially in the city, has roused tension and jealously. Intense competitiveness and aggressiveness is now common place among Koreans. As a consequence, the demand for healers and shamans has increased, not so much for physical cures, but for the spiritual healing of those distraught over materialistic misfortune.

*References*

Bureau of Cultural Properties Management. *Minsok Yesul Sajon* [Dictionary of Folk Art]. Seoul: Bureau of Cultural Properties Management, 1979.
Ch'oe Kil-song. *Hanguk Musoknon* [Survey of Korean Shamanism]. Seoul: Hyongsol Ch'ulp'ansa, 1981.
Hanna, Judith L. *Performer-Audience Connection*. Austin, TX: University of Texas Press, 1983.
Kim T'ae-gon. *Hanguk Musok yongu* [A Study of Korean Shamanism]. Seoul: Chimmundang, 1981.
Lévi-Strauss, Claude. "The Sorcerer and His Magic," *Structural Anthropology*. New York: Basic Books, 1967.
Murayama, Chijun. *Chosen no fuken* [Korean Shamanism]. Keijo: Chosen Sotokufu, 1932.
Yi, Chong-sok. "Panmannyonui hunggwa mot" [The Beauty and Emotion of Five Thousand Years], *Chungang Ilbo* (June 14, 1988).
Yu In-sok. "Soure mudang hakkgyo" [The Shaman School in Seoul], *Kyonghyang News* (January 16, 1987).

# Usha Devi Rudola

# A Garwhali Bakia

## by Alok Saklani

People in Garhwal (Himalayas) go, in times of theft, litigation, spirit possession, illness, or family dispute, to *bakias*[1] who then perform the functions of shamans, however, there are not many *bakias* left. The only practicing *bakia* of Srinagar[2] happens to be a frail, ordinary looking woman who is forty-one years of age. Her name is Mrs. Usha Devi Rudola. The other *bakia* in Srinagar is an old lady of over seventy years of age who has virtually abandoned her practice due to ill health.

Usha Devi Rudola is a housewife who takes care of her husband, her six children, and her parents-in-law. None of the children are employed, some are still in school. Therefore, Usha's husband finances the household with his small earnings from a tea shop. The Rudola belong to the Brahmin caste[3] and own a double-storied, mud and concrete walled house with six to seven small rooms of which some have been rented out. Some land is used as a kitchen garden. The living room is sparsely furnished with a cot, an old sofa set, and a ceiling fan. The family does not own any vehicle other than a bicycle. They lead the life of average Garhwali in the Himalayan hills and, compared to nearby cities, rank within the low income group.

Usha is about five feet tall which is the average height for Garhwali women. She has a wheatish complexion and dark brown eyes. As is common among Indian women, she wears her hair long. Her voice is soft and she has a matching disposition. Although illiterate, her convictions run deep and strong. Born into a Brahmin family (considered to be spiritually higher than other castes), Usha admits to having been a "conscious child with religious inclinations." She is a vegetarian because Hindu consider eating meat an obstacle to spiritual growth. Since her early life, she has been severely depressed when goats and bulls were sacrificed at Chandrabadni, a temple close to her maternal home. During her childhood, Usha claims to have seen visions of a deity in the form of an old woman or a small girl in red and yellow clothing (both colors are held to be divine). One year following her marriage[4] at seventeen, Usha began to become possessed by a deity.

As time went by, Usha's possessions became more and more frequent. During possession, she shivered violently and talked incoherently. She often walked out of the house at midnight and during the small hours of the morning and became increasingly indifferent to her health and her duties. In the meantime, she gave birth to a daughter and a son but her neglect of duties became intolerable to her husband and parents-in-law. The family's resentment grew and so did the deity's wrath which reportedly led to inflicting misery after misery upon Usha and her family. The struggle between the deity and the family lasted almost a decade during which Usha and her family's health suffered greatly. This forced the family to seek counsel of learned pundits who are well versed in Vedic hymns and holders of great knowledge, i.e., Brahmins. On their advice, rituals were held to "tie down" the deity. But the pundit who tied the deity developed a severe illness and soon sent a messenger to Usha. When she saw him, possession occurred again and the deity identified herself to be Dhari (a manifestation of Durga).[5] Usha reports that the deity also informed the pundit that his illness was caused by her wrath and that, on his request to be forgiven, his health will be restored almost instantly.

Shortly after, Usha and her daughter were swept away by the fast flowing Ganges. They almost drowned but escaped miraculously. Later, when Usha was possessed again, the deity explained that it was a warning to Usha's family no longer to oppose the deity's possession. The family was too terrified to object any further and decided to accept the fact. Subsequently, the deity demanded that a drum session be organized because she wished to dance.[6] Usha's husband refused since, in his opinion, it was not appropriate for his wife to dance (in India, it is not considered in good taste for women to dance in public). This annoyed the deity again and led her to cause pain in the chest and stomach of Usha's husband. Only when the husband learned of the true cause of the pain, he relented to the deity's wishes, on the condition that the deity would arrange for the drummers[7] at the dance. Usha reports that, within a day or two, drummers arrived on their own and declared that, in a dream, they had been directed by the deity to come to Usha.

## Initiation

According to Usha, the deity wanted her to perform (as a shaman) to assist the common "miseries" of the people, her husband reluctantly submitted under the condition that arrangements about the initiation should be made by the deity. A pundit, able of holding the ceremony, did indeed appear on directions given by the deity in a dream. The pundit showed Usha how to invoke the deity as well as how to conduct the ritual connected with the invocation. Possessions continued and Usha became adept in handling them. She also commenced to speak at great lengths while in trance. Her family and many others (neighbors, relatives) became impressed with some "true predictions" she made during trance. Within a few years, her shamanic consultations and healing had become part of the household.

## Shamanic Practices

Usha wakes up early each morning (around 5:00 a.m.) and bathes at least once a day. Prayers are held at 9:00 a.m. and in the evening around 6:00 p.m., lasting about an hour at each occasion. During this period, Usha sings devotional songs, accompanying herself with a *ghanti* (bell). Meals are partaken at the end of the prayers and on session-days only at the end of the sessions. Usha fasts about seventy-five days each year at different occasions.

Having been a practicing shaman for about seven years, Usha holds her shamanic sessions in her *puja* (worship) room, after her prayers on Tuesdays and Saturdays. During the prayers, Usha enters into a trance[8] which begins with hissing sounds caused by heavy breathing. Her eyes look differently and her voice turns sharp. She may rub her head and usually loosens her hair so that it covers partly her face. Thereafter, the first visitor is asked to open his/her "rice pack" and place the contents on the copper plate so that the consultation or healing can begin.

Usually five to ten visitors may come to Usha, on some days the number may be higher and on rare days there may be no visitor at all. The people seeking Usha's help may hail from neighboring villages as well as from Pauri and Tehri (20 up to 50 kilometers distant from Srinagar, respectively). Occasionally, there may be visitors even from more distant areas who are generally Garhwalis from outside the region. Some of the visitors may come to Usha only for a *darshan* (to come into the presence of and pay respect to the deity) but a great majority comes for alleviation of pain or misery. People of all castes, income levels, and walks of life (farmers, teachers, students, businessmen, etc.) approach Usha with their problems.

Usha attends to the visitors' wishes on a first-come-first-serve basis. The visitors are generally expected to bring a handful of rice from their home for purposes of divination. Although no fee is charged, virtually all of them put small change (10-30 cents) on top of the rice. Usha mentions that the rice is not a pre-requisite for divination and that the deity simply loves to play with it during sessions. Further discussions, however, reveal that while she holds the rice on her palm for inspection, she takes cues from the number of kernels (whether odd or even) and quality (whether broken or whole). At the same time, Usha claims that the deity "sees all" so she does not need the help of rice. Perhaps, Usha is correct that, although she is aware of what is transpiring during trance, she really does not know how divination is carried out. Visitors are not expected to reveal the problems which have led them to Usha. She is supposed to do so with the deity's help. Usha is further expected to divine the cause of misery. Sometimes, she also makes remarks on the source of the rice (whether fetched from home, a neighbor's or relative's house or the market). One can also obtain relief by sending rice through a proxy, provided the carrier is aware of the circumstances of the sender. Usha is believed to know just by looking at rice packs whether a visitor has come on his or her own or as a proxy.

The session is carried on in the local dialect (Garhwali) and visitors address Usha as "mother" (or goddess), even though some of them may be her own relatives (brother, sister, mother, father, husband, etc.). It is believed that the person speaking during trance is not Usha but the goddess herself. Thus the visitors may bow in front of her and plead for the removal of their misery or fulfillment of a wish. During off-trance periods, however, Usha is treated as an ordinary being. Further, each visitor is supposed to express agreement or disagreement with every statement made by Usha, although the consultation is more or less a long monologue except for an occasional sign of affirmation or negation made by clients. Sometimes, however, a visitor may be more emphatic and expressive on a disagreement. Usha normally speaks continuously for about ten to fifteen minutes once she held the rice of a visitor in her palm. The statements made may generally refer to the deity's limitless ability to help devotees in distress, and to the positive characteristics of the visitors, but rarely their negative traits. Thus, in the first few moments, Usha assures visitors that their misery can be alleviated by the deity and invariably flatters their "ego. Other *bakias* have also been observed to follow the practice of putting visitors "at ease," except that some may try to win their confidence by making efforts to "correctly divine" their circumstances in life. Subsequently, Usha may briefly discuss the nature of the visitor's misery and the causes thereof which may generally be one or more of the following:

1. *negative feelings of somebody (e.g., evil eye),*

2. *having displeased a god/goddess,*

3. *spirit possession,*

4. *sorcery,*

5. *fate or unfavorable planetary constellation.*

Often the problems are removed with the help of rituals, e.g., worship of planetary deities, annulment of sorcery/evil eye, or appeasement of a spirit, neither of which is performed by Usha. Initially only temporary relief is brought to gain the confidence of a visitor. For that purpose, a handful of rice is "energized" by Usha who will rub it between her palms and blow on it. The rice is then to be taken orally,[9] a few kernels at a time and/or to be placed on the forehead. Usha may shriek piercingly when energized kernels are handed over to a visitor. Once having benefitted and being satisfied by the preliminary treatment, a devotee returns to consult about the "permanent" cure. Some of those who believe that their problem has been altogether removed, may bring a gift (usually clothing) to Usha as a sign of gratitude.

Comparing with relationships of other *bakias* with their clients, the conversation between Usha and her visitors is mostly one-sided. This may be so because Usha's non-stop monologue does not provide her visitors with enough opportunity to affirm or deny the accuracy of her statements. Visitors can be seen to break down in tears during the sessions of other *bakias*, but such sight is extremely rare at Usha's sessions, probably because the visitors participate to a lesser degree and are given fewer chances to "open up" to her. Judging by the number of visitors at Usha's sessions, it can be said that she has average success.[10]

Usha states that the deity is always hovering around her

and, on certain occasions, when the interview for this study was in progress, she reported that possession had begun only by mentioning the deity's name. Usha also claims that the deity can cause barley to sprout, just by holding it in her palms when in trance. Preliminary tests conducted with Usha do not indicate psychic abilities,[11] but more detailed studies may have to be carried out in the future.

## Notes

1. The term *bakia* possibly comes from the word *bak,* meaning speech. It indicates the ability of a medium to converse with the spirits. Reports of mediumship or possession are frequent in the region, but most mediums are not capable of carrying on a conversation during consultation. Therefore there are only a few *bakias* in Garhwal.

2. Srinagar, part of the District Pauri in U.P., India, is situated in a small valley on the bank of the upper Ganga (Ganges). It comprises an area of about 9 square kilometers and has a population of approximately 9,000.

3. Garhwalis, being Hindus, are divided into two main classes, i.e., *bashisht* (superior), comprising *Brahmins* and *Rajputs,* and the *Dom* (low caste). The *bashisht* interact freely among themselves but the *Dom* (former untouchables) still constitute the artisan class. *Vaishya,* another caste, ranking third in the caste system, cannot be found in Garhwal.

4. On questioning why possessions commenced only after marriage, Usha replied that some of her (husband's) family did not appreciate her religious fervor. The goddess then decided to intervene. Because one does not become a *bakia* of his / her own choice, Usha ventured the opinion that the deity chooses people who are naive.

5. In mainstream Hinduism, Durga is a ferocious manifestation of the Hindu goddess, Parvati, the consort of Siva. Durga is foremost known for subduing the buffalo demon. In the Himalayas, it is believed that Dhari was an *avatar* (manifestation) of the goddess Durga, born to a family in Garhwal hundreds of years ago. She became a favorite with her parents because of her noble thoughts and deeds which gave rise to jealousy among her brothers. Therefore, one day, she was killed by them and thrown into the river Ganga. As the story goes, her head flowed down the river and stopped at the banks near Srinagar where it stayed for about six months. At that time, Dhari instructed a boatman (*dhunar*) in his dream to retrieve the head which had turned into stone. In another dream, a pundit was directed to place the stone into a temple.

6. On demand of a deity, a *mandan* is held in the village with drummers beating their drums. Any one of the spectators may become possessed by the deity and begin to dance.

7. The drummers are low-caste professionals who alone can play the beats during a *mandan.*

# Profiles of Contemporary Shamans

8. According to Mrs. Rudola, during trance her body becomes like a flower. Her forehead will be full of radiant light and "human" feelings are lost though consciousness remains.

9. The healing neither involves laying on of hands, nor psychic surgery, nor diet control, nor herbal mixtures, it appears to be more of a "verbal" treatment.

10. On the basis of the number of visitors they have during one session, *bakias* may be divided into three categories:
   i. unsuccessful, with an average of 1 or 2 visitors, often none,
   ii. average success, with 5 to 10 visitors, and
   iii. highly successful, with 20-40 or more visitors.

11. Some of the experiments are described in greater detail in the *Journal of the Society for Psychical Research*, No. 811 (April 1988):60-70.

# Elizabeth Cogburn

# A Caucasian Shaman

## by Sarah Dubin-Vaughn

From a mud-walled house near Taos, New Mexico, Elizabeth talks about her "calling."

*There have been many calls, or actually something like "waves of calls." But even before those, I can look back to the entries in my mother's journals when I was between a year and a half and two years old..." Betsy's having visions again tonight" and at another date, "Fairies came and took Betsy away again tonight when I was getting her ready for bed." Those were the first indications that there was something different about my life. In many ways, I was very isolated as a child. School was a nightmare. My peers seemed to be afraid of me and scornful of me, and it was as if I was too much, too strong, too active, too intense, too excited; my eyes frightened people. However, I never felt alone, because there were myriads of unseen people who came to play with me. And also animals. I was given to understand by my parents that I was somehow different, and somehow special. And every-*

*thing in my young life corroborated that. I never fit
into the patterns of ordinary life.*

Elizabeth Cogburn is best known for re-claiming the
heritage of sacred ritual dance for Westerners. The ritual long
dances she created celebrate each of the eight points in the
cycle of the year, i.e., the solstices, equinoxes, and the four
midpoints between them. In doing so, she has earned a unique
position among teachers and ritualists. She has led the New
Song Ceremonial Sun Dance at the summer solstice for the
past seventeen years. The dance was well established long
before white people became interested in Native American
sun dances.

She was "called" to dance, i.e., she developed her own
"natural" dance in a quite innocent way, with no hint that this
would lead her to an almost forgotten tradition of sacred
dance. In addition, she was also "called" to carry the Western
interpretation of the shamanic Qabalah tradition. In an ongoing creative process, she leads New Song ceremonials
which combine ecstatic dance with practices on the Tree of
Life (the teaching glyph of the Qabalah).

Mircea Eliade (1964) said that the "sacred" is "an element
in the structure of consciousness" and not merely a "state" of
consciousness or part of the contents of human consciousness.
A major task for our times is to discover ways to re-activate
this element in a culture that has, for the most part, until
recently disdained anything that speaks of spirit, the sacred or
religious feelings.

Elizabeth talks about having been "programmed" or prepared generally for the "call" by both her illustrious frontier
heritage and her childhood experiences. To explain what she
means by "programmed," she offers a fundamental philosophical explanation:

*Our sacred ceremonial theater is always enacting in
a variety of ways "the stories the people live by." Of
course, one of the major tasks of our contemporary
work, is the re-membering, re-formulating, the conscious choosing of the stories we are living by. I see*

*this as integral to...a mystical expression for the perfection, completion, wholing of the Self and the manifestation of earth of ever more highly evolved expression of the One Intelligence, which is the core purpose of all phases of our New Song Ceremonial Theater.*

*...We have all chosen our parents and our life circumstances in council with our guides and teachers even before we were born, because these are exactly the next teachings the Soul needs in Its evolution toward completion....The name of the game (what I call "High Game") is to claim the whole life, the pathology, dysfunction, and wounding right along with the wholesome values, support, and accomplishments.*

*...Transmuting the energy of these woundings into mutual empowerment and service to the celebration of Life is the task of the apprentices seeking initiation into higher consciousness; this is the work which comprises Rites of Passage.*

Reflecting on her own early childhood, Elizabeth says,

*When I look at the chaos I was born into, grew up in, and struggled to create a viable life out of, I can now see that all those wildly contradictory and intense varieties of experience were appropriate and necessary schooling and preparation for the "call" I feel assigned to carry out.*

All of her known ancestors were "different and special." She spent her childhood with well educated parents living a bohemian life style, going from city to country and back again to repeat the cycle. Through her maternal grandmother alone, she

*can count four generations of bright, passionate, strong-minded, independent, tough and beautiful women, beginning with Mary MacClean MacDonald of the isles of Iona and Mull, who risked the high seas and the wilds of Georgia Bay, Canada, with her husband and eight kids rather than be herded into "crofts" under a British policy that parallels ours with Native Americans.*

Not so much is known of her paternal ancestors except that "they were builders (and masons) across Kentucky, Missouri, Iowa, and Nebraska," but her "paternal grandmother was another strong-minded woman who passed along to me many valued hints about being a 'feminine' woman."

*In the early 1960s, after a couple of years of improvisational dance work with the Mary Whitehouse group in Berkeley (my husband was teaching at the University of California and I had just taken my master's degree in psychiatric social work), I was told that my natural dance—very undulating, round, flowing, strong, sensual—resembled Polynesian and Middle Eastern women's dance forms and I was encouraged to explore more disciplined training in one of those forms. I began training with Jamilla, a great Middle Eastern dance teacher; and working with her was like coming home. The dance permeated my dreams, visions, and waking life as a great woman's prayer dance, the dance of the daughters of the Feminine Divine Creatrix giving form, substance, and birth of Life in the manifest world....I learned to hold the images of life I sought to create...as I danced and as I taught the dance to others.*

The assassination of John F. Kennedy in the fall of 1963 caused her husband to realize that he couldn't face thirty years living and teaching in Berkeley. He, therefore, resigned from a desirable position in the Statistics Department of UC Berkeley on the eve of his tenure appointment. They left Berkeley in the summer of 1964 with two daughters, ages five and three, taking only what they could carry in and on their VW bus. Elizabeth's aging mother, Kathleen Summitt, joined them in the adobe house in Taos which became their home base for the next six years. In 1970, both Cogburns decided that their creative work and the education of their daughters required the "addition of a more urban base." Her husband went back to full-time teaching and research in mathematics and she wanted a dedicated circle of dancers. Her husband was offered a tenure position in the Mathematics Department at the University of New Mexico and they settled in Albuquerque, keeping the adobe house in Taos.

The years in Taos had set the stage for further initiations that took her back to the earth. Elizabeth often says, "In my mother's milk I was given the wisdom of my earth connection." Kathleen, her mother, living from her earliest years on the prairies of South Dakota, passionately loves the earth,

*the smells of river mud and driftwood fires of willow, cottonwood, everything that was natural and native. The ways and wisdom of the native people were much more akin to her soul than the starched linens, Haviland china, and polished sterling of her town life. As a young girl, she figured out how to cut school, leave her petticoats and long black stockings in a bundle under the board sidewalk and hike down to the Sioux camps behind the Indian school. There she spent many happy days in the tipis and tents of the Sioux people who welcomed her, were very kind, and taught her many things. It was from them that she learned to "put your troubles in your Sacred Middle and sleep on them" and things will come out all right. Mamma added that "the Holy Ghost will take care of them" from her own conviction and experience—this was a time when local whites had little or no respect for Indian ways or wisdom.*

Elizabeth continues,

*In my lovely isolated grade school years back in Chicago, one of the best entertainments for me and my brother was to open Mamma's old treasure chest in her sunny upstairs room and she would draw out one old album or artifact after another and tell endless stories from her life and those of our people. The best part for me was when she unwrapped what she called*

*her "medicine bundle" and spread out her treasures
that had been given her by her Sioux friends, i.e.,
porcupine quill bracelets, beautifully beaded baby
moccasins, a little brass wedding ring (probably trade
goods) which I later wore till it split in two. But the best
part for me was the medicine pipe. She had only the
bowl and said it never had a stem. I don't remember
her telling how she came by it, but I certainly absorbed
how much it meant to her as a treasured symbol of
earth/life-connected prayer that included the trees
and flowers and birds and animals and winds and
clouds and the unseen. We used to have what we called
our "Indian-pioneer camp" in the apple orchard
where Mamma taught us to build fires and roast corn
and potatoes and we made up all sorts of stories about
who we were and the adventures we had. And sometimes we held pipe councils to settle pretended disputes and prayed real prayers for all creatures.*

In the 1960s, Elizabeth, her husband and her mother often
took the two little girls to the Pueblo dances where the kids
learned to sit extremely still so that the *koshare,* sacred
clowns, wouldn't come around and poke fun at them. Respect
for the sacrality of Native American dances is strictly enforced
and the *koshare* are the enforcers. She kept asking herself,
"Where are our dances? Why can't we dance like this?"

"Don't forget," Elizabeth says emphatically,

*My father was an Episcopal priest! And even though
he had a nervous breakdown and had to be committed
to a mental hospital for a time when I was quite young,
and even though he was totally unrelenting in his
abuse of me at times, I was brought up with an intense
sense of the sacred. I can still remember what a master
of the Mass he was and how my brother and I served
as acolytes. I took care of all the linens, candles,
flowers, incense, bells, book changes from one side of
the altar to the other during services, and all of our
vestments. He was wonderful at the high Mass. He had*

75

*a rich voice, deep passion for the liturgy and cel-
ebrated Mass as if it was the first day of the world. For
me the heavens opened and I joined the spiralling
choirs of angels before the throne of God! At age
seven! Doré's etchings of the Bible and the hymnal
which I knew by heart came totally alive for me in these
visionary ecstasies during which I sometimes fainted
and missed my acolyte cues. At these times, in contrast
to how he was at other times, my father was unfailingly
kind and tender in ministering to me. I know that a gift
I carry from my father is an absolute sense in my cells
of what real living ritual might be!*

She adds that the dogmatic form of Christianity has always
been a problem for her but, deep within herself, "the essential
truths and the feeling of that essence of the Western tradition
are what I've been able to take out of that part of my cultural
heritage."

Chief Seattle reportedly said the white man might destroy
the red man but the red man would come back, in the white
man's skin. Elizabeth has heard a similar story attributed to the
last chief of the Arapaho. She also likes a saying by Brooke
Medicine Eagle: "All are Native Americans who have been
here long enough to be made of the dust of their ancestors'
bones." Questions whether she was trained with Native
Americans or which Indian tribe she is affiliated with, irritate
Elizabeth. Like for shamans all over the world, her training
came from guides in dreams, both waking and sleeping.

*They're always near, waiting to slip in another piece
of instruction or image, when I am open to it....People
of European ancestry—and I'm one of them—don't
understand. They think the lineage is handed down in
some direct, external, linear way. But that's not the
way it happened for me at all. For instance, while I was
living in Taos, in about 1968, I had a visitation. It
wasn't from an Indian guide at all; and maybe that's
why I didn't get fixated on trying to be like the Indians.
I was wide awake, standing on my feet, but in a vision
state, when this entity came into the room and de-*

*clared to me that he was here as my guide on this journey. At another time, he came to me and embraced me and said, "all right, now it's time to begin the deep work."*

I asked Elizabeth, "Weren't you scared when this guy showed up?" "Remember...when I was a kid...I spent an entire year in a room by myself?" When she was eleven, her father decided that the schools weren't teaching her anything and tutored her himself at home. During this time, she was rarely allowed out of the confines of her own room. "Well," she continues almost impatiently, as if I should know this part of the story already for it is so familiar to her. "This guy had been there all the time. I cannot remember any time in my whole life this guide wasn't there." The tone of her voice changes as she remembers another phase in her life:

*But when I got married, and was having the kids, that all receded for a period. There just wasn't time for interaction with the spirit world then. I was totally taken up with Bob, the first true friend I'd ever had, and then with the babies.*

Elizabeth was married four years and suffered several miscarriages before her first daughter was born, and since she and her husband had wanted children so much, there was little room for much else during those years. But then,

*he leaped back into the room, and in a way, I was embarrassed by it. I was taken totally by surprise, and I wanted to say to him, "don't talk so loud; somebody might hear you! Don't just come walking back into my life like this! Be more circumspect!"*

Elizabeth explains that she recognized the entity as her spirit guide, a spirit partner or lover, referring to Eliade's remarks that quite commonly shamans have both an earth mate or partner and a spirit partner, each of whom serves a specific function in a shaman's life.

In 1970, in Albuquerque, the guide significantly appeared in a dream:

*We were both in a boat, in a storm, and the waves were strong; we were trying to get to the shore, when I fell out of the boat and was washed up on the sand, just lying there trying to recover. I looked up, and he was coming in a Van Gogh kind of boat. He looked like what we now think of as the Hermit [of the Tarot]. He was wrapped in the Hermit's robe, and he was holding in his left hand the negatives...and he knelt beside me and said, "I've got them, I've got them....It's all right, you just rest; I've got the negatives." These negatives or blueprints were the imprints of those master patterns, i.e., the Tree of Life.*

Elizabeth took up the study of the Qabalah but did not fully incorporate it into her dances until well into the 1980s.

The Sun Dance in Taos has very simple, almost casual, origins. At first, there were "mudding" parties to resurface the Taos house. There were corn feeds and big dances at the harvest times, then there was the bringing of prayers into the dances. There was an urge in the community "to do ceremony, a desire to drum and dance and sing in a sacred manner." Elizabeth knew that if the community could improvise with the dance, as they had already been doing, then they could also improvise with their voices. Without a hundred years of tradition behind them, they knew they'd have to find the "new song."

At about the same time, Elizabeth was also moved to "getting to know the drum." (She now considers this another wave of the "call" to develop skills necessary for her work as a shaman). In native terms, the drum is a sacred "being" with whom one builds a relationship, entering into an agreement to combine human efforts with the drum's essence and thereby co-create the sound field for the dance. As if by magic, a drummer appeared and served as her teacher. He said, "Why don't we go out on this barren cliff over the Rio Grande and just drum." This was like sixteen hours straight of drumming a steady pulse beat. Elizabeth says, "We used to greet the full moon rising over Taos and drum straight through to sunrise." At that time, there were no women drumming. "This is where we really started," she says, "this man gave me images of women drumming in the streets of Morocco. He put a drum in my hands and gave me instructions." During those early moon rituals, she learned the truth of the drum: "All the songs of the universe are contained in the one-one-one-one beat; the drum will show the way to the dance and the song." Today, the ceremonial drum is the key instrument in all her dance rituals.

At the second year's Sun Dance, she began to put up a pole because there was a need to have something "to focus on."

*Gradually I attracted a group of people who were willing to hang in over the years, year after year, discovering from our own meditations and dreams and reflections on dance events what we needed. It's always been a collective image—in no way can I claim to be the solitary envisioner/creator of our form and structure; the cues, clues, and basic impetus to direction have almost always been an interweaving of vision from within and the input from the community.*

About the relationships between the New Song Ceremonial Sun Dance and Native American sun dances, Elizabeth says:

*I have never been interested in imitating Indians either as to life styles or ceremonial forms. I have learned a great deal about ceremonial process from careful observation of Indian rituals in this country, Canada, Mexico, and Guatemala. I have also studied ceremonial process among Tibetans, Nepalese, and Balinese. But I believe that imitating the forms of other peoples is inappropriate and misses the whole point of living ritual which must rise and evolve out of our own life experience and felt needs. It seems to me that ultimately the Ageless Wisdom, the Mystery Teachings, the Perennial Philosophy flow from one source and appear in myriad cultural forms. I believe it can always be discovered anywhere anytime by dedicated seekers.*

*My experience leads me to believe that there are certain archetypal forms coded in the collective con-*

*sciousness of the human race—forms such as the
Center Pole, the Tree of Life, the spiral, the circle, the
orienting wheel or mandala—and that these forms
will spring forth spontaneously in dedicated working
ritual groups. What native people have given me that
I most treasure is confirmation and encouragement to
claim and express deep inner knowings about the
oneness of all life, the existence of unseen powers
beyond the human, and the desirability and possibility
of rich communication with them, and the power and
joy of sacred ceremonies in maintaining a balanced
life and evolving beyond present states of consciousness.*

Elizabeth carries a medicine pipe, the most sacred of all
objects to the Native American Indian. The pipe first appeared
to her in a dream. She then went to Pipestone, Minnesota,
where Native Americans have always gotten their pipes. After
looking at all pipes on display and not finding the one she'd
seen in the dream, she asked if there might be other pipes. The
woman in charge showed her the complete storehouse of
hand-carved pipe bowls and, indeed, there was the pipe she'd
dreamed off. It had been carved by a woman. During her
discussion over the pipes, she learned that, in the old tradition,
one always dreams the pipe s/he is to carry.

Elizabeth kept the pipe for a couple of years and then, in
another dream, the pipe spoke to her and said, "I want you to
really take me up or really put me down." Elizabeth answered,
"I would be happy to pick you up, but I don't feel qualified."
And the pipe came back, "I am the New Song Pipe and will
teach you what I want you to know and do." The pipe has been
carried in a sacred manner, honored, revered, and treated with
great respect since that time. It has also been confirmed and
blessed by esteemed Native American pipe carriers.

When I pressed her further about Indians among her
guides, Elizabeth remembered an early dream in which the old
woman at the back of the forest, back of the mountain, began
to appear to her. This was in 1968 when she wanted so much
to dance. The old woman turned out to be Fannie Flounder,

one of the great medicine women of the Yurok people. She was a dancing medicine woman who said emphatically and with sincere assurance to Elizabeth," Oh my dear, you will dance!" Elizabeth says, "She really scared me!" Later she was able to corroborate the stories of this late, revered old shaman with a nephew of Fannie Flounder.

Elizabeth's full initiation as a shaman didn't come until 1975. It required that she perform and endure a lengthy ritual dance sequence which was uniquely hers.

*I was called into training for a year to prepare these dances, and all that I was given was a phrase. I was told that when I was able to fully "indwell," to dwell within the field of consciousness...the choreography would occur spontaneously....the understanding was that these were my investiture dances, my enmantling dances. And they took place on a sand bar in the Rio Grande on May 20, 1975. Those were my initiation dances.*

*After they had reviewed my year's work, which was the spiritual practice of dancing every day to Bach B-Minor Mass, they asked me what I wanted and I said, "I want my wings." They said, "Very well, you will be given your wings when you take up your sword." I protested that I didn't have anything to do with swords, and they said, "It's not the way you think. We'll show you your sword; we'll teach you and show you how to use it."*

*Then, driving through a remote part of Arizona with Bob and another shaman companion, I suddenly leapt up from the back of the van and said. "Stop! Stop! Stop! My sword is out here! My sword is out here!" Because my bladder was filled to bursting, I went running up the slope beside the road, too much in a hurry to look for the sword first. As soon as I was out of sight of passing cars, I squatted down with great relief, and right there in a perfect sunburst was this yucca plant with a bunch of magpie feathers right in the middle of it. At that moment, something clicked,*

81

*and I knew that this was the sword. It has no blade, it's one of those yucca swords! It has a point instead of a blade, and it works like a prod!*

*It took me years to learn that. The dance then condensed into "Take up your sword. And when you have really taken up your sword, you will your wings" ....the whole point of the dance was an exercise in learning that one must fall on one's own sword, and part of the essence of it was to withdraw the adversary projection; the adversary is within, so you fall on your own sword. Well, I fell on the sword.*

*It was my birthday, and my mother sat in a beautiful willow shrine to the east; my mother and the two shamanic companions who attended me had all agreed that whatever happened, including if I died, they would not intervene, they would simply be there. I had been instructed earlier, back in February, to assemble a circle of twelve dancers in Albuquerque that I had worked with, and I taught them a whole series of dances.... they played instruments at certain points, they sang at certain points, they did choral dances outside the ring where I was dancing at certain times, and when I fell on the sword, they told me later, nobody moved for 15 minutes—they were all so deeply in the inner life that was happening. I passed out...into a deep trance....*

*I knew I was in the underworld, and there were certain people I was concerned about, and I could see the shapes and textures and contours and states of their souls. I knew what they needed. And I knew where I was, and I was in total bliss. At the end of the whole thing, I came to and we went off the dance ground and had time for recovery. Then there was a great sweeping dance of the wings. "You will your wings." My mother came and laid upon me a white silk mantle, and as she did so, she pronounced my shamanic name which is from the Qabalah. The name had been given me earlier in a dream by a shamanic guide who was semitic. He came to me with those burning eyes and announced my name. I said, "So, who are you?" And he said, "Well, I'm here to guide you. I'm one of your guides, in particular realms and regions." So this was my initiation as a shaman and I was told, "These are your initiation dances and your next assignment will follow."*

Elizabeth continued to lead ritual dances in New Mexico and, in 1977, affiliated with Jean Houston as a teaching associate. Through Jean Houston's recognition, confirmation, encouragement, and the invitation to work with her the national connection was made. In June 1978, for example, Elizabeth staged a one-day Sun Dance ritual in New York.

Since that time, the New Song Sun Dance has been held exclusively in the west: New Mexico, Utah, and Colorado. From 25 to 40 participants come from all over the country for the two weeks in the wilderness. Ages range from one year to ninety. The ritual itself is made up of a series of ceremonies that pertain to the life of all people. The entire event serves to train each individual in greater knowledge of the Self. Living with a group in such primitive conditions serves to teach participants to cooperate at all levels of community life. The habits of one's normal life are suspended by necessity, and everyone shares in the physical work of the camp, ranging from digging and maintaining latrines to constructing the Sun Dance Lodge and the music pavilion to preparing the food in a communal kitchen to assuming active roles in creating the ceremonies. Celibacy is practiced, so married couples sleep in separate tents. There are long periods when normally practiced social interactions are suspended and silence prevails. Extensive psycho-spiritual practices on the Tree of Life take up the mornings of the three preparation days, the afternoons, following siesta, being devoted to practices in drumming, instrumental sound fields, body movement, and vocal work.

The Sun Dance itself takes place after the first week's work and continues for three or four consecutive days and nights, during which time neither the drumming nor the human movement stop.

*The "practice" is the ceremonial dance theater of the Tree of Life. Take the Tree of Life as a unified field pattern and a method for healing human consciousness and moving toward what we call wholeness. It is not irrelevant to remember that the Tree of Life in the Garden of Eden is said to bestow everlasting life, and that the leaves on the Tree of Life in the heavenly Jerusalem of Revelations are for the healing of the nations. We're concerned with the image of the Tree of Life with its roots in the earth, addressing ourselves as earthlings, and all that being native human implies—being touched with organic instinctive belly wisdom. As well, we're concerned with the Tree of Life with its roots in heaven, as an image of our knowledge that the universe is mental.*

Elizabeth understands theater "as a place of enactment... [where] we are enacting in our partly formal, partly improvised dance dramas aspects of the stories we live by."

*The stories of each person's soul journey are shared in council and elaborated in the dance. As in all great sacred ceremonial dance traditions, the inner work of self-examination and re-patterning that precedes and follows the main dance event are of utmost importance to the personal transformation process and the creation of depth, richness, and intensity in the dance. The aim of our practice is.... the perfection of the Self and the manifestation of more evolved and harmonious life for all beings.*

The ceremonies and rituals of which the Sun Dance is the ultimate enactment, serve the community in many ways, but essentially, effect deeply felt healings of wounded souls. Elizabeth's views of herself as a healer are

*that the greatest root cause of dis-ease is blocked creative energy. One of the greatest gifts for healing that can be given to the people is the opportunity to create—to create ourselves, to create something that is beautiful for all of us, and to do this in a communal and corporate way. And this is what's happening in the dance. Then each person creates him/herself all throughout the year and can come back with good hunt stories; this begets a whole flow of life as a work of art. The individual is the artist, the creator that gets this flow going. And this is how I feel I serve as a healer.*

One of the driving forces that kept Elizabeth going was her own healing. Through regular ritual celebrations, artfully created and continuously practiced around the cycle of the year, she and her people maintain their equilibrium, find and maintain points of balance for themselves. Participants in the ritual dances report that they not only heal old wounds, but they also learn how to live their lives throughout the year, accepting challenges, which often tend to depress the spirit, as sources of meaning and causes for celebration.

In shamanism, emphasis is often placed on the healing of individual illness, either psychological or physical, but another function of a shaman is also the healing of the group by revitalizing the human spirit through the use of ceremonies and ritual. Then, art is returned to its original function and life seen in larger terms. Human consciousness is trained to multi-track, i.e., to know that there are two distinct ways of being, that the "involved self" and the "witness self" are present simultaneously. The attainment of ecstasy is, furthermore, as basic a human need as food, drink, and sleep. If the expression of ecstasy is denied and not guided toward life-creating functions, it will erupt in violence and lead to pathology and/or war.

# Jerzy Grotowski

# A Shaman Director

## by Etzel Cardeña

> *We do not demonstrate action to the viewer,*
> *we invite him...to take part in the "shamanism"*
> *in which the living, immediate presence*
> *of the viewer is part of the play acting*
> Jerzy Grotowski (1986:49).

In his preface to Jerzy Grotowski's collection of essays, *Towards a Poor Theatre* (1968), Peter Brook, one of the most innovative and successful theater directors of the century, concluded the presentation of his Polish counterpart by stating that "The intensity, the honesty and the precision of his work can only leave one thing behind. A challenge. But not for a fortnight, not for once in a lifetime. Daily." These words, written while Grotowski was still engaged in theatrical innovation, are both prophetic of my own reaction to my experiences with a Mexican theater group working along the lines of Grotowski's own inquiry, and a subtle introduction to what would come later in the Polish director's career, i.e., a program to alter the basic consciousness, social and cultural structures that we have inherited along with the belief that they are immutable, to create an "active culture" where dichotomies, such as process/product, actor/spectator, are overcome.

Grotowski, first in the small scale of theater audiences, later in the vast expanses of natural settings in Europe and other continents, has pushed the thin thread between life and art to its breaking point, so that participants have the possibility to reacquaint themselves with their bodies, their surrounding and their fellow human beings, in a different way than they have exercised to that point. His goal is not the induction of exotic states of consciousness for their own sake, but to "cleanse the doors of perception" so that a direct contact with physical and organismic reality can be established without the mediations of conceptual filters or psychological defensive strategems.

Calling a theater director, no matter how successful or creative he might be, a shaman of the twentieth century, requires explanation, lest the term becomes nothing more than an extravagant compliment. Art, with its obvious invitation to question and even subvert the conventional interpretation of reality, has been the activity of many visionaries who, given communal support and other cultural circumstances, might have become shamans in hunter-gatherer societies. Shamanic traditions, either as a historical starting point or, paradoxically, as a utopian goal for twentieth century avant garde, have exerted pervasive influence in the arts, particularly in those forms (e.g., theater, performing arts, dance) in which the artist is his or her own medium. But Grotowski's claim to a shamanic robe (including the ability to induce changes in conscious states for the healing of the shaman's community) is stronger than that of almost any other artist or, for that matter, of any Westerner. A brief review of some landmarks in his development support this contention.

Born in 1933, Grotowski was the enfant terrible of Polish theater throughout his studies and first productions. In addition to being influenced by Stanislavsky and Meyerhold, common for individuals involved with the theater, he undertook a two-month trip through Central Asia in 1956 where, among other things, he saw a mime who would later compel him to describe some of the clear motifs of his work, namely nature and universal patterns embodied in unique individuals. "Nature—changeable, movable, but permanently unique at the same time—has always been embodied in my imagination as the dancing mime, unique and universal" ("Ekran," Grotowski, 1986:18). Around the same time, he must have been involved in extensive reading of Eastern philosophical and psychological books because he gave, in 1957, sixteen lectures on "The Philosophical Thought of the Orient," including Yoga, Buddhism, and Taoism. These lectures exemplify two other important strategies in his path: the recourse to non-Western traditions and, as indicated by his interest in Yoga and the later writings of Stanislavsky, the use of physical disciplines to produce changes in the ordinary modality of consciousness and ways of relating to one's body and the world at large.

During the 1960s, Grotowski saw his role change from that of a theater director of a small experimental theater group in Opole to, arguably, the most influential theater developer of new acting techniques and forms of representation of the second half of the century. Although heavily criticized in Poland, during the second part of the sixties, Grotowski's outstanding productions earned him enthusiastic praises from some of the most important theater figures in the world, e.g., Peter Brook, from England; Jean Louis Barrault, from France; Joseph Chaikin, from the USA, etc. A number of young and eager theater groups took the collection of his articles edited in *Towards a Poor Theatre* (1968) as the method of acting and performance creation. This vertiginous ascent in Grotowski's fame can be explained in many different ways, but certainly some of the elements that contributed to his impact in the world are:

1. *the incessant and uncompromising concern with the basic themes of human existence, among them, the nature of madness ("Kordian," produced in 1962), the search for meaning and salvation in the era of extermination camps ("Akropolis," produced in 1962) and the feasibility of human dignity*

*and purity even amidst intense suffering ("The Constant Prince," produced in 1965);*

2. *the development of an honest and valid encounter among humans, at first explored through the use of the audience as a close, in every sense, and intimate element of the production (for instance, in the production of the "Tragical History of Doctor Faustus," 1963), the audience members were treated as guests to a banquet offered by Faustus), later in the fostering of spontaneous communal rituals.*

3. *an extraordinary program of actoral training that, instead of the conventional accumulation of skills, proposed a methodical and totally committed liberation of the actor's body and psychology through the exploration and exposure of any form of self-deception and limitation. The final product of the exploration of the actor's spontaneity and direct reaction/perception was a total commitment to every action during the performance, a "total act" unmediated by the conceptual apparatus and personality distortions and defense (the foremost example of this approach might have been Ryszard Cieslak in "The Constant Prince," in which his performance was commonly described as involving an altered state of consciousness that allowed him to endure the incredible physical and psychological demands placed upon him).*

4. *closely related with the above, Grotowski's proposal of a "poor theater" that, in contrast to the increasing technicality of commercial ventures, requires only the direct contact between the, literally, self-sacrificing act of the performer and an audience willing to partake of the communal ritual of atonement and purification.*

Despite the evident acclaim and success of his activities of the sixties, Grotowski decided to take much further his "statement of principles" (1968), which included a need to learn with others what our unique experiences and organisms can teach us, to eliminate the constant self-deception and social strategems involved in common relationships, to go beyond the limitations created by ignorance and cowardice, "to fill the emptiness in us." In the late 1960s, thousands of people—both inside and outside of the theater—in different countries were eager to experiment the intimacy, honesty and intensity of Grotowski's work increasingly, he saw that even the decreasing distinction between performers and audience was still a limitation to an honest encounter among the people wanting to establish a sense of community among themselves and with nature.

In the 1970s, Grotowski abandoned any new projects framed within performance conventions and initiated a number of "paratheatrical" events, with names such as "Holiday" and "Project: The Mountain of Flame," in which participants met for a number of days and nights to explore the possibilities of being human in a setting minimizing hierarchical and verbal interaction. In these events, people from many parts of the globe met in a specific place, maybe a forest, and with minimal, frequently non-verbal, guidance from Grotowski's associates, explored the sense of freedom and re-encounter with other human beings, with the natural place and, ultimately, with themselves. These goals were sought through the blossoming of ritual activities initiated by any participant(s), then continued by other spontaneous, "organic" (in the sense of directly physical, spontaneous, non-conceptual) patterns of individual and group reactions.

In the late 1970s and through 1983, Grotowski decided to explore more methodically the common forms of "natural," organismic expression and ways of liberation found in different traditions, to investigate the "sources" of creativity and consciousness expansion. With a multi-national core group of thirty-six people (from India, Haiti, Poland, USA, etc.), he explored traditional techniques utilized among the Huicholes in Mexico, the Haitian Voudun practitioners, the Yoruba of Africa, and the yogis of India. This stage in Grotowski's work was designed the "Theater of Sources" and provided the basis for his current work on "Objective Drama" being carried out at the University of California, Irvine.

In his latest endeavor, Grotowski has unified his long-standing interest in rhythmic motion and sound patterns that, presumably, have a direct effect on biological functions and conscious experience, with his leading toward a rigorous, systematic approach. In ongoing work with traditional "master" performers and ritualists from various traditions (for instance, a Sufi dancer and Haitian ritualists), Grotowski's "technical specialists," accomplished and versatile performers, learn and record the movements and sounds of the traditional "masters" and later perform and teach those patterns to others.

In recent years, Grotowski has concentrated on the technical education of future performers, both at the University of California, Irvine, and at his Center in Italy (Grotowski, 1987:30-41). While his research on specific human actions (e.g., physical movements, songs, etc.) that help to transform the human nervous system and expand conscious capabilities has continued, he recognizes that these techniques are fraught within specific cultural traditions that cannot be fully taught or learned by an outsider. These techniques—what he calls *organons* of *yantras*—can nevertheless be discovered/developed/explored within one's own performing tradition to allow the display of what is both deeply personal, unique, and historical, and ahistorical, biological, continuous.

In his extraordinary career of three decades, the Polish director/shaman has come full circle to the origins of theater: the elimination of the illusion of disconnectedness (with one's body, with human-made and natural rhythms, with others, with the Universe at large) through shamanic performance and communal rituals, and back to the specialization of master performer/shamans who use their artistry to wage battle with inner and outer demons to reveal the joys and terrors of the human condition. Grotowski, himself austere, has combined an uncomprising shamanic quest with the role of a trickster par excellence. The theater director and shaman who, while not in view as a performer, creates the possibilities for transcending human limitations and, from his corner, directs fellow travelers.

## References

Grotowski, Jerzy. "Tu es le fils de quelqu'un" [You are somebody's son], *The Drama Review,* 31:3 (Fall 1987):30-41.

_____. "Playing Shiva" [produced appr. 1959], *Grotowski and His Laboratory,* ed. Zbigniew Osi'nski, transl. & abridged by Lillian Vallee and Robert Findlay. New York: Performance Journal Publications, 1986, p.49.

_____. "Ekran" [produced 1959], *Grotowski and His Laboratory,* ed. Zbigniew Osi'nski, transl. & abridged by Lillian Valley and Robert Findlay. New York: Performance Journal Publications, 1986, p.18.

# Three Urban Shamans in Southeast Asia

The following three profiles are based on my fieldwork in Southeast Asia in 1960, September 1971 to September 1972, summer 1975, June 1978 to June 1979, and spring 1987. I selected urban shamans to prove the emergence of new shamans when needs become so strong that people begin to look for shamans. I chose Southeast Asian shamans not because there are no shamans to be found in the big cities of the West but because I want the reader to experience urban shamans against a background not so close to home.

Of the 2.65 million people living today in the city state of Singapore, 76 per cent of them are Chinese (either Hokkien, Teochew, Cantonese, Hainanese or Hakka), 15 per cent Malay, 6.5 per cent Indian, and 2.5 others (Eurasians and Europeans). Singaporeans have, therefore, not only different ethnic backgrounds but practice also different religions. Malays are predominantly Muslims, Indians either Hindus or Sikhs, and the various Chinese groups go to Buddhist or Taoist temples and may go to Christian churches, too. Some even have converted to Christianity without giving up their visits to shamans and spirit mediums.

The other large Asian city I chose is the capital of Thailand. Bangkok has over six million inhabitants; 80 per cent of them are ethnic Thai, 15 per cent Thai-Chinese, 4 per cent are Malay, and 1 per cent either Indian, hill tribe or other minorities. The majority of Thai are Theravada Buddhists but some Thai-Chinese practice Mahayana customs, too. Thai-Malay are Muslims and Thai-Indians either Hindu or Sikhs.

1. In my first example, *an altar called for a shaman and a shaman was looking for an altar*.

When, in 1970, brushes and trees around Sembawang Shipyard in Singapore had to be cleared, a tractor broke down and brought the work to an unexpected halt. Looking for the reason of this unexpected incident, workers found in the bushes, right in front of the stalled tractor, a Hindu altar. Questioning the residents in this area, it was learned that Indian troops had camped at this site during World War II and had erected an altar on a snake-ridden hill. After the troops had left, Indian workers, living nearby, had taken care of the altar. Thus, a community formed before a shaman appeared.

Two years later, a simple Tamil dock worker dreamed of the altar. First, he could not find the altar in the area around the shipyard, but dreams kept urging him to continue his search until he was successful. The "voices" told him to stay on the hill, everything would be taken care of. The young man waited for weeks but nothing happened. In desperation he kicked the altar and injured his right foot which remained crippled.

Then, Hindu gods began to manifest in his body and, since 1972, every Tuesday and Friday evening, Hanuman (the monkey king who helped Rama to win back the abducted Sita), Rama (the seventh incarnation of Vishnu, see photo 13), Murgam (Siva's son), and the goddess Mahakali speak to a growing community of Tamils, Bengalis, Sikhs, and Chinese. Whatever god manifests, the deity calls those who seek help to the front. Speaking through the body of a humble dock worker, the god blesses, exorcises, heals, alleviates and solves personal problems without needing to listen to the worshipper's plight. In other cases, spiritual powers can be addressed directly or with the help of a translator, here the "divine voice" is the only one heard during the "manifestation."

At the end of each session, the shaman puts burning benzoine in his mouth to purify the channel through which the gods will depart. Afterwards, he distributes the donated food among those present. On other weekdays and on weekends, he advises without falling into trance, i.e., without calling gods into his body. Being a true shaman, he has access to the Divine whenever necessary.

Some years ago, a British colonel donated the roofed platform built around the hill and the altar. It offers protection for up to two hundred followers. The shaman himself lives in a little shed next to the hill. He leads an ascetic life and distinguishes himself from his entourage through his charisma, kindness and modesty. His helpers and assistants, who formed a community before the shaman appeared, respect him only when a god speaks through him. Outside the rituals, they treat him rather roughly. For example, when the shaman gave a lottery number to a follower and the number subsequently won, the winner shared the money with the shaman who used it to visit India. After his return, he was literally tied up by his assistants because he was enjoying himself too much. The assistants apparently fear to lose their means of income. I saw them frequently "borrowing" money out of the donation box.

People from different ethnic groups and with different religious backgrounds come with questions about their health, their career or business or problems within their family. For example, women want to know how they can win back their philandering husband. Mothers may ask how they should treat their vagrant son. When people find their requests answered or their wishes granted, they write their name into the donation book. Donors will then bring a meal on "their day," usually rice cooked with honey and raisins. On week nights there may be sixty followers, on holidays up to two hundred Singaporeans sitting in front of the altar.

The codification of rituals has already begun. Though performed by predominantly "casteless" people, the shaman's assistants emulate brahmin behavior. For them, it is important to perform rituals "correctly." Though there is actually no other authority than the gods themselves to give directions through the shaman, the assistants have become dogmatic and insist on the imitation of certain brahmanic rites.

When I returned to Singapore six years later, in 1985, the hill with the altars had been leveled. The government had finally re-enforced the expansion of Sembawang Shipyard and I was also told that the medium had died.

2. The second case describes the *development of shamanic networks* in an industrial environment.

On October 16, 1978, I was invited to participate in the birthday celebrations for a shrine which had been built near the gate of a ballbearing factory in Jurong, a satellite town of Singapore. It was also the 1105th birthday of the shrine's spirit. Surrounded by the workers of the ballbearing factory, two shamans entered into trance and offered incense and fruit to the spirit.

The main shaman told me later that three years ago, neighbors had warned the factory owner that a spirit was residing at the roots of a certain tree. The area around the tree had already been levelled and an answer to the problem had to be found fast. At that time, the head of the Sales Department introduced the constructor to a group of shamans who then talked with the spirit and, with the help of the monkey god, obtained an answer. (The Chinese monkey god is a mythological being who, in the sixth century A.D., accompanied the Chinese monk Xuan zhang on his journey to India to locate Buddhist scriptures.) The spirit expressed his willingness to move into a new shrine and the constructor was advised to spend, on three consecutive days, some time on the hill. He told me later that once, when he stood on the hill, something moved in the bushes. It turned, however, out to be a stray dog.

Other events took place simultaneously. Wanting to buy a motorboat, the constructor suffered severe burns when the engine exploded on the trial run. Skin transplantations became necessary and he lost the faculty to walk. When the head shaman visited him in the hospital to discuss the construction plans for the shrine, he touched also the feet of the constructor. The next morning, to the great surprise of the hospital staff, the engineer was able to walk again. Without words being exchanged, the traumatic consequences of the accident had been removed by a shaman.

The tree was cut down ceremoniously and earth from the site was put into an urn donated by the constructor. The urn was then ritually installed in the new shrine and the factory workers, who had built the shrine, continued to offer daily flowers and fruit.

This attracted the attention of outsiders. One night, the urn containing the spirit disappeared from the shrine. The shamans were called again and they found out that a second shrine had been built behind the wall of the factory on the opposite side of the street. A cleaning woman had stolen the urn at night and it had been installed in the new shrine. The head shaman talked with the woman who had been stricken by an inexplicable illness after the theft. She returned the urn and asked the spirit for forgiveness. That she recuperated immediately afterwards did not surprise anybody. She had relieved her conscience by making up for her wrong behavior.

Who were these urban shamans? In 1978, the head shaman was a forty-year-old "Straits" Chinese (the term indicates that he and his parents had been born in Singapore). His grandparents, however, had come from Canton. During the day, he worked as a bookkeeper in a sewing-machine factory. Not feeling himself bound to Chinese tradition, he had converted to Catholicism when he was twenty. Already early in life he discovered that he had "good hands" to massage and so he began to experiment with herbal potions as well, studying with a Taoist priest who tried to convince him to commercialize his gift. This was not acceptable to him and he continued, therefore, his studies with Buddhist monks. The most important insights, however, came to him during meditation.

At the age of thirty-three, he began to advise and to heal people after work every weekday night and on Sundays. Saturdays he goes to the Singapore Mental Hospital where patients voluntary come to him. Many have been abandoned by their families. He talks to them and gives them blessed water to drink. Sometime he takes patients into his house. After they have become accustomed to the life outside a mental hospital, he finds work for them. One former patient now drives a truck, others work in factories or in the harbor. Focussing his attention on his patients not their symptoms, this shaman does what modern physicians, psychiatrists or social workers have no time to do.

He is called also in cases of "mass hysteria." Female

Malay-Muslim factory workers are occasionally possessed by spirits. This seems to be connected to the fact that orthodox Muslim societies do not allow women much freedom of movement and expression. Suppressed and repressed emotions are often augmented by frustrations accompanying labor disputes. Spirit possession then gives the women an opportunity to draw attention to their plight in a cultural acceptable way. After having been the focus of an exorcism during which their repressed feelings are brought to a catharsis, these women have no difficulty with reintegrating and returning to their everyday life. The exorcised spirit had been responsible for the possession not they themselves.

Young men have asked this shaman for training. They meditate and fall into trance under his supervision. Some of them are already allowed to bless patients (see, photo 14), others assist with the rituals. Their motives are altruistic. All of them work during the day, as car seller, bookkeeper, nurse, or student. Whatever donations accumulate, the money is spent for patients or hospitality offered to visitors on weekends and during festivals. The donations are anonymously left in small red envelopes on the altar. None of the shamans knows what has been put into the envelope, e.g., a small coin, a dollar or bigger sums. Clients determine themselves how much the advice and help they received are worth to them.

3. The third case describes *how modern Thai acquire shamanic skills.*

I met the shaman I am going to discuss in Bangkok through his secretary who took evening classes at Mahidol University together with my Thai assistant. The shaman was holding a high position in the Ministry of Education and told me, in 1978, that approximately sixty to seventy shamans like him can be found in Bangkok, many of them in high government positions. He added also that they have a long waiting list for those who want to be trained by this group. I do not mean to say that membership in this shamanic group is expected of high government officials or that shamanic training is desirable for those who want to hold certain offices like membership in a masonic lodge was for high officials in the United States in its formative years.

In general, urban Thai rarely inherit their shamanic faculties nor do they receive a "call." They decide themselves to become shamans. Before training, they occupy already high positions in their society, so shamanic faculties don't raise their social status but their mental and spiritual powers certainly increase. Their claim is that they are motivated by their concerns for their and their fellow citizens' well-being.

Because ninety per cent of all Thai are Buddhists, this official was no exception. He wore several Buddhist amulets on a necklace underneath his shirt. The amulets had been given him at different occasions by Buddhist monks. He showed me how he determines the power of these amulets by testing their temperature. He attributes his own success as shaman to meditation practices in his present and former lives.

This shaman's training consisted of seven days concentration exercises which included the teaching of breathing techniques. During two additional days, he learned four mantras to shamanize and four mantras to call the spirits. When he talked about spirits, he used the Thai word *winyan* (spiritual essence) or Phra Phrom (Lord Brahma, a generic term for high-ranking spirits, not Brahma of the Hindu trinity).

People come to him when their houses are haunted or when they want to know where to put the poles for a new house or where to place a new Buddha statue. He remembered a case where the spirit of a small baby was thirsty. He told the parents how to help this spirit and, out of gratitude, a lottery number was revealed which subsequently won.

Born in 1929 from Thai-Chinese parents, he decided early to become a businessman. Later, in 1957, he chose to be a school teacher. He advanced to the position of district director and was soon called into the Ministry of Education. At the age of thirty-seven, he began to shamanize in his free time. His clients belong to the middle and upper classes in Bangkok, but he is also called to "work" in other parts of the country.

One of the shamanic sessions I attended was held in a Thai-style house, made of teakwood and standing on poles approximately a yard above ground. A colleague put on a white garment, because he was to serve as medium. We sat down on the floor in front of the altar with Buddha statues from different periods next to Indian gods. On the walls were photos of monks, one showing the present Thai king in monks' robes during the few weeks he spent in a Buddhist monastery shortly before his coronation. Candles were lit and the official "called the spirits." The white-clad colleague meditated and prepared himself for their arrival.

After a few minutes, his facial expression changed and the Indian god Vishnu began to speak through him. Vishnu announced that he lived in the sixth heaven of *kamaloka* (the World of Desire) where another language is spoken. Vishnu, however, spoke for us in Central Thai and used once in a while Pali terms known to every Theravada Buddhist. The shaman thanked Vishnu for his appearance and the god made room for the spirit of a legendary monk, Phra Narai. The third spirit to appear was Somdetch Toh. In the middle of last century, he had been *Sangharaja,* the highest representative of Buddhism in Thailand. The spirit of this well-known personality delivered a sermon on the Four Noble Truths, the basic teachings of the Buddha. He also blessed some Buddhist medals (see, photo 15).

Shamanic rituals will have a Buddhist touch in Buddhist countries. Shamans may use the "Buddhist connection" to legitimize their practice and Buddhist practitioners may feel the necessity to resort to shamanic practices. The explanation given is that the Buddha has entered *nirvana* and can no longer be addressed by mortals. Appeals can, therefore, be directed only to spirits of the Middle Realm who act as mediators between the world of spirits and the world of man.

There may also be nature spirits residing in trees or mountains. They personify untamed nature, and it is advisable to stay on good terms with them (e.g., the mountain spirit of Doi Suthep near Chiang Mai). All these superhuman powers can be propitiated to serve mankind. It is also said that good deeds on earth improve the spirits' own *karma* (the results of their thoughts, words, and deeds, as has been explained above).

With these three cases I attempted to document the appearance of shamans in Southeast Asian cities. They illustrate shamanic activities in an urban environment. One shaman received a "call," one discovered shamanic faculties and cultivated them, and the third decided to become a shaman and sought the appropriate training.

# The Oracle of the Dalai Lama

John F. Avedon (1984:191-217) has given us a detailed description of a Tibetan tradition which provides for "oracles" who are consulted in important matters of state.

He reports that, for example, on February 14, 1981, 6:00 a.m., the Dalai Lama was sitting on his throne in the Central Cathedral of Daramsala which had become his residence after his flight from Tibet to northern India in 1959. The "oracle" had undergone special meditation practices for two days and had also avoided to eat impure food (fish, pork, garlic, onions). He was assisted by four monks in putting on bulging red brocade trousers, a red silk shirt, two heavy robes "covered by a thick piece of brocade with an opening for the head," and knee-high white leather boots.

After the oracle had been driven to the Cathedral, he was helped into a triangular jacket and a type of backpack which supported four flags with three victory banners.

*The flags, made of doubled-up brocade, hang from flexible metal poles and run the full length of the monk's back; the banners, shaped like a roll of umbrellas, ascend from mid-thigh to above the head and are crowned with golden points. His sleeves are now bound with strips of red cloth; the left one, padded for archery, is stitched with three more scarlet eyes. Then a front piece of exquisite yellow, gold and red silk, its base exploding in hundreds of rainbow-hued threads, conceals all. At its center lies a golden mirror, the cardinal points dotted by clusters of turquoise around an amethyst, its polished silver core emblazoned with the Sanskrit* mantra *of a tantric deity. A three-foot-long silver sheath and sword are buckled on the left side, a golden quiver filled with arrows on the right; a golden thimble, used when drawing back a bow-string, is slipped over the right thumb. These are the accouterments of an epic Tibetan warrior, a hero from the days of Gesar of Ling, Tibet's great legendary king. But, despite the martial nature of the uniform, the monk is not going into combat...in a few minutes' time...his consciousness will be cast aside in trance and replaced with that of Dorje Drakden...chief spirit minister and bearer of counsel for the State Oracle of Tibet (Avedon, 1984:192).*

The actual event starts with the blast of long horns, the music of cymbals, drums, and the chanting of monks. The "oracle"

*can barely walk. Altogether the eight layers of his clothing weigh more than one hundred pounds, the helmet...another thirty pounds. But it is not only his costume that makes it difficult...to move unassisted. He is already starting to enter the first levels of trance. A slight quivering rolls up and down his body. His breathing is short and loud...his eyes are tucked in on the shelf of the skull and have a wild and startled look.*

Then

*The whole countenance becomes clear and pure. The medium assumes a piercing, distant look. He is immersed in the visualization of himself as a tutelary deity standing at the center of a celestial mansion; without this meditation, he is unsuitable for possession (Avedon, 1984:193-194).*

The Dalai Lama whispers secret questions into the "oracle's" ear. Each question is answered quickly. Cabinet ministers, the Chairman and the Vice-Chairman of the People's Deputies join and an official petition is read. Composed "in verse, it requests the revelation of specific aspects of the Dalai Lama's, the Tibetan people's and the government's future. It contains no more than three questions." Questions and answers are this time heard publicly.

Another medium may enter the scene, e.g., the medium of the Gadong Oracle, sometimes called Black Vulture Hat. He is also a minister and one of the protective deities of Tibet, Pehar Gyalpo.

*Unlike the Nechung mediums...those of the Gadong monastery are not monks. The mediumship is passed in a lay lineage from father to son. The present medium is a man in his mid-thirties employed as a secretary in the Dalai Lama's private office (Avedon, 1984:197).*

Avedon maintains that "Tibet's chief oracle has been consulted by the nation's leaders on virtually every key decision of state" for 1,300 years.

The twelfth medium of Tibet's State Oracle was born to a family of middle-class shopkeepers in Lhasa on January 5, 1930. Divination by a well-known lama led the mother to sent the boy to Nechung Monastery where, at the age of ten, he suffered a strange illness, and "his ravings seemed to impart a logic of their own." He was sent to Ganden Monastery where he "started to experience genuine trance on a daily basis," culminating in the message that the Chief Protector "Dorje Drakden will take possession." He was, however, asked to leave Ganden. When he was sixteen, he retired to a cave. Though he fulfilled

*the daily quota of recitation, there was still no discernible change in his condition....one morning, in the middle of the retreat, he woke feeling well for the first time in years....A messenger now arrived bearing the startling information that...the Nechung kuden had died. The day of the medium's death had been the very day on which Lobsang Jigme's illness disappeared (Avedon, 1984:209).*

The Gadong medium announced that "a child of fifteen, born in the Year of the Iron Horse; his name, Lobsang Jigme" would be the prospective *kuden.* Although during the three hundred years of Nechung Monastery's existence, none of the eleven mediums had been selected "from the ranks of its own monks," several tests confirmed the announcement.

*The need to thoroughly test the authenticity of the Nechung kuden had, for centuries, been a critical concern of the Tibetan government. As the most delicate policies of state, both domestic and foreign, were involved with the oracle, the possibility of a leak, either from a malignant spirit taking possession (and subsequently relating information via another medium) or from the medium himself retaining some trace memory of the trance, was ever-present. So, too, was the danger of a garbled or mistaken transmission. To protect against the latter, the level of the medium's trance was closely observed, a complete possession, inducing unconsciousness, being the ideal state. Such a possession could occur only if the 72,000 channels upon which, according to tantric theory, consciousness is mounted in the human body were clear of all obstructions (Avedon, 1984:211).*

Early in 1945, Lobsang Jigme became officially the new medium of the Tibetan State Oracle. His position is precarious. Previous kuden have been executed for revealing secret government information or have been fired because their meditation practice deteriorated. However, Lobsang Jigme has had close relationships with the Dalai Lama since the latter's boyhood and throughout the political unrest in Tibet. He followed the Dalai Lama into his exile at Daramsala.

For more detailed descriptions of the rituals around the state oracle, the history of state oracles, and the life of the oracles themselves, I refer the reader to Avedon's book, *In Exile from the Land of Snows* (1984).

When Buddhism entered Tibet in the seventh century A.D., indigenous spirits were allegedly tamed by the Indian tantric master Padmasambhava. They pledged to support Buddhism and Tibetan Buddhist sages then incorporated the earlier deities in the Buddhist pantheon, transforming the fierce spirits into protectors of the *dharma* (the Buddha's teachings). Indigenous images and customs have, therefore, been deeply ingrained in the Tibetan Buddhist fabric from the beginning.

# Shamanism and Law

How did shamanic knowledge enter the practice of law? Carol, the lawyer I will be talking about, does not necessarily travel to the spirit world to obtain information but she attempts to connect with different levels of consciousness. On one hand, she went through formal university training to become a lawyer and, on the other hand, she studied and practiced traditional shamanic healing with several teachers in California. One of her support groups is

> refining and redefining a traditional Native American ceremony used in conjunction with rites of passage and various stages of initiation. Traditionally, the ceremony requires at least twelve persons to perform, including the patient. The participants are each assigned to hold a position on a medicine circle. Each position represents a part of the psyche. The "patients" tell their personal story while facing the person sitting in the south....The personal myth is then mirrored back in both its light and dark aspects by each of the positions on the wheel, each speaking to the patient in the first person from the particular part of the psyche their positions represents. The ceremony takes several hours to perform and involves following a very precise choreography and invocation of the spirits.

In "handling the energies of the ceremony," participants understand "the essence of the healing process," so that they can heal themselves and also apply elements to their own work as therapists, consultants, teachers, landscape designers, accountants, and lawyers.

Carol considers herself to be a "holistic lawyer" who operates "as a bridge between inner and outer reality" and facilitates "individual and mass paradigm shifts."

The "other reality" was "close at hand" already during her childhood. She would manage to take a cooking pot

> out into the yard, gather grass and leaves and make a brew....I was convinced that, if only I could remember certain formulas, I could create a transmutation of these green materials. An inner debate persisted throughout my childhood as to whether it was more important to develop the faculty of visualizing and believing that the transmutation would take place or remembering or rediscovering the precise steps of combining ingredients and speaking certain words.

She decided to become a lawyer when she was about fifteen.

> I saw that it was lawyers who were the wheels within the political system, and that the political and social situations needed a lot of change. So I needed to...at least acquire the skills of a lawyer...[whose function it] was to serve other people and bring about positive changes for society. With this naive idealism firmly rooted in my consciousness, I sailed through the rest of my academic career studying psychology and philosophy knowing that I would get plenty of the pragmatic nuts and bolts in law school. I graduated and commenced the practice of law at twenty-four, still largely believing that lawyers generally shared my human concerns. My entire experience relating to the goal of acquiring the skills of a lawyer had up to this point been a lot of fun. I had not had to bend, fold, spindle or mutilate myself to don the garb of a lawyer.

Her profession brought her into contact with lawyers

> who definitely did not share my values....I learned that there were some lawyers who genuinely cared about

*their clients' well-being and many who did not. In the course of my private practice in which I was basically my own boss, I became convinced that the standard mode of practicing law was not serving peoples' interests and was perpetuating negativity which injected more conflict and disharmony into society. The more acutely aware of this I became over the course of my first year of practice, the more motivated I became to quit the practice of law entirely.*

*...I had been consciously working on waking myself up through meditation, self-hypnosis, psychotherapy and dream work since my college years...I entered into a deeper sense of independence and interdependence... and now have a systematic way of accessing a deeper level of truth....I saw that most people were trapped in realities that society had programmed them to experience. They were cut off from themselves, the deeper source within them and their access to God and the rest of the universe. They had not had sufficient experiences or positive conditioning to trust the information that came from within themselves.*

*I also observed that the clients I saw and the attorneys with whom I worked had various systematic habits of regimenting themselves (drugs, alcohol, addictive relationships, addictions to money, consumerism and work), so as to keep their inner voices from "getting to them." Further, I observed that it is not the practice of attorneys to listen to their clients nor give them a chance to define what they want.*

Carol's motivation to redress the situation led her to review how she had overcome her own "programming," her hesitation to change and fear of the unknown and how she had recognized her denial to determine what she really wanted to share deep down. She had to decide whether she wanted "to practice law and guide those who came" to

*a territory that was mined with negative programming and experiences that reinforce the tendency to stay in*

*a prison of reality defined by fearful deference to the
"truth" of others?*

Carol studied, for seven years, the shamanic and healing
practices of Native American, African, Asian, and pre-Chris-
tian European traditions. One of her teachers, "Grampa Rob-
erts," rarely performed ceremonies with his patients and when
he did, "he never did it the same way twice." His foremost
principle was the "understanding of universal energy as un-
conditional love."

To work within the legal system, she had to find new
modalities and she had to "walk" her talk. She says,

*People are burdened by fears which prevent them
from fully expressing who they are, what they are here
to share and what they want.*

*Fear is maintained by our false belief that we exist
separate from the spiritual outside of ourselves.
Therefore, when we believe that we are not part of a
spiritual dimension, we experience ourselves as finite.*

*Not being aligned with the truth of our oneness with
the spiritual realm, we generate conflict and disharmony.*

People are largely afraid "to cooperate or to share." There is
a

*need to control and hold onto energy and resources
out of a fear of not having enough and in an attempt to
feed the emotional void that the sense of disconnectedness creates....They really never get enough of what
they don't need.*

She postulates:

*We create what we believe to be true.*

*We have been collectively creating a reality of separa-
tion from the spiritual realm which causes us to see
ourselves and the world as finite. If we knew the*

*infinite source within us, we would relax.*

Her objective of counseling individuals on legal problems, aside from assisting in removing the negative impact of the problem, is to provide an experience in which they are put in touch with their own wisdom and where they begin to trust this information. "The basic way I accomplish this is by inviting them to find their own answers to the questions they present to me. One simple process which I use to accomplish this involves getting them to first define their ideal outcome for the situation." The process works as follows:

*I ask the clients to pretend that there are no limits, and for the moment, we do not have to consider the possible demands of others involved in the situation.*

*I restate to the clients what they have defined as essentially valuable to them. The practice of restating involves a form of active listening in which I attempt to state what it is I have heard they really feel and want until they agree that I have correctly heard them.*

*I ask the clients to define what they believe is possible given their perceptions of the demands of others in the situation and available resources.*

*The clients and I explore the possible assumptions in their perceptions of others and their beliefs in the limitations of resources with which to create.*

*A strategy is then co-designed with the clients. I provide the information concerning the limitations and requirements of the legal or business context in which they are operating and the clients are otherwise encouraged to act in a manner which is consistent with the essential values defined in the first step of the process.*

Carol says that the "magic" comes in when clients identify with what they really feel and want so that she can suggest

*a simple and direct way that it can be implemented*

*which was not apparent upon the initial presentation of the problem. The result is that people are immensely happy that they get to do what they want rather than be imposed upon by the rules of someone outside of them. They are also validated in their own underlying sense of what "should" be done.*

Fears, hesitation, doubts about acting from their own information are dispelled and a strategy on external referents is build up. Carol gives some examples:

*David had come to see me after a year's hiatus. I had helped him with some letters and paperwork to reduce the child support order by which he was bound. He wanted to do as much of the work as possible on his own....he was not successful, however....his concerns were not about money, but rather his loss of contact with his daughter...His daughter had been taken out of the state by his former wife without consulting him or even advising him of her phone number. He had written the child, but was uncertain if and how his cards were presented. He had been living with this situation for some time, so I did not have to respond to a sense of crisis. I did tell him very briefly that it was legally possible to obtain regular contact with his daughter....avoiding giving him any details of how this might be accomplished....*

*We next discussed the process of how it was that he came to me at this time. He was about two and one-half years into his process of recovering from workaholism and alcoholism. He began to identify his pattern of avoidance, of not following through, of becoming distracted from the things that really fed his existence....We explored his relationship with his parents and found a family pattern of abandonment....We then focused on the little girl inside of him. I gave him an exercise to make contact with her as distinguished from his physical daughter....a way he could make contact inside....We adapted the form of inner dia-*

*logue to his practice. I gave him questions to work with: What does your little girl want to receive from/ give to you? What does your daughter want to receive from/give to you?*

At that point, Carol suggested

*that he could begin the healing and deeper bondage process straight away by allowing to see himself at a sacred lake with his former wife and then with his daughter. He could take them into the healing waters and release any recriminations or lack of forgiveness....I asked him for his daughter's birthday. He...answered that it was that day (the Fall Equinox). I suggested that he celebrate her birthday with her at the sacred lake and that he re-image her birth, helping and welcoming her into the world...*

*He came for his follow-up appointment twelve days later. He reported a good birthday celebration and some clear sense of communication with his daughter on her needs. He understood that his daughter needed the chance to work out her feelings and issues on the father-daughter relationship as well. He saw that his own wholeness was dependent on the relationship with his inner and outer little girl/daughter. He had identified more of his old patterns, the compatibility of his and his former wife's addictive behavior, container-izing his relationships by limiting his available time, keeping the flow of his income unstable so he would be prevented from acting fully or consistently. He stated that he believed he was ready to take the step of committing to a regular therapy process, and I offered three names of psychotherapists particularly skilled in the area of recovery.*

*We then moved to translating this new clarity into action in the material plane. He wanted to begin with regular phone contact and wanted his former wife to cooperate in facilitating this. He hedged a little on how much he was willing to impose on her, and I reminded him that a gentle but clear statement of his needs would also serve her to confront her part of the denial in the overall pattern. Something felt incomplete to me....I spontaneously recalled a portion of our previous session where he had described his fear that his daughter believed that he did not care for her because of the absence of contact and that he felt he was doing everything he could. I went to my notes and read these lines back to him, infusing them with the feeling tone with which I had heard them. He saw that he needed to act more directly, more convincingly for his daughter's sake....I then described concrete legal options or contacting his former wife on his behalf. He elected instead to write his own letter advising his former wife of his intent to visit the child and his desire for phone contact. He would practice this task, finding his balance between using strength to threaten and coerce and compromising his need to ask for less than what he wanted. I remained available to him for feedback on his process of learning to express this balance point.*

Mediation is another process Carol uses as an alternative mode of conflict resolution or problem solving. During this process, she assists clients in arriving at their own solution.

*I use much the same communication process as I do on the one-to-one counseling in the presence of two or more parties to the mediation. The energy that is available for change and growth in the counseling process comes from the emotional charge people experience when they finally identify and articulate what it is that they really care about....I have experienced dramatic transformation of participants as they discover and reveal what they really want to their "adversaries." They often see some way in which they are valued by the other person and/or a way which they can now give where they thought the other person was closed to receiving from them....*

*The alchemy of mediation is very appealing to me. You bring together conflicting elements, move through a process of integration by deeply articulating the individualized, often polarized viewpoints, accomplish a discharge of the tension and arrive at a basis for future relationships free of animosity....the synthesis is not possible until each party has really "come clean" and spoken the truth of what is seen from their viewing point and what they want. The alchemy does not work when people are operating from a place of denial of their needs where peace is defined only by the cessation of conflict. So again, my fundamental task is to promote open and honest communications....*

*The greatest potential of my involvement in the process is connecting the present experiences of pain and turmoil of my clients with deeper unresolved issues of their childhood and/or their fundamental concepts of self and the world they inhabit. If this linking is made, there is the opportunity to release the old pattern of reality-making based on the finite model. They also gain an experience of effectively having their needs met in a way that addresses the deeper self instead of placation of the superficial concerns....*

Talking about her work in general, Carol says

*Healing ourselves and bringing harmony to this planet at this point in time of unfolding collective consciousness requires to focus especially on being ourselves. Making ourselves available to the moment...I have to transcend my own programming which predisposes me to control my client's process and to preconceive a "good" result....My job is to get myself out of the way so that the spirit may move what needs to be moved in any given situation....As we live this way, each one of us comes to realize that we are a communicating part of an infinite being or spirit that has chosen to create itself in the diversity of many individualized personalities....Each has a part to be played that is needed by the whole.*

*If I had neither the skills nor processes I have described, I could still support the expression of each person around me by validating their feeling and knowing, helping them see their dreams more clearly, not letting them make my knowing more influential than their own, and simply by allowing them to feel the beauty I experience in knowing and loving them. This, I propose, is the foundation of how "urban shamans" approach the people they serve.*

# What Did We Learn From These Profiles?

S hamans are actively and successfully working in the modern world. Shamanic practices are, therefore, not confined to "backward" or underdeveloped areas but flourish in all cultures, even those that pride themselves on their sophistication. Shamans may hold a Ph.D. degree (Max Beauvoir) or other positions of power (e.g., government officials in Bangkok). We can no longer maintain that shamanism is only practiced by the uneducated or powerless. Shamanism is also neither a prerogative of the educated nor those with high intelligence but originates in a different part of being, i.e., the shaman's heart, soul, and spirit. Intellect is not the "source." It is the container but not what is contained. Intellect reflects on the shamanic work and can assist in refining techniques and approaches but it can also block the doors to other realms.

Shamanism, moreover, should not be confused with "black art" or any form of sorcery or satanism. When shamans do become agents of harm, it is said that the source of energy is polluted. It will lead to catastrophes and a dishonorable and painful end of the unethical shaman. Purity and responsibility of the shaman are essential and expected, because shamans have to be deserving of the trust of their clients.

Shamans will always stress that they are only the vehicles, the servants and mouthpiece of a higher source. They put the benefit of others before their own needs.

Shamanism often shows elements of performing arts and

other aspects of entertainment. When some shamans prefer quiet places and are content with performing away from the eye of the public, dramatization and public display may be expected from others. Dramatization, however, is not the goal but the means to focus effectively the attention of the clients and to translate the ineffable into ritual action.

Presently, shamans have to face new problems. The curiosity about this traditional form of dealing with the supernatural, raised by ads in the papers and television publicity, also carries the danger that shamanism may become a "performance art" and "tourist attraction" outside of its original function of fulfilling specific needs for a community. Nami, Ch'ae, and Oksun are examples of shamans who work together with political, and sometimes even religious, leaders (see, photo 10).

Art has been religious at its origin. The perfection of shamanic art in the twentieth century may either lead society back to its source toward spiritual renewal or vulgarize, and thereby adulterate, the shamanic matrix beyond recognition. However, there is still hope, the preconditions for becoming a shaman, in the case of the Korean shamans, for example, who suffer an initiatory illness, go through a prolonged training to study and memorize elaborate rituals, have not yet changed.

**Photo 1**
*Automatic Writing
(Singapore)*

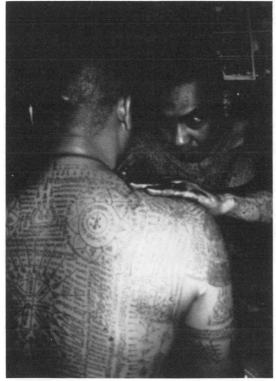

**Photo 2**
*Thai shaman, applying
protective tatoos (Central
Thailand)*

**Photo 3**
*Thai-Malay shaman after tiger possession*
*(Pattani, Southern Thailand)*

**Photo 4**
*Malay-Muslim horse possession*
*(Singapore)*

**Photo 5**
*Malay shaman, calling the spirits
(Kelantan, Malaysia)*

**Photo 6**

*The black flag on an altar in front of a house
indicates that a shaman is performing inside the temple
(Ord Bridge, Singapore)*

**Photo 7**

*Max Beauvoir, the Haitian houngan, in front of a
temporary altar preparing for the ceremony to open an exhibition*

**Photo 8**
*Vusamazuu Credo Mutwa, the Zulu sangoma,
in the courtyard of his compound*

**Photo 9**
*David Kaonohiokala Bray,
the Hawaiian kahuna,
wearing the sacred whale
tooth pendant and his
shaman amulet on which an
opal is surrounded by a nine-
pointed star, the rising sun
with 23 rays, the full moon
and another star. The band
on David's forehead holds the
sacred kukui nut*

## Photo 10

*Nami, the Korean mudang, "taming" the knife blade on which she is going to dance during a ritual for National Television (Seoul, Korea, August 1981). The Chinese characters on the boulder in the background read "National Reunification"*

## Photo 11

*Elizabeth Cogburn, the Caucasian shaman, with her power staff and sword*

## Photo 12
*Jerzy Grotowski, the shaman director*

**Photo 13**
*Hindu shaman,
possessed by the God
Rama (Sembawang
Shipyard, Singapore)*

**Photo 14**
*Chinese shaman,
blessing a client (Upper
Serangoon Road,
Singapore)*

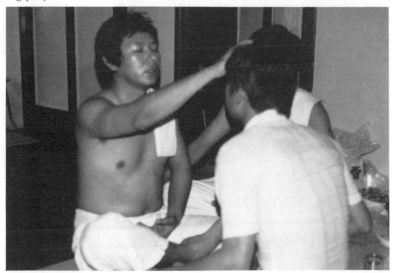

**Photo 15**
*Thai shaman,
blessing amulets
(Bangkok,
Thailand)*

**Photo 16**
*Chinese shaman,
falling out of trance
(Pegu Road, Singapore)*

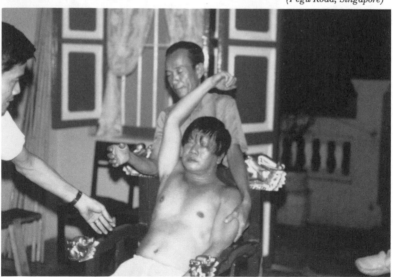

## Photo 17
*Chinese shaman,
possessed by
a sea goddess
(Changi,
Singapore)*

## Photo 18
*Chinese shaman,
fighting demons at the
birthday celebrations of
her guardian spirit
(Upper Thompson Road,
Singapore)*

**Photo 19**
*World tree (bai si), used in a nag khwan (spirit) ceremony on the eve of ordination (Chiang Mai, Thailand)*

**Photo 20**
*Chinese shaman, blessing new equipment in a factory (Singapore)*

# Part III

# Diversity and Individualization

## *Historical Overview*

To understand the diverse forms in which modern-day shamanism presents itself, we have to go back in history and look for developments which caused changes, may they be either shifts in focus or in paraphernalia or both. Most of all, we have to look at those who provide us with information about shamans so that we can recognize the personal biases researchers have introduced to the data. In doing so, we may also find out whether there are any connections between modern shamans and the shamans of the past.

For hundreds of years, shamanism has been denounced by Church authorities in Europe and abroad and shamans have been persecuted as heretics. Aside from the records of witches' trials, descriptions of shamans in Europe can, therefore, only be found in the myths and tales of the people.

An early report on Central Asian shamanism was written by the Franciscan monk Vilhelm av Ruysbroeck who had been sent by King Louis IX of France for two years to the court of Mongolia in 1253. It was as late as the seventeenth and eighteenth centuries that European settlers crossed the Ural Mountains where shamanism flourished in less accessible areas of Asia (see, e.g., Siikala, 1978:77-78).

Ethnographic reports on Siberian shamans caught the interest of European scholars not before the second half of the last century. These accounts appeared to be more reliable than the observations of missionaries and world travellers who spoke of superstitions and strange folk practices. With the growing number of scholarly reports around the turn of the century, shamanism was recognized and became a legitimate topic in academia. Bogoras (1910) and Jochelson (1905-1908), not necessarily trained ethnologists when they started to collect data, became experts on local traditions during the period of their political exiles. It was they and scholars like Popov (1923), Shirokogoroff (1923), Nioradze (1925), and others who provided us with greater insights into the "shaman complex." Siikala speaks of studies of a "theoretical nature" appearing "side by side with publications of material or texts aiming at pure description. General works, chiefly phenomenological analysis, increased in number, especially from the 1930s onwards, as more and more publications of material appeared to provide a sounder basis for comparison" (1978:18-19, 82-87).

Later, Ohlmarks (1939) and Bouteiller (1950) were among those who further advanced our knowledge on shamanism. A drawback came in the fifties, when Siberian shamans went into self-imposed exile. Whatever anthropologists working for one of the ethnographic institutes of the Soviet Academy of Sciences collected was kept secret in the central archives. The turning point came for the USSR in the 1970s when shamanism was proclaimed to be an "early form of religion" or "social consciousness" and was no longer considered to be a superstition alien to Communist ideology (Hoppál, 1983:3).

The general consensus of Western scholars was that the shamans living between Lapland and the Chukchee Peninsula belong to a large unit (Findeisen, 1957:7). Thus "Western" scholars tended to take the North Asiatic shaman as a model and possible prototype of early shamanism. However, despite the overwhelming amount of data from North Siberia, we really do not know whether Siberian shamans represent the oldest form of shamanism. The reports on shamans in other parts of the world cannot always attribute the appearance of shamans outside of Siberia to diffusion, this forces us to consider simultaneous origin as an alternative. Shamans emerge in any group who has a need for them.

The debate whether "black shamanism" (i.e., full possession) is the oldest form of shamanism (Schmidt, 1931; discussed by Schröder, 1955:850-855) has still not been put to rest. Schmidt stated that "black shamanism" developed in an agrarian culture and dealt with spirits of the Lower World while "white shamanism," dealing with spirits of the Upper World, was a later form which developed in a pastoral culture. Eliade went even further in declaring the magical flight and the conscious travel of shamans into the Upper World to be the only true forms of ecstasy. He refused to consider possession trances to be valid shamanic experiences (1974:507). Archaeological findings, esp. the cave drawings in southern France and northern Spain, however, draw our attention to the possibility that possession trances might have been known already in hunting and gathering societies.

The hypothesis that the mind-expanding/magical flight trance became available after methods to enter and exit possession trances had been developed, is confirmed by my field data. Mind expansion offers itself in the periods between possessions and makes possession less necessary later on. Eliade thought that

> *"possession" could develop from an ecstatic experience: while the shaman's soul...was traveling in the upper or lower worlds, "spirits" could take possession of his body. But...once the spirits have taken "possession" of the shaman, his personal ecstasy—that is, his ascent to the sky or descent to the underworld—is halted....there is a certain "facility" about "possession" that contrasts with the dangerous and dramatic shamanic initiation and discipline (1974:507).*

133

Eliade's opinion has been disproven, among others, by the shamans I worked with. One said casually that she goes on a "magical flight" while her body is possessed by the spirit of a deified general. She has recall of the magical flight but not what the spirit says or does while he uses her body.

In my opinion, it is as dangerous and dramatic as the magical flight when shamans allow a spirit to use their body; that means, they know how to evoke and how to send a spirit away. The "magical flight" experiences of shamans appear to be a bonus for simultaneously producing a manifestation of the Divine (see, Trances, later in this Part of the book; also the profile of Max Beauvoir in Part II).

There are areas in the world where full possession is still culturally expected, e.g., from Chinese spirit mediums in Singapore or from Voodoo, Udamba, and Candomble practitioners in Middle and South America (see also, the description of the possession trance of the Dalai Lama's oracle in Part II).

Shamanism started as an oral tradition which did not produce any written records. Shamanic paraphernalia were and are, with few exceptions, made out of perishable material. What proof do we have? When we want to look at physical evidence for the development of shamanism, we are referred to neolithic caves in Europe. Studying these cave drawings, anthropologists deduced that hunters and gatherers, that is, nomadic cultures, may have known of shamans. The anthropomorphic figure on the famous painting at Lascaux is lying in front of a wounded aurochs. The man's penis is erect which could indicate an ecstatic state, while a bird, perched on a nearby staff, could be interpreted as a symbolic representation of the soul, a messenger, or a guardian spirit. (Carbon-dating places this drawing of a prone shaman between 14,000 and 12,600 B.C.) Similar petroglyphs and pictographs have been discovered also in Africa and in southern China.

Cave drawings can be used like Rorschachs test where viewers project their own perceptions into the drawing. Lommel spoke of early people who, "still firmly anchored in their 'world-view,'" were totally unable to explain pictures which did "not correspond to, or directly depict, this world-view; they seem only to see that which their world-view and their mythology encourage them to see" (1967:134). We are not familiar with the world views of people who lived over 16,000 years ago, so when we attempt to reconstruct their thoughts, we have to be aware of the subjective character of our twentieth century interpretation. Nevertheless it may be the only way to intuit at least some of the content of these drawings.

Most of the cave drawings found in northern Spain (e.g., Altamira), southern France (e.g., Lascaux, Trois Frères, Teyat, Dordogne;), and the USSR (e.g., Lake Onega, eastern Siberia), date from the same period and indicate hunting magic and states of ecstatic "possession."

We recognize early concepts of life after death and a possible feeling of guilt about the killing of animals which was necessary for human survival. The hunted animals were propitiated and invited to sacrifice themselves. They were promised that their journey to the "other world" would be sped up and they would be given a place of honor in tribal rituals (see, e.g., the bear ritual among the Ainus). Animal bones were, therefore, collected after slaughtering and ritually put together again.

Is there any connection to the initiation rituals reportedly performed in North and South America, Africa, and Indonesia (Eliade, 1974:53-58). We are told that the bodies of neophytes were ritually dismembered and reassembled so that they could emerge as shamans (Findeisen, 1957:27-28).

Looking at initiatory rituals worldwide (see, Human Relations Area Files), less than 50 per cent of shamans go through a dismemberment experience. At least none of the shamans profiled in Part II and none of the 122 shamans I worked with during the thirty years of my field research experienced dismemberment during initiation. Though a restructuring of the psyche occurs when a new shaman begins to emerge.

We may find images of dancing skeletons on murals, and bones adorning shamans' robes and paraphernalia. In many cultures, bones remind of the precariousness of human existence and symbolize for the initiate (whether in shamanism or Tibetan and Mongolian Buddhism) processes which lead to transformation. According to Eliade, such thinking "belongs to an archaic, pre-Buddhist stratum of spirituality, which was based...on the ideology of the hunting peoples (the sacredness of bones)" (1974:435). Animal as well as human bones were equally considered to be sacred.

Anthropologists tell us that, in totemic societies, animals are seen as ancestors, however, animals are not always the teachers in these societies. Animals as teachers and guardian spirits seem to appear predominantly in the earliest form of shamanism, i.e., in hunting and gathering societies. The North American Indians, in spite of heavy attacks by missionaries and social pressure and persecution they suffered from the U.S. government, have retained these beliefs. Only fairly recently has an act of Congress (the Native American Indian Religious Freedom Act in 1978) returned freedom of religious practices to them.

The shift to the worship of nature gods (Sun, Moon, Sky, Wind, Mountains) occurred when some tribes began to cultivate gardens. Shinto in Japan, for example, is a belief system typical for horticulturists. To this day, the Huicholes in Mexico and most people in Southeast Asia still live in horticultural societies.

In other areas, people began to till the soil and formed agricultural societies. These more permanent settlements changed the needs for shamanic intervention. The necessity for hunting magic, for example, was superseded by the need for making rain or stopping floods.

In different geographic areas, where soil conditions and lack of water did permit neither horti- nor agriculture, nomadic pastoralists (e.g., the Evenki in North Siberia and the Hungarian horsemen) also developed belief systems with society-specific forms of shamanism (Goodman, 1987, 1988).

Most of all, after the establishment of permanent settlements, shamans moved from their leading role in a tribe to the role of specialists. With more complex and hierarchical social structures, division of labor became necessary. We now find deified heroes among the guardian spirits, e.g., in Folk Taoism. Unchanged remained the shamans' role of being the mediators between the spiritual world and that of humans.

The rulers of some countries, however, continued to retain and exercise shamanic faculties. The crowns of Korean kings of the Silla Dynasty (third to fifth century A.D.), for example, show shamanic symbolism (antlers, trees). Furthermore, during the Middle Ages in Europe, the sick would approach kings and queens, believing they could get well when a royal hand would touch them. They believed that, during the anointment of a king, divine powers were installed in the royal body. In Europe it was accomplished with the help of an archbishop, whereas in South and Southeast Asia rulers became god-kings (*deva rajas*) through the services of Hindu priests. Similar beliefs can be found among Muslim. Malay chronicles in the archives of Singapore National University recorded that, until the middle of the nineteenth century, Malay sultans were still practicing shamans.

If we want to find examples in the twentieth century, we can look at Iran where the Ayatollahs are believed to have access to transcendental powers, a tenet which is upheld by Shi'ites to this day. How can anybody contradict a man who receives direct messages from God?

## *Is Shamanism a Religion?*

At this point, the reader may ask whether shamanism is a religion. Siikala (1978:11-13) discussed the opinions of Uvo Harva, Gottlieb Georgi, Hans Findeisen, and Vilmos Diószegi because they talked about shamanism to be the old ethnic religion of Siberia.

But we have first to clarify what we mean when we use the word "religion." Etymologically, "religion" comes from the Latin word *"religio"* (*re-ligere,* which literally means "to tie together again," i.e., to reunite the creation with the creator).

The difficulty to explain "religion" arises from different frames of reference, i.e., whether the term was defined by theologians or sociologists or anthropologists. The anthropologist Geertz spoke of religion as

*(1) a system of symbols which acts to (2) establish powerful, pervasive and long-lasting moods and motivations in men by (3) formulating conceptions of a general order of existence and (4) clothing these conceptions with such an aura of factuality that (5) the moods and motivations seem uniquely realistic (1972:168).*

The sociologist Bellah (1972:37) found a brief definition "considerably more difficult than a definition of evolution" and the anthropologist Hultkrantz's view (1973) "of the autonomous position of the shamanic complex as a segment of various religions" is of no help because it requires qualification. Hultkrantz fails to talk about the origin of shamanism which appears to be rather the prototype of all religions than a segment of later religions which allow folk beliefs to exist in their framework of legitimacy. Also, during later developments, partly to increase the effectiveness of their performances and partly to be tolerated by the locally dominant religion, shamans absorbed and reinterpreted elements of belief systems with which they had come in contact. This proves rather the resiliency of shamanism and does not necessarily make the "shamanic complex" a "segment of various religions."

Culture has been seen as

*an integrative process through which people identify themselves in relation to a pattern of life histories, experiences, actions and artifacts....People translate their world according to the "social facts" rendered in the social collectivity of ideas. Participation in a belief system gives the person authenticity in the context of the established institutional norms of behavior (Blundell, 1984:89).*

and religion has been an intrinsic part of the culture in each ethnic group from the beginning.

I hesitate to define "religion." The word means so many different things to different people. Common usage seems to imply that religion constitutes a codified body of sacred scriptures and a priestly hierarchy which cannot be found in shamanism. But when we include contact with the metaphysical and the belief in the survival of the soul, then, despite the lack of doctrine and the lack of institutionalization, shamanism is a religion. Shamanism is, in fact, the proto-type underlying all established religions. Furthermore, it were shamans who kept the belief in divine protection alive.

To give one example of the turning point where shamanism and religion began to take different routes, I refer to K.C. Chang who recently advanced the hypothesis that "shamanism played a strategic role in the development of early Chinese political culture" (Keightley, 1989:1).

> ...the ancient Chinese could be seen as particularly preoccupied with the Heaven-Earth intercommunication. The shamans—religious personnel equipped with the power to fly across the different layers of the universe with the help of the animals and a whole range of rituals and paraphernalia—were chiefly responsible for the Heaven-Earth communication (Chang 1986:414-418).

Chang is using a passage in the *Chu yu, xia* section of the *Guo yu*. These "Conversations of the States" tell us about historical events during the Zhou dynasty, 1122-256 B.C. The relevant passage in the *Chu yu* has been paraphrased by Derk Bodde as follows,

> *Anciently, men and spirits did not intermingle. At that time there were certain persons who were so perspicacious, single-minded, and reverential that their understanding enabled them to make meaningful collation of what lies above and below, and their insight to illumine what is distant and profound. Therefore the spirits would descend into them. The possessors of such powers were, if men, called* xi *(shamans), and, if women,* wu *(shamanesses). It is they who supervised the positions of the spirits at the ceremonies, sacrificed to them, and otherwise handled religious matters. As a consequence, the spheres of the divine and*

*the profane were kept distinct. The spirits sent down blessings on the people, and accepted from them their offerings. There were no natural calamities.*

*In the degenerate time of Shao Hao (trad.xxvi cent. B.C.), however, the Nine Li (a troublesome tribe like the Miao) threw virtue into disorder. Men and spirits became intermingled, with each household indiscriminately performing for itself the religious observances which had hitherto been conducted by the shamans. As a consequence, men lost their reverence for the spirits, the spirits violated the rules of men, and natural calamities arose. Hence the successor of Shao Hao, Zhuan Zu, charged Chong, Governor of the South, to handle the affairs of Heaven in order to determine the proper place of the spirits, and Li, Governor of Fire, to handle the affairs of Earth in order to determine the proper places of men. And such is what is meant by "cutting the communication between Heaven and Earth" (1961:390-391).*

Chang dates this passage as having been written in the fourth century B.C. and considers it

*the most important textual reference to shamanism in ancient China [providing] the crucial clue to understanding the central role of shamanism in ancient Chinese politics. Heaven is where all the wisdom of human affairs lies....Access to that wisdom was, of course, requisite for political authority. In the past, everybody had had that access through the shamans. Since heaven had been severed from earth, only those who controlled that access had wisdom—hence the authority—to rule. Shamans, therefore, were a crucial part of every state court; in fact, scholars of ancient China agree that the king himself was actually head shaman (1983:45).*

The passage from the *Guo yu* speaks of the shamans' magical flight, a form of shamanism which was practiced in the northern provinces of China, closer to Siberia, while other sources, e.g., De Groot (1910) tell us that in the southern provinces of China the spirits would enter shamans and "possess" them. Keightley finds that

> ...it was only because the xi and wu had such powers that the spirits were said to have descended to them. It was not the descent of the spirits that conferred the powers. There is no talk here of the kind of trance, possession, or fresh insight generally associated with shamanism. For whatever purpose the spirits came down...it was not to confer knowledge of..."what is right in the upper and lower realms," because the shamans already had that knowledge before the spirits arrived (1989:9).

Basing his statements on the work of I.M. Lewis, Sivin says that

> the experience of possession depends...upon the social and political status of the one possessed....There are two main types of "the seizure by divinity." One is found among those in the central religious cult of a people. This possession is pregnant with moral significance, and accessible only to an elite commissioned by the gods to exercise divine authority over other mortals. The other, found in cults peripheral to the conventional order, is open in principle to all who wish to take part, and is marked by general religious enthusiasm—a direct benediction from the gods, rather than one earned through sanctioned conduct and dispensed in measured ceremony by a high priest or monarch (1979:73).

Social distinctions are made between, "the controlled, sanctioned, earned, elite kind of 'seizure by divinity' as opposed to the general, populist one" (Keightley, 1989:11). The textual reference seems to indicate a turning point.

> It either demonstrates bureaucratic resistance to the idea of a free flow of communication between Earth and Heaven, or it implies the existence of yet a third

*kind of shaman—the shaman-cum-bureaucrat, the shaman-cum-moral metaphysician and strict ritualist, who engages in neither flight, possession, nor ecstasy. In this view, for example, the Shang king, as the mediator between his people and the spirits, might have been a xi; he would not have been a shaman as the term is generally understood (Keightley, 1989:29-30).*

Religious practitioners, undoubtedly, played a major role in the genesis of the early Chinese state. When, around 200 B.C., Confucianism became the belief system on which the Chinese Empire was built, shamans were left out of the mainstream development. The situation became even more problematic with the arrival of Buddhism four hundred years later. Early philosophical Taoism had shared beliefs with shamanism. Taoist philosophers invited each individual to become self-sufficient and stay connected with the "Tao" (the Infinite Source). Folk Taoism then restored belief in continued revelations and people began to look again for shamans who would produce manifestations of the "divine" and who could convey the "divine" messages.

Shamans never had difficulties when they had to operate in multi-ethnic and multi-religious states. From Singapore, I can report that Overseas Chinese may convert to Catholicism but they may also invite Taoist priests to their shamanic celebrations because ordained priests are needed for certain functions. I saw Taoist priests frequently conducting evocative rituals at the beginning of shamanic festivals, even some Buddhist monks were invited to chant blessings (see, Festival of the Nine Imperial Gods, Singapore, Heinze, 1988:183-206). In spiritual emergencies, however, they all will consult shamans.

Looking at the profiles in Part II, the voodoo practitioner, the Hawaiian *kahuna,* and the Zulu *sangoma* as well as the Hindu shaman and the Tibetan oracle operate inside the framework of the religion of their country. For the other shamans, early local beliefs syncretized. They have been and still are tolerated and practiced in the framework of world religions.

Symbols and paraphernalia of the Tibetan oracle (see, Part II) carry features of the Bon religion prevalent in Tibet before Buddhism arrived. Another example are African slaves who, after having been brought to Brazil, were forced to use Christian names under which they continued to practice old rituals to evoke their African gods. They incorporated even indigenous Native American elements into their Afro-Brazilian customs. Southeast Asian shamans, who all claim to be either Muslims, Taoists, or Buddhists, draw legitimacy from world religions, too (see, e.g., the profile of the Bangkok shaman in Part II). We should, therefore, not be surprised when, in Asia, even representatives of world religions participate in shamanistic rituals.

*Concepts seem to move in a circular fashion—local beliefs are reinterpreted and codified by the elite and then, in a more elaborate form, superimposed on the original beliefs. Thus, on the one hand, local beliefs gain legitimacy through acceptance by the elite and, on the other hand, normative religions are kept alive by local practices (Heinze, 1982:xi-xii).*

Wanting to look at levels where new forms are emerging, the reader is referred to the Caucasian shaman and the Polish director in Part II. Elizabeth Cogburn, for example, created the New Sun Dance Song ritual inside a growing community of Westerners in the United States and Grotowski invites his audiences wherever he goes to co-create with him.

## Different Forms of Shamanism in Different Countries Reported by Different Researchers From Different Disciplines

Since those early Siberian studies, more data on Eurasian shamanism have been provided by Diószegi (1968), Edsman

(1967), Michael (1963), etc. For a more extensive discussion on research in Eastern Europe as well as North and Central Asia, the reader is referred to Siikala's (1978) and Hoppál's (1983) surveys which mention, among others, the history of Buryat shamanism collected by Mikhailov and the terminology on Buryat shamanism by Manzigeev. Hoppál lists also a monograph on early forms of religion among the Turk people of Siberia by Alekseev, the records at the Moscow Ethnographic Institute as well as numerous other field studies, e.g., on the Voguls, Ostyaks, and the Finno-Ugrian people, Basilov's study on Central Asia (1976), and Heissig's study on Mongolia (1980).

Ethnologists, psychologists, and historians of religion conducted research in different countries, e.g., Baeckman and Hultkrantz (1978) on Lapp shamanism; Blacker (1975) on Japanese shamanism; Halifax (1979, 1982) and Neihardt (1961) on North American shamanism; Heinze (1988) and Spiro (1967) on Southeast Asian shamanism; Kakar (1982) on Indian shamanism; Kendall (1985), Lee (1981), and Youngsook (1979) on Korean shamanism; Harner (1977) and Metraux (1959) on South American shamanism; and Peters (1981) on Nepalese shamanism. They report of shamans who differ considerably in paraphernalia, technique and worldview. The most quoted book, however, is Mircea Eliade's comparative work on shamanism as an archaic technique of ecstasy (1946, 1974). Eliade was a historian of religion and a philosopher who, with the help of graduate students, compiled one of the most comprehensive collection of reports on shamanic activities all over the world. His only shortcomings were that he used secondary sources, i.e., he did not conduct fieldwork on shamans himself and he did not believe in "spirits."

On the initiative of Rob Wikan of the Finland-Swedish University and the Donner Institute for Research in Religious and Cultural History, in September 1962, forty scholars from four Nordic countries as well as H. Diószegi (Hungary) came together for a symposium on shamanism held in Åbo. Nine of the presentations were later edited and published by Edsman, 1967. Nearly twenty years later, in September 1981, a symposium was organized by Mihaly Hoppál in Hungary, in cooperation with the Ethnographic Institute of the Soviet Academy of Sciences (e.g., Basilov). The discussions focussed on Eurasian shamanism. Most of the forty-two contributions were edited and published by Hoppál in 1983. This symposium was followed, in fall of 1981, by a colloquium on shamanism in Paris, organized by Robert Hamayon from the University of Paris (Nanterre) who had invited mainly French participants. In 1982, another symposium was held in Manchester, England, on "Shamanism among Lowland South American Indians," organized by Joanna Ofering Kaplan from the London School of Economics. Hoppál then called, in August 1983, again scholars from Austria, Canada, Chile, Finland, France, Hungary, Great Britain, Italy, Poland, Sweden, Switzerland, the USA, the USSR, and West Germany to participate in a three-day symposium on shamanism in conjunction with the XIth International Congress of Anthropological and Ethnological Sciences (ICAES) in Vancouver B.C. (Canada). He organized a similar three-day symposium again in conjunction with the XIIth ICAES in Zagreb (Yugoslavia) in July 1988.

At the 1983 symposium in Vancouver, participants expressed interest in continuing the discussions the following year in California. Therefore, the First International Conference on the Study of Shamanism was convened in San Rafael, California, on the Labor Day weekend in September 1984. The aim was to integrate recent studies on shamanism and stimulate further research. Participants came from Canada, Hungary, Italy, Peru/Finland, Philippines, the United States, and West Germany. During the conference, participants went one step further and investigated contemporary forms of shamanism which included "urban shamanism." The need for a broader approach led to inviting 77 colleagues from Italy, Peru/Finland, the United States, and West Germany representing the disciplines of anthropology, art history, art, education, history of religion, hypnotherapy, parapsychology, philosophy, psychiatry, psychology, psychoneuroimmunology, and psychotherapy to attend the Second International Conference on the Study of Shamanism the following year in fall 1985, again at the St. Sabina Center in San Rafael, California. Theoreticians met with experientially oriented experts and gravitated toward the investigation of shamanic elements in the process of healing. The Third, Fourth, Fifth, and Sixth International Conferences in San Rafael, 1986, 1987, l988, and 1989 respectively, were then devoted to the study of shamanism and alternate modes of healing. The proceedings of these conference, containing from thirty up to forty contributions as well as the transcripts of the discussions, are now available in print.

Drawing from available publications, my own fieldwork, and the profiles in Part II, differences and similarities in calling, initiation, training, trances, paraphernalia, rituals and symbolism between European, Asian, American, and African shamans, will now be discussed in the following chapters. I will also point to diversities among each group.

# 1. Call, Initiation, and Training

According to Eliade, the term "initiation" refers to

*a body of rites and oral teachings whose purpose is to produce a decisive alteration in the religious and social status of the person to be initiated. In philosophical terms, initiation is equivalent to a basic change in existential condition; the novice emerges from his ordeal endowed with a totally different being from that which he possessed before his initiation; he has become another (1958a:x).*

With some local variations, all these criteria pertain to shamanic initiations during which a candidate is transformed from an ordinary human being into a vehicle for the supernatural. This re-connecting to the supernatural appears to be the most important factor in each initiation.

*From the fact that man was created and civilized by Supernatural Beings, it follows that...his behavior and activities belong to sacred history; and this history must be carefully preserved and transmitted intact to succeeding generations. Basically, man is what he is because, at the dawn of Time, certain things happened to him (Eliade, 1958a:xi).*

Eliade himself asks whether the re-creation of the original myth is still important in the twentieth century. "Modern man" perceives himself as a "historical" being while the "man of archaic societies considers himself the end product of a mythical history." Modern man sees, indeed,

*in the history that precedes him a purely human work and...believes that he has the power to continue and perfect it indefinitely, for the man of traditional societies everything is significant—that is, everything creative and powerful—that has ever happened took place "in the beginning," in the Time of the myths (Eliade, 1958:xi).*

In other words, modern man believes in evolution and the creation of new forms. The repetition of ancient rituals like baptism and confirmation are now more social formalities than actual transformations. Only Bar Mitzvahs seem to have retained features of the original initiation ritual during which the candidate enters the religious community as an officially recognized member and is also consciously reconnected to the Divine Source.

Initiation rituals for shamans are less dramatic in our times. Sometimes, the process of initiation can extend over several years (see, Elizabeth Cogburn, Part II), however, connecting with the "universal source" is still important.

In contrast to other rituals, each shamanic initiation has to be preceded by a selection process. Individuals can become shamans

1. *when they are called to serve,*

2. *when they inherit the role, or*

3. *when they decide themselves to become a shaman and look for a teacher who will train and initiate them.*

147

To gain an understanding of present conditions, we have to look at first-hand data, i.e., information collected in the field. Ethnographic data on North Siberian shamans reveal that many of the shamans in the past refused to accept the "call" because human sacrifices were required to complete their transformation into shamans. It is, for example, said that for each bone of a shaman the spirits ask for a human substitute to be taken from among the shaman's relatives (Findeisen, 1957:61). Even when it was considered to be ethical when an individual wanted to protect his relatives from this fate, the shamans who refused to follow their call were punished severely by becoming blind or suffering other dehabilitating illnesses even death (Findeisen, 1957:35). Such demanding conditions were allegedly not only set by ancestor spirits but by the "helping spirits" of the ancestors as well because, when spirits become "masterless" after the death of a shaman, they have to look for a new individual through whom they can become active on the earthly plane (see, Findeisen, 1957:37; and my observations in Southeast Asia, 1982, 1988).

My research, however, did not yield any reference to human sacrifices in connection with shamanic initiation. In Southeast Asia, I found that, in the past, people have been killed and buried under the gate posts of a city, so that their spirit would protect the access to this urban center (Heinze, 1982:131). This speaks of the power of spirits whose body suffered an untimely death, but has nothing to do with shamanism.

In sum, individuals can become shamans

1. *being called by an ancestral spirit who has been a shaman during his/her lifetime, or*

2. *being called by a shamanic spirit, although there have not been any shamans among ancestors on his or her father's side, or*

3. *being selected by nature spirits (of a mountain or a water course) who want to manifest in a human body, or*

4. *being selected by a spirit from a higher realm who needs a body to assist the people on earth, or*

5. *because the soul of a deceased has been nourished on the "shaman's tree" in heaven so that it can be reborn as a shaman, or*

6. *because a man from heaven looks for a wife on earth and their child becomes a shaman, or*

7. *because a mystical union between a heavenly and an earthly being is sought (see, for example, Spiro, 1967, on Burmese nat marriages), or*

8. *because an animal mother carries the soul of the selected individual into the underworld to be nourished and trained, or*

9. *because illness has been brought by demons who abduct the soul of an individual and carry him/her into the underworld so that s/he learn to take on the characteristics of these demons, or*

10. *because an individual decides to study with another shaman (Findeisen, 1957:47, and Heinze, 1988:55, 278-282).*

Folklorists all over the world have elaborated on the belief that when children show unusual faculties, are growing faster than their peers, and display a greater sensitivity toward people and events, they are supposed to become shamans. They may faint easily, have hallucinations, and speak with spirits. These are very general criteria. Recent research (including my own observations and personal communications of colleagues), reveals that even in the United States many children have "imaginary companions" without telling anybody about their fictional playmates. Virtually none of these children will become a shaman later on. The "imaginary companions" vanish one day by themselves when the need for their presence has faded away. In cases of future shamans, the opposite is happening, spiritual entities continue their dialogue with their human companions and make their wishes known as soon as the candidates are adult enough to handle the vocation (see, e.g., profiles of the Garhwali shaman, Elizabeth Cogburn, and the Tibetan oracle, in Part II). I don't believe that shamans are "fantasy-prone" individuals. Their "calling" touches much deeper levels than any fantasy can do. It is also important to note that in all cultures shamans are allowed to practice only after they have passed the age of puberty.

Black Elk's initiatory vision came when he was nine years old, but it was not until he reached the age of seventeen that he (even then precociously) was able to admit his vision to another shaman who helped him to understand its meaning. It took several more decades until Black Elk entrusted Neihardt (1961) with the legacy of the vision.

Lame Deer experienced the attention shift at sixteen, but it was not until midlife, and after "getting drunk and going to jail," that he was able to integrate the visions into his "surface" mind (1972). Katz also confirms, "Between the ages of approximately twenty-five and forty, the question of whether a person will become a healer is usually settled" (1982:145). Cordova was fully initiated at twenty-five but it was not until midlife that he began to use his powers to help others (Lamb, 1975).

The majority of shamans in my sample began to practice when they were in their thirties, that means, after they had fulfilled their duties toward society, e.g., married and had children or had been successful in their profession (1988:45-46). There seems to be a connection to mid-life crises, i.e., those periods when individuals begin to restructure their life and attempt to discover its purpose (see also, Heery, 1987:182). Becoming a shaman in mid-life is predominantly found in multi-ethnic and multi-religious societies where the choices of life patterns are so manifold that individuals grope for the right one by the method of trial and error. Another possible explanation is that in the twentieth century the resistance to accepting the "call" and the reluctance to becoming a shaman is stronger than in previous times. Shamans hesitate to surrender because acceptance of the "call" means unrestricted commitment. They have to relinquish any ego-centric goals and be ready to serve at any time. Shamans are, furthermore, not recognized by professionals in the medical and psychiatric sciences and shamanic rituals are not considered to bc valid treatment procedures. "Professionally spoken," shamanism is seen as being based on scientifically unsupported superstitions. It will require more research to substantiate the success of shamans in scientifically acceptable terms so that these prejudices can be removed. The research suffers, though, from the difficulties to obtain complete medical records of a client before s/he was treated by a shaman and then a medically approved clean bill of health after the cure. And it is not the shamans who resist to cooperate in research but the clients.

Going through dismemberment, death, resurrection—the whole concept of shamanic illness—was a necessary preparation for shamans, especially in North Siberia. It is not a prerequisite in other societies with different belief systems. What are then the first signs for an emerging shaman?

Before I started my fieldwork in Asia, I read in De Groot that Chinese mediums, for example,

> *must be of a nervous, impressionable, hysterial kind of people, physically and mentally weak, and therefore easily stirred to ecstasy. The strain on their nerves cannot be born for many years, and hence they all die young (1910, VI:1296).*

Elliot made similar statements about Singaporean mediums when he found that youth under the age of twenty

> *are the most suitable candidates—particularly those whose horoscopes...do not include a proper weighting of the more stable elements. Such people are expected to lead blameless but unhappy lives, and to die young (1955:46-57).*

Furthermore,

> *Chinese and Thai traditions tell us that individuals may accept the "call" to prolong their lives. They believe the time they spend in trance is added to their*

*life span. Also, in "serving" they feel spiritually pro-
tected (Heinze, 1988:47).*

From my own research, I can report that less than ten per
cent of the 122 shamans I worked with were suffering from
poor health before they accepted the "call." Ninety per cent
felt they had been "selected" on account of good behavior in
previous lives. In other words, their conduct during previous
lives had prepared them for "becoming vehicles for the
divine." All ten Malay *bomohs* and two of the seventy-seven
Chinese *tang-ki* had inherited their faculties, the two Chinese
shamans and the two Malay *bomohs* in Singapore from their
grandmother or their uncles from their mother's side, the eight
Malay *bomohs* in Kelantan (Malaysia) and Pattani (southern
Thailand) from their grandfather on their father's side. No
previous occurrence of shamanism was known in the families
of the remaining 110 shamans.

I repeat that we have to be careful whom we want to call
a shaman. When women in northern Thailand, for example,
are entrusted with the care for the clan spirits, this does not
necessarily make them *ma-khis* (vehicles of the spirits,
Heinze, 1988:55).

All shamans and mediums I worked with experienced
visions at the beginning of their career and only one of 122
decided on his own to become a shaman (see Part II, the
Bangkok shaman).

While the majority of shamans and mediums I worked
with were solely advised by spiritual entities, only a few
Chinese and Thai but none of the Malay and Indian went
through any formal training or spoke of official initiation.

Let us now look at how shamanic tendencies manifested
in the lives of the shamans profiled in Part II and how they
were "called, initiated, and trained."

Max Beauvoir, the voodoo shaman, resisted "losing his
conscious and rational control during ceremonies" until he
was approximately thirty-five years old. He accepted the role
of a shaman, after he had discovered that "being possessed
increased his conscious awareness and gave him new capabilities." He followed, however, the traditional pattern of his

ethnic group, although he felt also motivated to "bridge the distance to the Western world."

Vusamazulu Credo Mutwa, the Zulu shaman, was exposed to traditional ways already as a child through his grandfather on his mother's side. His calling and initiation were gradual but he had to undergo a purification ceremony before he could be trained as a *sangoma* and become a custodian of Zulu traditions.

David Bray, coming from a line of *kahuna* priests who had served the kings of Hawai'i for twenty-five generations, was raised by his aunt who herself was a *kahuna*. He inherited a sacred stone and cane from a famous *kahuna* teacher. David Bray was also very much concerned about teaching the Hawaiian "ways" to Westerners.

Nami, the Korean shaman, began showing signs of spirit possession at the age of fifteen. She claims that she did not suffer any particular illness but had insomnia and nightmares. She was initiated when she was seventeen and had, with nineteen, learned enough to officiate village rituals and to lead twenty other shamans during the performances. Although, Ch'ae, a Los Angeles student, went to Korea with the intention to become an shaman, Oksun, the third shaman discussed in Part II, emerged again from the traditional framework of her culture.

The Garhwali shaman Usha had already visions when she was a child. She became "possessed" for the first time one year after her marriage when she was seventeen, but she and her family resisted the "calling" for almost a decade. Health and fortune of her family improved only when she declared herself ready to be initiated by a pundit. After it had been officially determined that she had been selected to become a receptacle for "divine" intrusion, a learned *brahmin* taught her how to evoke the deity as well as how to conduct the necessary rituals. From then on she was on her own.

Elizabeth Cogburn, a Caucasian, speaks of herself as a "red face shaman," because she was "called" to follow the shamanic path. (In Native American beliefs those who inherit the profession are "black face shamans.") Elizabeth went through long periods of gradual initiation and was taught by several spiritual guides. They came to her while she was awake or while she was dreaming. She had also been prepared for her calling by her heritage and during events in her early childhood. During communal events, she became aware of her vocation. After she had discovered the power of the drum and found her medicine pipe, she continued listening to her inner voices. It took her one year to prepare for her initiatory dance which she performed in front of witnesses. Afterwards, she continued to create and lead ritual dances in a communal setting.

The calling, initiation and training of Grotowski, the Polish director, is hard to assess. He gradually developed his faculties to transform and to trigger transformation, especially after his trip to Asia.

Among the three samples I cited from my research in Southeast Asia, the first shaman was called, initiated and taught solely by Hindu deities, the second discovered shamanic faculties and cultivated them on his own, when he outgrew the teachings of Buddhist monks and Taoist priests. The third Southeast Asian shaman decided to be trained and, after the rather brief training period of nine days, was initiated and relied on his own intuition later on.

The life of the Dalai Lama's Oracle followed the traditional pattern. Already as a child, he experienced visions which indicated his propensity to enter possession states. However, he had to wait until the previous oracle died so that he could officially step into the "office" his religion had prepared for him.

The last profile in Part II, a Western lawyer, does not mention any calling or initiation but speaks of training in many fields related to shamanism. The lawyer was born with the propensity to shamanize and then cultivated her faculties whenever an opportunity offered itself. She is only one example for the many occurrences of shamanistic activities in other professions as well.

In the United States, we find a great number of weekend workshops announcing training in shamanism. The quality of such training is seldom put to test. It does not seem to be appropriate to attempt a revival of shamanism by combining "core elements" from different cultures. Such attempts start on the wrong foot, because core elements may be part of shamanic rituals, but do not constitute the essence of the ritual. They are vehicles of expression but not the message itself. Shamans go beyond the performance of rituals. They respond and fulfill the immediate needs of others and will select rituals and paraphernalia according to such needs. Shamanic techniques may be effective means for self-exploration, however, experimenters should be taught the pitfalls of psychic openings which require closing. They have to be convinced of the necessity to properly sending away the energies which they evoke during the process.

Shamans emerge where needs arise. Shamans usually appear in a community which has formed before them (, e.g., see Part II, the Hindu medium in the Southeast Asian example). Shamans begin to step into the expected role and tune in to higher dimensions so that they may secure a solution for an acute problem.

An Ojibwa medicine woman said recently,

*I'm a messenger and a guide. And that's my purpose in the world. I gather information for people and guide them on a spiritual path. I give them an idea of where to look; then I give them a little push, and they're on their own (Glasser, 1989:41-42).*

Humility and the awareness of being servants of the community and mediators between the sacred and the secular is lacking in many "workshop-trained" shaman candidates.

The same Ojibwa medicine woman warns about the dangers when insufficiently trained individuals conduct ceremonies,

*Some people just watch what other people do at ceremonies, and they imitate the actions. They run into problems because they haven't been taught....they can bring in a lot of forces or spirits they don't know anything about. They may not be able to handle the consequences of other people freaking out or the presence of spirits they can't see. They might lose*

*control and lose touch with reality, as well....Maybe*
*you won't die or lose your mind, but you may become*
*crippled, or be plagued by some major illness for the*
*rest of your life. The training program requires humil-*
*ity of going to someone and asking for guidance,*
*serving an apprenticeship, going through the sweat*
*lodges, and doing whatever else is necessary*
*(Glasser, 1989:45).*

Most shamans have undergone prolonged periods of
physical, emotional, intellectual, and spiritual training during
which their ego becomes service oriented so that they can
become the vehicles and translators of transcendental knowledge. They reconnect their clients to the infinite source and,
because circumstances and the condition of the clients differ
each time, each shamanic event is unique. Shamans also stress
that their training never ends because they keep receiving
instructions from the "higher" source. A clear distinction has,
therefore, to be made between

1. *methods and techniques for self-exploration and*
   *self-cultivation using shamanistic methods and*

2. *shamanic practices themselves.*

(The reader will note that the term "shamanistic" is used when
a non-shaman uses certain techniques for self-exploration and
empowerment while the term "shamanic" indicates practices
carried out by a "professional" shaman.) Mastery of methods
and techniques for self-exploration and getting in contact with
the sacred are preconditions for becoming a shaman, but other
conditions have to be present too. All of them are service
oriented.

To become a mediator between the sacred and the profane
and to fulfill the specific needs of one's community are serious
commitments. The length of such commitment depends on the
"contract" with the spiritual world. It can be either for a few
years or for the rest of a shaman's life (Heinze, 1988).

# 2. Trances

The word "trance" is being used rather indiscriminately. I found that the term "shamanic trance" can refer to a wide range of distinctly different states of consciousness. Felicitas Goodman distinguished between states

> *that occur principally in response to biological cues, such as sleep or orgasm, and those induced primarily with the aid of cultural signals, such as the meditative states, hypnosis, or the religious or ritual state...(1986:83).*

Rouget saw trance

> *as a state of consciousness composed of two components, one psychophysiological, the other cultural. The universality of trance indicates that it corresponds to a psychophysiological disposition innate in human nature, although, of course, developed to varying degrees in different individuals. The variability of its manifestations is the result of the variety of cultures by which it is conditioned (1985:3).*

To talk meaningfully about trances is so difficult because we don't have a commonly agreed upon definition for the so-called "normal" state of consciousness. Consensus about what the "norm" actually is may vary considerably between different ethnic groups (see, Ackerknecht, 1971:63-64, and Benedict, 1934, 1972).

The "everyday" state of consciousness can best be defined negatively as differing from hypnotic, sleep and dream states as well as hypnagogic (preceding sleep) and hypnopompic (preceding waking) states. Many of us have only a vague idea of what it means to be "fully awake." *Vipassana* meditation teaches us to be conscious of every thought, word, and deed. Now, some researchers keep telling us that less than 8 per cent of our perceptions are consciously registered and processed. If this is true, this may be one reason why shamans say they have to shift the attention of their clients to different levels of experience.

Eliade calls the shaman a master of ecstasy and sees this ecstasy unfolding during "magical flight." In religious literature, we read about "ecstatic" states of prophets and saints. The word "ecstasy" itself is derived from the Greek *ekstasis,* "being put out of place and carried away by a powerful emotion, a state of extreme emotional exaltation." Here we have landed in the middle of a controversy. Eliade, who studied the phenomenology of shamanism, clearly stated that not any ecstatic can be called a shaman. For Eliade, "The shaman specializes in a trance during which his soul is believed to leave his body and ascend to the sky or descend to the underworld" (1974:5). Eliade and Harner reject that shamans can also become possessed. Possession seems to imply that an intrusion occurred and a spirit has become the "actor," but Findeisen (1957) and other scholars, especially those who conducted extensive fieldwork, found that shamans are capable of doing both. Almost each shaman can go on a magical flight and can become possessed, too. Eliade considered possession a later, "degenerate" form of the magical flight and saw "the incorporation of spirits and possession by them" to be "universally distributed phenomena" which did not necessarily belong to shamanism (Lewis, 1971:49).

As mentioned above, I observed the development going into the opposite direction, i.e., from possession to magical flight (see also, Cardeña, 1989). In Singapore, for example, people may fall into deep possession trances unexpectedly. It can happen when they enter a temple or while they are watching the possession of a medium or even while they are doing their daily scores. They will then go to an experienced medium and be diagnosed whether they require exorcism or whether they have been "called to serve the gods." An exorcism becomes necessary when it is said that the individual has broken a taboo, e.g., has stepped inadvertently on offerings, lives in an apartment house which has been built on cemetery grounds or when mischievous, earthbound spirits want to draw attention to their plight. It then suffices to perform an exorcism during which offended spirits are appeased and made to promise an end to the affliction. Those "selected to serve the gods" are either trained by experienced mediums or begin to follow the instructions of the possessing spirits.

After they have served as vehicles for the gods for some time, their possession states may move from full possession to more and more monitored possession, eventually reaching states where possession is not used that frequently anymore and the mind of the shamans begins to "expand" (see also, Max Beauvoir's self-report in Part II).

Before I discuss this issue further, we have to look at "altered states of consciousness" (ASC) in general. An ASC has been defined by Tart as an individual feeling of a clear

> *qualitative shift in his pattern of mental functioning, that is, he feels not just a quantitative shift...but also that some quality or qualities of his mental processes are different. Mental functions operate that do not operate at all ordinarily, perceptual qualities appear that have no normal counterpart (1972:1-2; see also, Bourguignon, 1973; Ludwig, 1968; Peters and Price-Williams, 1980; and Prince, 1968)*

I prefer the word "alternate" instead of "altered" because the term "altered states of consciousness" carries negative connotations and implies intrusive or artificial "altering" while the term "alternate states" better describes the progression of states which an individual experiences in descending or ascending order.

The following diagram

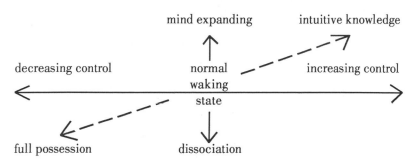

shows that states of consciousness may become increasingly dissociative and less controlled to the point of full possession (e.g., multi-personality disorders). Or individuals enter increasingly mind-expanding states which they learn to control to the point of "intuitive knowledge" or just "being" (Heinze, 1988:94).

From the above, the reader can deduce that I disagree with Harner (1980) and Goodman (1988) who say that there is only one "shamanic" or one "religious" state of consciousness. My field notes document that most shamans pass through a series of alternate states during one session until they reach the level on which they operate best.

We find descriptions of different states of consciousness in the manuals of world religions because the need to come into the presence of the "Divine" is deeply rooted in the human soul. (To give one example, the Buddhist Abhidhamma lists over 108 different states of mental cultivation.) During my fieldwork, I was told over and over again that people do not have the time for intensive cultivation and that they, furthermore, are unable to reach higher dimensions. However, because it is essential for them to witness the manifestations of the "Divine," they need shamans who serve as "vehicles" or "mouthpieces of the gods."

It is believed the "Divine" has manifested when a spirit has entered the body of a shaman, in other words, when the shaman shows visual signs that s/he has become "possessed." The process of passing through possession states of increasing depth may last from a few minutes to half an hour. It is said that the shaman's ego detaches itself from the body to make room for the "intruding" spirit and may either fully merge with the spiritual energy or go on a magical flight at the same time. One medium in Singapore told me in great detail what she had experienced on her magical flights, but she had no memory of what transpired, when her body had been used by a deified general at the same time (personal communication, 1979).

To repeat, we have to recognize shamanic states where shamans go on a "magical flight" and explore the upper or the lower worlds. They remain fully conscious and monitor all experiences in the spirit world. During possession states, however, shamans allegedly have no control and later no memory of what transpired. Furthermore, even experienced shamans will go through periods of temporarily flooding, i.e., they allow the possession to run its course without any interference because when they were taught how to trigger possession states, they also learned how to exit these states, on their own or with the help of assistants (see, photo 16). Assistants will either sprinkle blessed water on the medium or physically close the "Third Eye" (on the forehead, between the eyebrows) with their thumb.

Some ethnic groups have developed terms for different possession states. Cardeña (1989), who conducted fieldwork in Haiti, speaks of a disorganized, transitional stage, followed by a state where depersonalization occurs and a different identity appears. Frigerio reports that the Umbandistas of Argentina recognize three levels of possession: *irradiacion, encostamiento* and *incorporacion* (terms borrowed from Portuguese).

> Irradiacion *(irradiation) means that some of the entity's energy is reaching the medium, but does not have full control over his body; the medium may experience strange sensations in certain body parts, or may have intuitions about certain problems, but is still basically himself.*

> Encostamiento *(to be beside) means that the spirit is leaning against the medium...touching him and in this way controlling his body. It may also cause the medium to forget some of what he is witnessing. In daily usage, these two terms, irradiacion and encostamiento, are frequently used interchangeably, to denote a state of half-way possession.*

> Incorporacion *(incorporation)...means that the entity has fully entered the body of the medium and he is therefore completely possessed (1989:2).*

Frigerio discusses at length how important *incorporacion* is for mediums because clients expect to talk to the god and not the person of the medium. Mediums may, therefore, claim to be fully-possessed not to disappoint their clients, even when the depth of their possession states is fluctuating during the session (see example below).

Rouget thought that trance consists "of a series of events that can only be described by those who have lived through them" (1985:3). Because trances are subjective experiences, he found it more productive to look at the "external manifestations" of trances. He suggested to analyze the context during which trances are observed and to investigate "the representations of which they are the object" (1985:3). Rouget defined possession as a "radical alteration of the embodied self" and distinguished between

ecstasy *[which can be equated with magical flight]: immobility, silence, solitude, no crisis, sensory deprivation, recollection, hallucinations;*

possession: *movement, noise, in company, crisis, sensory overstimulation, amnesia, no hallucinations (1985:11).*

I was present when a Meo shaman in northern Thailand went on a magical flight. Although the reason for the ritual was of rather minor importance (she had been called to heal a child from a severe cold), she went through all motions of the ritual without leaving out any of the expected parts. She sat down on a bench in front of the family for which she was performing this feat, using the bench like a horse. She blindfolded herself and began to ride through the spirit world, shaking two iron rings from which several metal objects were dangling. Once in a while she would curb her horse, jump up, and greet the spirit she had just met. After having briefly talked to the respective spirit, she would sit down again, bobbing up and down on the bench like on a horse, until she met another spirit. She certainly was not immobile and silent in her ecstasy and she performed in full view of the people concerned. Rouget's distinctions, therefore, need to be tested in each case and require qualification before they can be applied.

More helpful is Cardeña who, in a paper on the "Variety

of Possession Experiences" (1989b), distinguishes (1) transitional states from (2) states with discrete identity, and from (3) states with transcendent qualities,

1. *transitional: dizziness/light headedness, precarious equilibrium, somatic alterations, cognitive disorganization (common to state transitions: sleep, anesthesia, hypnosis; pre-reorganization);*

2. *with discrete identity: change of one identity to another, co-identities, unusual behavior and experience (multiplicity of being, dissociation, expression of forces/entities);*

3. *transcendent: total involvement, consciousness expansion, energy, organismic (breakdown of self/body; alternate modality of experiencing).*

Cardeña's "transitional" state corresponds to Frigerio's *irradiato* and *encostado* states. Cardeña's second state is described by others as "full possession" and Cardeña's "transcendent" state can be compared with "magical flight" and other "mind-expanding" experiences.

I found in Southeast Asia that trances in Malaysia, Indonesia, Thailand, and Singapore differ considerably from the trances of Siberian shamans. The masters of alternate states of consciousness in Malaysia seldom go into full possession trance, except during horse or tiger possession. The trances in Indonesia, especially Bali, are part of community rituals which have shamanic features, but are mostly performed to bless and protect the whole community. Indonesian shamans practice on a one to one basis in their own homes. The trances of Thai shamans are often so light that physical changes are not visible to the ordinary eye. Clients of Singapore Chinese mediums, however, expect to come into the presence of deities, e.g., full possession. They want to "see" the deities, talk to them or be talked to directly.

When I witnessed the progression from full possession to controlled possession and studied the access to different states of consciousness in Southeast Asia, I found that a shaman's career began with strong possession trances which Frigerio would have called "incorporation" and progressed, in most cases, to more consciously monitored forms of trance.

It has to be mentioned here also that it is physically difficult to remain in a deep trance for a long time. Shamans, expected to dramatize the ritual process and making the invisible visible, do not hesitate to produce the expected manifestations whether a deity actually possesses them or not. As we all are creators of our own reality, they "create" the trance and may, eventually, during the performance work themselves into a genuine trance. Acting out a trance is as acceptable as a genuine trance. Clients who come with high expectations won't be aware of any difference.

Through my long-standing friendship with shamans, I am able to distinguish whether they are deeply in trance or working on intermediate levels or are not in trance at all. I will give one example:

A forty-year old housewife in Singapore called, in 1978/1979, the spirit of a general from the Three Kingdoms (third century A.D.) into her body every evening from 7 to 12 p.m. and twice on weekends. During onsetting trance her toes stiffened and curled. When the depth of her trance decreased, her toes released tension and uncurled. It was very interesting to observe how she monitored the intensity of her trance during a five-hour session. Her clients looked the god into his (her) face and did not pay any attention to his (her) feet. They could not "see" any difference. Toe curling was an indicator of the depth of trance for this particular shaman while other changes, e.g., different facial expressions, reversed breathing patterns, can be observed with other shamans. Such changes indicate either onsetting possession of a different spirit or varying depth of trance.

I saw Chinese mediums change their pattern of breathing when a possession was imminent. They began to swallow air and made vomiting noises. They rolled their head and sweated profusely. This checks with De Groot's description of the "descent of a spirit into a medium,"

*Drowsily staring, he shivers and yawns resting his arms on the table, and his head on his arms, as if falling asleep. As the incantation proceeds with in-*

*creasing velocity and loudness with the accompaniment of gongs and drums, "eye opening" papers are being burned. The medium suddenly jumps up to frisk and skip about (1910:1274).*

Techniques to go into trance differ considerably. Some shamans use meditation in solitude, some require drumming and chanting in public (Heinze, 1988:84-98; Jilek, 1982:326-243, Neher, 1962: 151-160). The role of rhythmic sensory stimulation has been studied already by Adrian and Matthews in the 1930s and in the 1940s by Walters and Walters (1949). The Walters are quoted by Jilek as saying

*rhythmic sensory stimulation of the organ of hearing as a whole can be accomplished only by using a stimulus containing components of supraliminal intensity, a steep-fronted sound such as produced by untuned percussion instruments (1982:327).*

Prince (1968) considered the possibility of auditory driving a "commonly used portal of entry in the dissociative state." Neher found that different sound frequencies are transmitted along different nerve pathways in the brain (1961:152-153) to which Jilek added that

*auditory driving responses were elicited at the fundamental of each stimulus frequency (3,4,6 and 8 beats per second), and also at second harmonics and second subharmonics of some stimulus frequencies (1982:327-328).*

Achterberg reports,

*The sound of the percussion instruments and the rattles are time-honored methods for consciousness altering, and are considered to have a numbing or analgesic effect....Several physiological facts support the role of sound....First, the auditory tracts pass directly into the reticular activating system (RAS) of the brain stem. The RAS is a massive "nerve net" and functions to coordinate sensory input and motor tone, and to alert the cortex to incoming information. Sound, traveling on these pathways, is capable of activating the entire brain. Strong, repetitive neuronal firing in the auditory pathways and ultimately in the cerebral cortex...could theoretically compete successfully for cognitive awareness. Other sensory stimuli from ordinary reality...could thus be gated or filtered out. The mind would then be free to expand into other realms (1985:42-43).*

Other techniques to reach alternate states of consciousness are: focussed suggestive attention, pain stimulation (pushing skewers through cheeks and tongue, e.g., Chinese and Tamil shamans in Singapore), hypoglycemia and dehydration, forced hypermotility, kinetic stimulation (dancing or rolling one's head), hyperventilation, hot or cold temperature stimulation, seclusion and restricted mobility, visual-sensory deprivation, sleep deprivation (Heinze, 1988: 85-87, see also, Jilek, 1982:335-339).

Some shamanic traditions employ sacred plants, i.e., hallucinogenic substances (see, Fürst, 1972; Harner, 1973; La Barre, 1938; Wasson, 1968). The fly-agaric mushroom has been used among Siberian shamans, peyote among the Huicholes and the Native American Indian Church, and Banisteriopsis vine (*ayahuasca*, also called *yage*) among Indian tribes in Central and South America. Achterberg quotes Prem Das, "a young man trained in both Yogic and Huichol traditions" who "views the sacred plants as an intermediate step only, and says that advanced practitioners no longer have need of them" (1985:37).

No hallucinogenic substances were used to induce trance by any of the 122 Southeast Asian shamans I studied. Although opium and hemp are easily available, these hallucinogens are considered to be recreational drugs. I remember one case where a medium in trance consumed large amounts of hard liquor (whiskey and sake) and continued to take opium. It was amazing to observe that neither alcohol nor drugs had any visible effect on his trance and he was completely sober when he returned to his everyday consciousness. Similar was the case of a diabetic woman who could not tolerate any alcohol in daily life but consumed large amounts of liquor with impunity when she was in trance and possessed by a general from the Three Kingdoms. Temple committee members explained that the deity was very fond of alcohol and had been placated to grant some wishes of the community.

These findings do, however, not exclude the possibility that sacred plants are part of shamanic rituals in other parts of the world.

When we look at the trances described in Part II, the Haitian shaman and the Tibetan oracle are expected to go into full possession trance on the cues their culture has provided for them. The trances of the Zulu, Hawaiian, Korean and Garhwal shamans don't indicate full possession though the audience may, at times, expect it. Caucasian shamans also work with trances, either generated by prolonged dancing and drumming (Cogburn) or dramatic involvement (Grotowski). Although both don't intend to create a new religion, they are examples for Felicitas Goodman saying

> *we have a biological propensity for experiencing both the ordinary and the alternate reality. In the long run...humans cannot tolerate ecstasy deprivation. The religious trance is an indestructible part of our genetic heritage. No amount of urban living can change that. If humans were no longer taught any religions, they would...spontaneously create new ones from the content of ecstatic experiences, combined with bits and pieces transmitted by language and folklore (1988:171).*

Bourguignon conducted a statistical study looking at trances crossculturally. Using data of the HRAF (Human Relations Area Files), her team found that

> *of a sample of 488 societies, in all parts of the world..., 437, or 90% are reported to have one or more institutionalized, culturally patterned forms of altered states of consciousness....It is clear that we are dealing with a psychobiological capacity available to all societies (1973:9-11).*

Anthropologists agree that ritual trance is known by many names and is practiced in many different forms by different ethnic groups. Goodman, quoting Lex (1979), confirms that trance "arises from manipulation of universal neurophysiological structures of the human body [and] lies within the potential behavior of all normal human beings" (1986:84). Goodman herself just finished a book on her study of the effect of body postures on the religious altered state of consciousness. She is using the sound of a rattle as trigger mechanism during her experiments.

When trance is an innate human faculty, we seem to lack opportunities to experience trance in the West. We can watch an evangelist speaking in tongues on T.V. But trance, in general, has been secularized and may be experienced at rock concerts or at football games which provide a cathartic release of emotions. These trances have retained the function of social mechanisms but do not necessarily connect the spectators in the football stadium to any sacred realm.

Trance is more than a conditioned reflex and a dramatization of the audience's expectations. The main feature of a shamanic trance is that the shaman shifts the attention of those present to a level where healing can occur and solutions to acute problems can be found.

I fully agree with Lommel who said

*In all accounts the shaman's psychical experiences during the trance are conceived as real experiences, frequently understood as miracles and spread abroad as such.*

*Of course, they are no less real because they are "only" psychic realities. Moreover, the shaman's trance produces a real effect in the psyche of the audience. The latter never remain mere onlookers, but are stirred to the depths by the shamanistic trance. They experience a process of transformation—a catharsis—a purification and ordering of the psyche, an increase in self-confidence and security. All this renders them better able to stand up to the dangers of everyday life (1967:106).*

## 3. Pathology

Some psychiatrists still maintain that shamans are suffering from some kind of mental illness (Devereux, 1956, Silverman, 1967). In the case of Siberian shamans, their trances have been diagnosed "arctic hysteria" (Aberle, 1952) and long discussions have been carried on about the epileptic nature of shamanic behavior. More evidence has in the meantime been accumulated. When epileptic seizures seem to be connected with spiritual experiences (see, e.g., Dostoevski's self-reports), epilectics seem to lack the ministerial, altruistic features of shamans (Findeisen, 1957:166). Jilek (1978:32-39) discusses at length the different erroneous theories starting with Kroeber's conclusion that "not only the shamans are involved in psychopathology, but often also the whole lay public of primitive societies" (1952). Jilek suggests that

> the classification of shamanic behavior and of native ritual, in terms of Western psychiatric nomenclatures, constitutes both a eurocentric and a positivistic fallacy: (1) eurocentric, because it elevates modern Western culture to an absolute norm against which other cultures and their institutions may be judged as abnormal, (2) positivistic, because it considers behaviour which does not fit into the framework of logico-experimental explanatory theory, as a departure from rational norm due to ignorance or poor reality testing (1978:34).

The 122 shamans I have worked with over the last thirty years go regularly and professionally into trance. They all have daytime jobs and lead a productive life which bears no indication that they have "supernatural" faculties or that they are "fantasy-prone" (see also, among others, Peters and Price-Williams, 1980). Only two of the 122 shamans went into early retirement to devote all their time to their altruistic vocation, all of the 120 work as book keepers, taxi drivers, sales persons, models, housewives, students. I found that it takes a healthy, rather robust mind to become possessed "voluntarily under controlled circumstances" (Lewis, 1971:56). Richard Noll (1983) compared shamanic states with the experiences of schizophrenics and found that there is not much correspondence. Roger Walsh (1989) quotes Eliade saying that "shamans remain functional throughout life while many schizophrenics may deteriorate." Bryce-Boyer (1964) conducted research among Apaches who show some schizophrenic features, however, the Apache shamans are the least pathological of the tribe. Furthermore, the conditions of a hysteric or schizophrenic will, at times, be uncontrollable and, in many countries, be diagnosed as spirit possession which require exorcism. Psychopaths are also egocentric and asocial by nature. They are easily excitable, incapable of judging problems and cannot develop feelings toward other. Selfless service is the least thing they are inclined to involve themselves. The trances of shamans, on the other hand, take place in a culturally acceptable framework and are controlled. Scientists have to admit that these are important differences.

To "evaluate the stages of consciousness people experience during a particular practice," Roger Walsh (1989) has begun to work on stage maps. He compares shamanic, schizophrenic, insight meditation, and yogic states, the latter two mean either the ascent through the seven chakras toward the union with the Divine in yoga or the seven *jhanas* of increased concentration over one hundred distinct states on the way toward *samadhi,* as listed in the Buddhist Abhidharma. According to Walsh, during the shamanic journey state

*it seems that shamans have some diminished awareness of the environment but still can interact with clients and the community. So it is not a complete reduction of external awareness. Concentration seems to be enhanced. Shamans...have control over their state and the content. In fact, they can move through various realms, to various places, at will. The level of arousal tends to be increased....so calmness seems to go down. Introspective sensitivity is increased. The self sense—the sense of identity—is usually, but not always, experienced as a separate individual being; identified not so much with the physical body but with the soul....Affect and emotion can vary from positive to negative, depending on what is being experienced. The content is usually dominated by organized, coherent imagery which reflects the world-view of the shamans, their understanding of the upper and the lower worlds, where they are going, who they expect to meet ....So there is a high degree of organization (1989:19).*

Walsh continues to say that in individuals suffering from schizophrenia

*awareness of the environment can be either increased or decreased. Concentration is drastically reduced. Schizophrenics have very little ability to concentrate and have practically no control over their states. Their arousal is usually high; they may be agitated and need tranquilizers for that reason. Calmness goes way down. Introspective sensitivity can be increased. The sense of self may disintegrate. Cognitive processes are so out of control, there is not enough cognititive coherence to maintain a coherent sense of self....Emotions are usually negative, often horrific, but occasionally can be ecstatic. The mental content is fragmented, often lacking a framework of coherence, except in cases of paranoia (1989:20).*

However, Insight meditation

*hones sensitivity, so awareness of the environment increases. On the other hand, in yoga, one goes inward and withdraws the senses—it's called* pratyahara—*so that awareness of the environment is drastically reduced. Concentration in insight meditation is somewhat increased but "momentary," meaning that attention moves from one object to another (this is also true of shamanic journeys). However, in yogic* samadhi, *concentration is dramatically increased, fixed and immovable meaning that attention remains fixed on a single object. Both practices de-*

*velop increased control of the mind. Whereas arousal for shamans and schizophrenics increases, in insight meditation usually it decreases and in some of the yogic practices dramatically decreases. Calmness increases in both Buddhist and yogic practices (1989:20-21).*

Walsh continues that

*Introspective sensitivity is dramatically increased in Insight meditation....The research data with tachisto-scopic studies show that Insight meditators probably have a greater degree of perceptual sensitivity and processing speed than has ever been recorded in human beings before....In Insight meditators, the sense of self is deconstructed...into its component stimuli—a thought here, an image a second later, an affect, another thought....At this sensitive level of perception these cannot be mistaken for a continuous sense of self or ego. It is like watching a movie. There is only one frame and then there is another, but with our usual limited perceptual sensitivity they look con-tinuous and in motion.....one deconstructs what is thought first to be a stable self-sense or ego into constituent components and finds ceaseless flux. On the other hand, in yoga, the end result is unchanging atman, purusa or pure consciousness, an unchanging transcendental self-sense (1989:21).*

I quoted so extensively from Walsh to support my point that we have to increase our efforts and continue to investigate the properties of shamanic states. As long as the DSM-III-R does not provide classifications of shamanic states, health practi-tioners will diagnose such states as pathological. The perpetu-ation of erroneous opinions blocks future research and de-prives us of valuable resources.

Furthermore, although there has been evidence that a "wounded healer" has developed insights and techniques which qualify him/her to become a shaman (Halifax, 1982, and others), the majority of the shamans in my sample never went through a psychotic state or showed any sign of pathology. For me, the "wounded healer" concept indicates that people who have completed the healing process consciously have, like shamans, a deeper knowledge of the ways how to deal with imbalances in the relationship between man and the universe but they may not necessarily become mediators between the sacred and the secular for their community.

## 4. Gender

Of the 122 shamans I worked with, 86 were men and 36 were women. Of the ethnic Chinese shamans 61 were men and only 16 were women, indicating that Confucian influence pushed female shamans *(wu)* from their prominent positions in earlier Chinese society into less respected roles (Eliade, 1974:546). Later shamans, who practiced in the framework of Folk Taoism, suffered when their messages from the "Lord High" were used to legitimize political uprisings. Among Chinese shamans today, gender discrimination is rare. A male shaman may become possessed by a sea goddess (see, photo 17) or a forty-year old housewife may become the vehicle of a deified general from the Three Kingdoms (appr. 300 A.D., see, photo 18).

Of the 31 ethnic Thai shamans, 17 were women indicating that female shamans retained a greater equality in Thai society. The predominance of middle-aged male shamans becomes obvious again when we look at the sample of ten Malay bomohs of whom only two were women. Among Hindu, shamanism is almost exclusively practiced by men, although, especially in northern India and Nepal, we find also successful female shamans (see Part II, profile of the Garhwali shaman).

The sex of a shaman, however, is not important to clients. They are attracted to those shamans who have the most powerful spiritual connections.

Across countries, we sense, furthermore, a tendency toward hermaphroditism. Among the Ngadju Dayak of southern Borneo, for example, the *basir* are priest-shamans. The term *basir* means "unable to procreate, impotent," which makes the *basir* hermaphrodites. They dress and behave like women and are considered to be the proper intermediaries between the feminine (earth) and the masculine element (sky), satisfying the need of abolishing polarities (Eliade, 1964:352).

During sessions, in northern Thailand as well as in Burma, shamans will select clothing which resemble women's attire. Shamans also may enter a marriage with their possessing spirit, female shamans with a male *nat* (e.g., in Burma) or male shamans with a female spirit which does not preclude that they have a "human" spouse too. Eliade informs us that the "mystical marriage of the shamaness to her tutelary god appears to be an archaic custom" (1974:463). He also notes that

> *among the Auraucanians, shamanism is practiced by women; in earlier times, it was the prerogative of sexual inverts. A like situation is found among the Chukchee: the majority of shamans are inverts and sometimes even take husbands; but even when they are sexually normal their spirit guides oblige them to dress as women; cf. W.G. Bogoras, 1904:450ff. Is there a genetic relation between these two shamanisms? The question seems difficult to decide (1974:125).*

He reports later that

> *Ritual transformation into a woman also occurs among the Kamchadal, the Asiatic Eskimo, and the Koryak; but in the latter case Jochelson found only a recollection of such a transformation. Though rare, the phenomenon is not confined to northwestern Asia; transvestitism and ritual change of sex are found, for example, in Indonesia, (the* manang bali *of the Sea Dyak), in South America (Patagonians and Araucanians), and among certain North American tribes (Arapaho, Cheyenne, Ute, etc.; 1974:258).*

> *A young man seldom becomes a* manang bali *[in Indonesia]. They are generally old or childless men,*

*attracted by the extremely tempting material situation....In Ramree Island, off the coast of Burma, some sorcerers adopt women's dress, become the "husband" of a colleague, and then bring him a woman as a "second wife,," with whom both men cohabit....This is clearly a ritual transvestitism, accepted either in obedience to a divine command or for the sake of woman's magical prestige (1974:351-352, note 48).*

Eliade recognizes that "ritual and symbolic transformation into a woman" probably derived from the ideology of an archaic matriarchy, but does not necessarily "indicate any priority of women in the earliest shamanism." The special class of men "similar to women" can also not be attributed to the "decadence of the shaman." It is a phenomenon which "extends far beyond the North Asian area (1974:258). The "clear traces of a feminine magic and a matriarchal mythology, which must formerly have dominated the shamanism of the Sea Dyak" is, for example, contradicted by "the fact that this *manang bali* class is unknown in the interior of the island," indicating that "the entire complex (transvestitism, sexual impotence, matriarchy)" may have come "from outside, though in distant times" (Eliade, 1974:352).

# 5. Paraphernalia

During my fieldwork, I found a large variety of paraphernalia used by contemporary shamans. Meaningful for the community around the shaman, such paraphernalia may be puzzling to any uninitiated outsider. I will first report on the most striking differences.

Malay-Muslim shamans practice in their daily clothes and use a minimum of equipment,

*1. water and flowers to be blessed while chanting verses of the Qur'an and to be offered to the spirits evoked;*

2. *limes* (limau nipis) *cut into four pieces for divination,*

3. *a wooden knife to be put between the toes of clients to diagnose their condition;*

4. *herbal medicine.*

Hindu shamans (see, Part II) wear a white loincloth, leaving the upper part of their body bare when they are male. They use limes to exorcise, *nim* (*margosa,* pomegranate) leaves to sprinkle blessed water, and *vibhuti* (cowdung ashes) to be applied internally and externally as medicine.

Thai shamans either wear daily clothes and, maybe, a scarf draped around one shoulder like a brahmin cord or, in the north, they don traditional Burmese clothes when "calling the spirits."

Most Chinese shamans require more elaborate equipment,

1. *a "dragon throne," (an armchair painted in red, carrying the insignia of the spirit and the eight trigrams of the* I-Ching, *see, photo 16);*

2. *flags of different colors (for the generals protecting the four directions), exorcist flags, etc. (see, photo 6);*

3. *skewers (applied to demonstrate the protection of the possessing spirit) as well as swords and whips used in exorcism;*

4. *an "apron" worn during trance, carrying the insignia of the possessing spirit;*

5. *blessed water;*

6. *red ink and brushes to write on amulets and charm papers;*

7. *divining blocks* (mu bei), *made out of kidney-shaped pieces of bamboo, between 6 to 8 inches long, split lengthwise into two halves, each with a flat and a convex side;*

8. *charm papers.*

The instruments used for rhythmic sensory stimulation or trance induction will be drums and rattle of various sizes. Rhythmic drumming is also often accompanied by vigorous chanting of temple committee members or loyal followers.

The important role of the drum is mentioned in the profiles of the Haitian, Zulu, Hindu, Korean, Tibetan, and the Caucasian shaman in Part II. I myself observed the use of the drum with all Chinese mediums whether in Singapore, Malaysia, or Thailand. Ethnic Malay, Javanese, and Balinese shamans will use a small gamelan orchestra of their own and northern Thai shamans have a traditional orchestra playing for them during trance. Frequently, there will be two orchestras alternating because a spirit dance may last a day or two.

Shamanic practices require a place where sacred objects can be placed and be protected from contamination. Because Islam does not allow any depiction of the sacred, Malay-Muslim shamans create a sacred place before each performance. For example, a yellow cloth is hung from the ceiling, different offerings are laid out, and a candle is lit to evoke the spirits (see, photo 5). Chinese mediums have elaborate altars on which Taoist deities stand next to statues of Buddha and Buddhist saints or even Hindu gods and the Madonna. There will always be some flower and fruit offerings, some incense burning, and small cups are constantly filled with freshly brewed tea in case the visiting deities are thirsty.

On photo 7 in this book, Max Beauvoir puts bottles of alcohol as offerings on a provisional table to prepare for the opening ceremony of an art exhibition and photo 15 shows an altar typical for a Thai shaman.

Other ethnic groups expect their shamans to wear certain insignia, a staff, a sword, a pipe, or a powerful amulet. Elizabeth Cogburn speaks of her medicine pipe as a portable altar. The pipe appeared first to her in a dream. After she had found her pipe in a storehouse, she learned of the tradition that one has to dream of one's sacred pipe. The pipe "taught" her what she needed to know and to do.

It should be mentioned here that Elizabeth's sword "manifested" in a yucca plant out in the Arizona desert. Swords have traditionally been used by shamans to fight fear and to battle with "demons" (see, photo 18), or to turn the sword against the shaman's own body to prove that s/he is protected from harm. In Singapore, Chinese mediums may hit their shoulders with prick balls for the same purpose.

On photo 9, David Bray is wearing his sacred whale tooth pendant as well as his shamanic amulet. It contains a nine-pointed star surrounding an opal. Depicted on his amulet are also the rising sun with twenty-three rays, the full moon, and another star. David wears, furthermore, on his forehead the sacred kukui nut. The history of the sacred stone Kukapihe is told in David Bray's profile in Part II.

The most elaborate paraphernalia are those of the Tibetan oracle (described in detail in Part II).

Ceremonial objects are used not only to please and to instill confidence in clients and to put on a "good show." Drums, bells, pipe are also used for more intrinsic reasons, that means, divine power can manifest in ceremonial objects. Especially drums and bells lend themselves to become the voice of spiritual power. Nothing is so powerful as the sound of a drum or, for example, the sound of Tibetan trumpets. The universe resounds and everybody present is imbued with these "vibrations."

In sum, paraphernalia and ceremonial objects follow either different local traditions in their expected appearance or are newly created by shamans when specific needs arise. Paraphernalia are diverse and individual in their material form but everyone of these objects and articles of clothing serves to make the invisible visible and thus represents spiritual power.

# 6. Rituals

Victor Turner sees in a ritual "prescribed formal behavior for occasions not given over to technological routine, having reference to beliefs in mystical beings and powers" (1974:19).

The structure of each shamanic session does, indeed, reflect the ritualized communication between shamans and the supernormal according to the belief system and the myths of the respective ethnic group (see, *Manifestations of the Sa-*

*cred,* Part I). Such a communication goes beyond the purpose of a prayer and is usually expected to be reciprocal.

There are seven steps necessary to complete a ritual:

1. *The shaman and all those who are invited and have expressed the wish to participate decide on the purpose of the ritual.*

2. *The shaman determines and consecrates the ritual space.*

3. *Before anybody enters the ritual space, the shaman and all participants are purified (using certain breathing techniques, water, incense, etc.).*

4. *The appropriate spiritual entities are evoked.*

5. *Communication between the sacred and the shaman occurs and all participants benefit from the presence of the Divine.*

6. *The spiritual entities are feasted and properly send away.*

7. *All leave ritually the sacred space and are reintegrated into the routines of daily life.*

In his *Rites of Passage* (1909/1960) which accentuate different stages in life (e.g., birth, maturity, death), Van Gennep speaks of the natural sequence of rites of separation and rites of reincorporation. After entering the sacred space (the state between separation and reincorporation), participants are in the "liminal" state which allows the "unusual" to occur. They come into the presence of the Divine.

We may, therefore, talk about preliminal, liminal, and post-liminal stages. There will also be seasonal and crisis rites (Turner's rituals of affliction, 1974:9) because all rituals are instrumental.

Focusing on shamanic rites, Findeisen's description of Siberian rituals offers more details for a healing ritual:

1. *The shaman gets in touch with a helping spirit;*

2.  *s/he learns about the cause of the illness and where the soul of the sick person can be found;*

3.  *the shaman calls the spirits to catch the soul of the sick person;*

4.  *the shaman chases the illness demon out of the body of the sick person;*

5.  *the shaman returns the soul of the sick person to its body,*

6.  *the shaman thanks the helping spirits for their assistance (1957:131).*

Siikala (1978:76) lists twenty-seven different items and eight distinct stages. The structure of a ritual may change with different purposes, e.g., (a) healing by sucking, laying on of hands, massage, herbal treatment, or other means, (b) calling back an errant soul, or (c) exorcising.

All exorcisms I attended seem to follow a pattern which has also been reported by anthropologists who conducted fieldwork in other parts of the world.

1.  *the possessing spirit is called while pouring blessed water on the victim. Sometimes the water is poured through the flame of a lighted candle. Sometimes certain substances—uncooked rice, charcoal, onions, parsley, sulfur, salt, and small green beans—are thrown on the possessed as well (see Heinze, 1988:272);*

2.  *the spirit is asked to state his/her name;*

3.  *the spirit is asked what s/he wants;*

4.  *the spirit is promised that his/her wishes will be fulfilled;*

5.  *the spirit is then asked to leave.*

6.  *If reluctant, the spirit is commanded to leave in very authoritarian terms.*

7.  *When all present feel that the spirit has been*

*satisfied and has left, the patient is reintegrated
into the community.*

A similar sequence is described in the *Rituale Romanum* of the
Catholic Church. The Church, however, only casts spirits out
and does not promise to fulfill any wishes of the "demons." No
agreement is entered because no spirits other than the officially recognized saints may be asked to assist with human
needs.

To demonstrate the development of news rituals, I refer to
Elizabeth Cogburn's New Sun Dance Song Ritual (see Part
II). This ritual grew out of her own and the experiences of the
community interacting with her.

Although there are no direct connections to the sun dance
rituals practiced by North American Indians, the following
comparison can tell us something about genesis and purpose
of rituals.

Jilek (1982:331) calls the Sun Dance "the most magnificent ceremonial of the Plains tribes of Algonquian, Siouan,
Caddoan, and Shoshonean stock." Tribes were furnished with
the opportunity to express emotions in rhythmic form. "It
involved complex group rites associated with medicine power
and mythological themes relating to warfare and bison hunting, drawing large numbers of participants, "dancers, singers,
drummers, and spectators" (Jilek, 1982:332).

While the Sioux celebrated the Sun Dance every summer,
the Blackfeet performed it at irregular intervals of two or three
years.

*Among the Plains Algonquians, performance re-
quired a vow or pledge, usually made by a chaste
woman, in order to ward off sickness from self or kin—
the ceremonial therefore had prophylactic significance. The actual dancing ceremony lasted up to four
days; it was preceded by three or four days of fasting,
thirsting, and preliminary rites, and followed by
games, banquets, and other celebrations, so that the
whole festive occasion might extend to almost a
fortnight....The traditional Sun Dance lost its major
function, that of securing supernatural support for*

181

*individual and collective success in warfare and the chase, when Indian resistance to "manifest destiny" was finally crushed by U.S. Cavalry....In a desperate last resort to supernatural means, most Indian peoples...turned to the Ghost Dance religion often following the example of preeminent Sun Dancers...This transformative movement...aimed at a total change in the supra-individual system and was inspired by prophetic visions experienced in altered states of consciousness....The Ghost Dance movement ended with the bloody suppression of the Sioux out-break of 1890.*

The shamans of the Shoshone then, acting upon inspiration, shifted the emphasis of the Sun Dance ceremonial to

*the curing of illness and alleviation of social misery....The ceremonial developed into a redemptive movement...with therapeutic aims of achieving a total change in individuals, to promote spiritual, emo-tional, and physical health and thereby benefiting the community.*

With the exception of the Kiowa and the Assiniboine, in the original Sun Dance ceremony of the Plains Indians

*the self-inflicted torture was a prominent feature of the public performance....Young braves would propitiate supernatural agencies by the sacrifice of their pain and at the same time obtain individual spirit powers as well as the recognition of their fellow tribesmen. The devotee's skin was pierced with sharp skewers at breast, shoulders, or back, and fastened by strong thongs to the center pole or to buffalo skulls. For many hours he would then dance while leaning back, his weight hanging at the pole, or, if attached to buffalo skulls, he would drag them around the entire camp circle....*

Previously outlawed by the North American government, the Sun Dance Ritual *experienced a spectacular revitalization when the changing Zeitgeist encouraged the native renaissance we are witnessing since the 1950s. By the mid-1960s the Sun Dance flourished again as the major indigenous ceremonial of the Indian tribes in Wyoming, Idaho, Utah, and Colorado, claiming more adherents than the Native American Church of the Peyote Cult....Since the Sun Dance was also revived among the Sioux around 1960, hundreds of participants and spectators again gather every August at the Pine Ridge reservation in South Dakota (Jilek, 1982:332-333).*

Jilek recognizes in the Sun Dance

*the characteristics of a shamanic initiation. It includes calling and instruction by dream visions, guidance and tutoring by a shaman, and enduring an ordeal with fasting, thirsting, and painful self-torture in the quest for a personal power-vision (1982:333).*

After the Native American Indian Religious Freedom Act of 1978, sun dances have been held more often. In California, Wallace Black Elk, the successor of Neihardt's Black Elk, even conducts a Sun Dance for Caucasians outside of Ashland, Oregon, every August. Although most of the dancers will be Caucasians, the drummers are tribal people and all the rules about fasting, thirsting, sweat lodge, etc., are followed. When I attended the Sun Dance in the Ashland hills in August 1987, my observations confirm Jilek's description.

*Moving four times in each cardinal direction, the dancers alternately charge toward and retreat from the treelike pole erected in the center of the Sun Dance corral. This center pole with the traditional paraphernalia attached to it is charged with a symbolism reminiscent of the archetypal arbor vitae, and is considered a source of power as well as the medium through which cosmic power is channeled. A dancer who has taken the sacred vow is tethered to the center pole by rawhide ropes. These are tied to one or two*

*skewers which the Sun Dance chief slides through the*
*supramammillar skin of the dancer's chest after mak-*
*ing incisions, often bloodless, with a knife reserved for*
*this ceremonial use. Blowing his eagle-bone whistle*
*and sometimes holding a power-staff for protection*
*and strength, the devotee may dance for hours and*
*continue tugging until he "breaks the flesh"*
*(1982:334).*

Piercing is not practiced during Cogburn's Sun Dance. After Elizabeth experienced catharsis in her individual initiatory dance, now all participants in the New Song Sun Dance experience catharsis in a community setting. Elizabeth's dancers connect with a higher source which, during their ritual dance, manifests in the center pole.

To compare practices at different geographic locations, the life, rituals and practices of Max Beauvoir, the voodoo shaman in Haiti (see Part II), can be compared with that of Akuete Durchback in Togo, because the traditions they follow have common roots in Africa. Voodoo ceremonies, wherever they are performed, include elements which underscore man's relationship to the earth. The main technique of spiritual practice is entering a trance state where spirits are experienced directly. Akuete demonstrated supernormal powers already as a small child when he appeared to be possessed by spirits. His family did not encourage his trance and sent him to study medicine in Paris. While pursuing his studies, the spirits dramatically re-entered Akuete's life so that he returned to Lome and established himself as a spiritual master and teacher. Max Beauvoir as well as Akuete gradually and reluctantly accepted the "call." Both were exposed to Western ideas and technology and both returned to the ways of the traditional shaman in their culture without forgetting what they had learned in the West.

# 7. Symbolism

Symbols have been interpreted as being either "referential" or "condensation" symbols.

*Referential symbols are devices of reference such as spoken words, writing, signs, emblems, and designs, all of which have accepted meanings and which serve as economical devices for transmitting ideas. These have developed consciously during the evolution of culture, and are not of themselves charged with emotion. Condensation symbols, on the other hand, are a "condensed form of substitutive behavior for direct expression, allowing ready release of emotional tension in conscious or unconscious form." Both are rooted in the unconscious and transmit an emotional quality to situations and behavior. The condensation symbols are probably older; the referential developed later as a result of "emotional denudation." Ritual appurtenances and acts include both. The singing, rhythm, and costume inolved in a ritual are basically referential symbols, but they become charged with emotion and feeling derived from the unconscious (Rogers, 1982:59).*

*While a ritual constitutes of a chain of symbolic acts which are performed in a symbolic setting, a ritual symbol is "the smallest unit of ritual which still retains the specific properties of ritual behavior" (Turner, 1974).*

In shamanism we find a cross-culturally recurrent symbol, that is the representation of the world axis (*axis mundi*) or the world tree, also called the Cosmic Tree (in Northern Siberia, the larch), a pillar or a pole.

Cosmic pillars were believed to support heaven and to open, at the same time, the road to the world of gods. The Rig Veda, one of the oldest books in the world, mentions already the *skambha* (I, 105; X, 89, 4). In Europe, we find examples of "cosmic pillars" among the Celts and some teutonic tribes before they were converted to Christianity (e.g., the Irminsul). Cosmic poles are known also to tribes in Indonesia and elsewhere. "The Kwakiutl believe that a copper pole passes through the three cosmic levels (underworld, earth, sky)" (Eliade, 1957:35).

Hindu and Buddhist mythology speak of Mt. Meru as the Center of the World. The Cosmic Mountain is surrounded by the continents. Different levels and realms of experience are layered hierarchically around its top.

The center of the world, this axis, is the place

*where the sacred manifests itself in space, the real unveils itself, the world comes into existence. But the irruption of the sacred does not only project a fixed point into the formless fluidity of profane space, a center into chaos; it also effects a break in plane, that is, it opens communication between the cosmic planes (between earth and heaven) and makes possible ontological passage from one mode of being to another (Eliade, 1957:63).*

The aborigines of Australia use language and ritual to convey the meaning of the physical landscape. They intend to ensure the survival of those traveling in the Outback; and they want to interpret the dreamtime so that individual explorations convey the collective wisdom. The Australian aborigines actually create spirit markers in both the landscape and the dreamtime at places of vital resources—food and water in the Outback—to establish connections to the visions discovered during dreamtime. "Aboriginal truth and the social organization which provides access to cultural wisdom are created and recreated by a relationship to time and space quite unfamiliar to European philosophy" (Michaels, 1985:505-510).

The shaman's vehicle to ascent to the Upper World can be a tree, a pole, a ladder or s/he may ride on a bench like a horse (see, the Meo shaman, p. 162). Sometimes, a shaman just uses sound, i.e., a drum which is then called the "horse" of a shaman.

*It is indispensable in conducting the shamanic seance, whether it carries the shaman to the "Center of the World," or enables him to fly through the air, or summons and "imprisons" the spirits, or, finally, if the drumming enables the shaman to concentrate and regain contact with the spiritual world through which he is preparing to travel (Eliade, 1974:168).*

Eliade discusses evidence of "mysterious objects found in prehistoric sites" which could be interpreted to be drumsticks. If we agree with this interpretation, prehistoric men may already have "used drums comparable to those of the Siberian shamans" (1974:503). Much more could be said about the symbolism of the drum which is so complex because it serves a variety of magical functions.

When we look at trees as vehicles for ascension, tree symbolism can be found all over the world. Tree spirits appear already on over four-thousand-year-old seals found in the Indus Valley and we can only speculate on the lore connected with Harappan trees. In India, the

*sacrificial post (yupa) is made from a tree that is assimilated to the Cosmic Tree. The priest himself, accompanied by the woodcutter, chooses it in the forest....The sacrificial post becomes a sort of cosmic pillar (Eliade, 1974:403-404).*

We find such posts and trees mentioned in the Rg-Veda, III, 8, 3, and the Satapatha Brahmana, V, 2, 1, 10. The world tree, in form of a bai si, still appears in animist rituals in Thailand, e.g., at a *nag khwan*, performed at the eve of an ordination to assure that the soul of the novice will follow him into the monastery (see photo 19).

In Turko-Mongol religion the "birch or the post with seven or nine notches symbolizes the Cosmic Tree and hence is believed to stand at the 'Center of the World'" (Eliade, 1974:403).

Germanic lore talks about the world ash, Ygdrasil, that sends its roots into the underground world and whose branches reach the upper worlds. With the Judeo-Christian tradition, the Tree of Life and the Tree of Knowledge in the Garden of Eden assume different meanings. The Caucasian shaman (see Part II) talks about the "Tree of Life" which she modelled after the Qabalistic tree to use it as a "cosmic map" (for further details on the World Tree see, Vastokas, 1977).

Another archetypal shamanic symbol is the Cosmic Rope that holds together heaven and earth. The "rope trick" of Indian fakirs is a more demonstrative variant of a shaman's ascent to upper worlds. Individuals, having had Out-of-the-Body experiences, report that they feel connected to their physical body by a silver thread and that they were afraid they may not be able to return to life if this thread should break. These explanations go beyond the comparison to the umbilical cord which connects an unborn child to its mother. From Tibet and other parts of Asia to the Eskimo and the Huichol Indians in the Americas we hear about the soul or life-force "connected to the body by a fine thread as thin as the silky thread of a spider" (Kalweit, 1988:50). I wrote a whole book on the *tham khwan*, a Thai custom to tie the soul of an individual to his/her body (1982). This ritual becomes necessary when an individual goes on a trip into different territory or his or her body is considered to be weakened by loss of soul (which may have occurred accidentally or through the acts of a sorcerer).

Other means of ascent and descent are stairways like the one used by the Buddha to descend from Trayatrimsa Heaven. This stairway is depicted, among others, on Thai murals and reliefs at Bharhut und Sanchi. An actual sword ladder is still used by Chinese or Korean shamans today (see, among others, Eliade, 1974:455, and Heinze, 1988). To give more examples from around the world: The Egyptian Book of the Dead speaks of the ladder leading to heaven. "The Russian of Voronezh bake little ladders of dough in honor of their dead, and sometimes represent seven heavens on them by seven bars" (Eliade, 1974:487, note 95). A ladder *(klimax)* with seven rungs is mentioned in the Mithraic mysteries and we should not forget Jacob's ladder mentioned in the Bible (Gen. 28:12). Mohammed, furthermore, saw a ladder rising from the temple in Jerusalem.

Shamans also use bridges to cross over into different realities (see, e.g., Heinze, 1988:60, 78, 191-192). We have been told as children of the rainbow being a bridge which connects heaven and earth. In "some Japanese initiations the candidates are made to construct a 'bridge' upon seven arrows and with seven boards," (Eliade, 1974:484), comparable to the sword ladder of Chinese and Korean shamans.

I did not discuss the symbolism of colors and numbers because diversity has led to too many different interpretations for the same color and number. There seem, however, to be certain numbers like 2 (polarity), 3 (trinity), 5, 7, and 9 which are of universal importance. The symbols discussed above have been selected for comparison with symbols of other ethnic groups, so that readers can train their eyes to recognize the underlying common meaning in their diversity. They are, indeed, the major archetypal, universal symbols.

# 8. Clients

The clients I met during my fieldwork came from all walks of life.

*Men as well as women consult shamans....They belong to all age groups. They have accompanied their parents when they were children and they are brought by younger relatives when they [are too old and] cannot come on their own anymore. I observed.., in 1978/79, that the age groups between eighteen and forty-five constitute the majority of clients.*

*Each society is composed of a wide range of socio-economic groups, the lower-middle and the working classes being the largest in number and professionals in the minority. The clients of a shaman show the same distribution....To whatever socio-economic group they may belong, all clients seek protection and help of spiritual powers manifesting in a shaman of their choice (Heinze, 1988:63).*

These and other field observations prove that not only old women, widows, and disadvantaged people seek shamans. This would underestimate the wide range of needs discussed in Part IV. Furthermore, existential needs can arise at any age and be felt by any individual equal of his or her sex, status, and income. It would be falsifying the data if I would attempt to outline a profile of a typical client of a shaman. My task is to point out that everyone of my readers may, in time, feel the need to consult a practitioner who goes beyond visible symptoms and penetrates to the core of a problem.

Lommel expressed clearly the expectations of the clients who go to shamans. Whether they are fully aware of the processes or not,

> *They experience a process of transformation—a catharsis—a purification and ordering of the psyche, an increase in self-confidence and security. All this renders them better able to stand up to the dangers of everyday life (1967:106).*

# 9. Emergence of New Shamans

The first sign for the emergence of new shamans is that their faculty to establish connections to other worlds, in brief, their spiritual powers manifest and are discovered by others.

As an example how traditional shamans began to work, I selected Lommel's report on an Australian shaman. (He added that the tradition of the Australian aborigines is dying out rapidly since the thirties of this century. We can be doubly grateful to him that he attempts to collect and preserve the lore of Australian shamans.)

> *The shaman can go down to the netherworld, the country of the dead, and enter into relation with the spirits of the dead and in particular his own dead ancestors, in order to become artistically productive.... If a shaman speaks with the spirits of the dead, this takes place by his soul leaving him while he is asleep.... At sunset the shaman's soul meets somewhere the shadow of a dead ancestor. The shadow asks the soul whether it shall go with it. The shaman's soul answers yes. The shadow of the dead ancestor then becomes his helping spirit. Then they go on together...*
>
> *The shaman's meeting with the spirits of the dead*

*proceeds according to a ritual....First the shaman covers his eyes with a leafy branch, in order not to see too many dead all at once, and sits down modestly among those present.*

*The spirits begin to sing and dance. The shaman must not take away the branch from in front of his eyes and watch the dances until the helping spirit that has brought him there tells him to. When the dance is over the spirits release the shaman's soul and his helping spirit brings it back to his body. When the shaman wakes, his experiences with the spirits seem to him like a dream. From now on he thinks of nothing but the dances which he has seen and his soul keeps on going back to the spirits to learn more and more about the dances.*

*His wife may then notice that his soul leaves the body every night....the shaman will tell her that he goes to the spirits to learn dances. Then he will first explain the dances to his wife and sing them to her, and after that he will teach them to everyone else. That is how the magnificent pantomimic dances of the aborigines come into being.*

*But it also happens that a shaman loses the gift of frequenting the underworld. He suddenly becomes incapable of making contact with the spirits and his poetic gift for creating songs and dances vanishes. In such cases all the men gather together to reestablish the broken link with the dead forefathers.*

*The shaman is laid on the ground. All the men sit in a circle around him. They begin to sing and as they sing they slowly rub the shaman's body. The men sing for hours on end on a regular rising and falling note: mmmmm nnnnn mmmmm nnnnn. The shaman gradually goes into a trance; finally his soul leaves his body and...roams about looking for the spirit of a dead ancestor. After long wandering it will finally come upon such a spirit.*

*The dead ancestors themselves send out one of their number to look for the shaman. They themselves have painfully missed the shaman's visits and the contact with their living descendants. They wish to reestablish relations with the living. The shaman tells the spirit of the dead that he no longer knows the way to the underworld and cannot "find" any more songs. The spirit of the dead—frequently it will be the spirit of his father or grandfather—promises to help him and to come for him in a few days.*

*After a time—it is perhaps one evening when the people are sitting quietly and talking—the shaman suddenly hears a distant call. It is the helping spirit calling him. He goes off by himself and converses for a while with the spirits (Lommel, 1988:15-18).*

In the twentieth century, all over the world, shamans usually begin to work inside their family. Initiation now mainly takes place on the spiritual plane. In an urban setting, for example, we do not find many other shamans "authorized" to confer such initiation. The reputation that a shamanic advice and access to otherwise unretrievable information, an exorcism or a cure, has been successful spreads fast. One satisfied client tells his relatives, acquaintances, and friends and the group of followers grows. (I want to add here, that among the shamans I worked with none ever accepted a case s/he could not solve. Success rates are hard to measure because it is impossible to interview clients who may not want to talk about their experiences. One can only assume that shamans are successful when the number of their clients keeps growing.)

During the second phase in the career of a shaman, a hierarchy develops among the assistants. Some have taken over the task of regulating the stream of clients, others interpret and explain what the spirits have said. Clients have to be told how to wear amulets, how to use the herbal medicine and the blessed water. Entourage and clients expect codification because the "correct" performance of rituals is considered to be vital.

The entourage usually also determines the fee for the different shamanic services and administers the incoming donations. Although it is generally believed that shamans will lose their faculties when they become greedy, in some cases, the wealth of successful shamans becomes obvious. In other cases, their modesty and frugal life style speak of their altruism.

In multi-ethnic societies, shamans often borrow from different traditions and constantly reinterpret the syncretistic elements of rituals. The vitality of shamanism rests in the shamans' faculty to integrate effortless features which enhance the effect of shamanic performances. The reason for syncretism is quite obvious. Different ethnic groups have brought their own religion and culture to the city and the effectiveness of their rituals has become known to all other ethnic groups. That means, urban shamans, as all their predecessors from the beginning, integrate elements of the cultures with which they come into contact and give these elements a new meaning according to the context of the ritual performed. All elements of urban shamanism are familiar to the shamans and their clients. All have been in contact with the respective traditions as insiders or outsiders. This does not exclude cases where shamans, indeed, shape new images and create symbols to convey the "formless" messages they continue to receive from the spiritual world. Paraphernalia and rituals will also correspond to the personality of a particular shaman and the needs of the people who consult him or her.

This wide range of shamanic forms is beneficial because it allows a wide range of explanations and fulfills a wide range of needs. Important for this investigation is that, without the legitimization of a certain culture and tradition, techniques and rituals develop and change to fulfill the needs of a particular segment of a city's population. Legitimization occurs after the successful shamanic ritual. Its codification may render future performances less flexible.

Laurel Kendall who did extensive fieldwork with shamans in Korea for over a decade was asked whether Korean shamanism has changed. She found this question difficult to answer and said, "Change relative to what?" (Kendall, 1988:2).

Shamans continue to fulfill the expectations of those around them. People want spiritual advice, protection, and healing and they want to experience the presence of spiritual power. These expectations then prepare the ground and open the gates for shamans so that they can touch their clients to either trigger their self-healing powers or give them otherwise not accessible information.

# IV. Conclusions

With different geographic, climatic, and cultural circumstances, we find different forms of shamanism corresponding to different local needs. The stereotype of the North Asiatic shaman should no longer block our view when we meet other forms of shamanism.

As mediators, shamans work, therefore, on a number of different levels.

1.  *Socially, they are citizens like everybody else,*

2.  *spiritually, they enjoy a higher position on account of their relationships to the "Divine,"*

3.  *during the shamanic ritual, they operate on intermediate levels, between the spiritual world and the world of humans. Normative rules of the social order are suspended, and the encounter with the omnipotent spiritual world is screened. On one hand, shamans protect the spiritual world from being polluted by human weaknesses and ignorance and, on the other hand, they channel spiritual energy in a useful way so that it does not overtax the capacity of their contemporaries.*

Therefore,

1.  *socially and culturally, the environment of contemporary shamans differs considerably from that of paleolithic shamans.*

2. *citizens in the twentieth century have also needs that differ considerably from those of our predecessors in early hunting and herdsmen cultures, but an individual in a big city may feel as alienated and isolated as a hunter in an early jungle. Considering their existential nature, the needs of contemporaries do not differ much from those of earlier generations.*

3. *The characteristics of shamans who enter into contact with the spiritual world are the same.*

When existential emergencies occur and show overwhelming dimensions, when politicians lose the confidence of their constituency, when priests do not consider the needs of their community, when physicians and psychotherapists treat the symptoms and not their patients, because they don't have the time or they feel constrained by "scientific" considerations, when underlying imbalances in an individual's physical, emotional, social, philosophical-moral-intellectual, and spiritual systems remain unattended, then the search for spiritual help begins and will produce new shamans.

Shamans will be consulted when and wherever an individual desires to "magically" change life conditions, be it an emergency of overwhelming dimensions or the simple wish "to be loved by a certain person" or the need to find a lost object or person.

Shamans reinterpret and, at times, re-create worldviews which they communicate in symbolic language and ritual.

Wherever we look, the diversity of shamanism has grown along with socio-political developments. Despite the almost infinite possibilities of shamanic expressions, shamans themselves always play "an essential role in the defense of the psychic integrity of the community" (Eliade, 1974:508), in this case, as has been said at the beginning of this book, we have to envision community more in a spiritual than a geographic sense. Each shaman accepted responsibility with his/her call and this responsibility is irrevocable. Having been called to become the mediator between the sacred and the secular, each shaman reminds us of our own responsibility as individuals toward our communities and, most of all, toward this earth and the universe.

# Part IV

# Needs Fulfilled by Contemporary Shamans

The environment of shamans in the twentieth century differs considerably from that of paleolithic shamans and so do the needs contemporary shamans have to fulfill. Prehistoric men asked for success in hunting while nomadic pastoralists asked for new pastures, and horticulturists as well as agriculturists needed rain or relief from floods. We can, therefore, expect that people living in great cities have needs which are not so much concerned with the weather or new hunting or grazing grounds.

Houses have always been built to protect against the inclemencies of the weather. City houses have even been equipped with thermostats and air conditioners to control the weather inside. So city people have been led to believe they have become independent of nature. Only at times of fire, hurricane, earthquake, and war, lack of shelter, and especially lack of food and water, can become fatal. Remembering the conditions during World War II in Germany, I keep, e.g., an ample water supply in my refrigerator. I did not forget that we can live without food for weeks but only a few days without water.

Although urban life is no longer at the mercy of natural forces, it stayed dependent on other powerful elements.

Among others, we have become dependent on the benevolence of politicians. No longer afraid of becoming the target of discontented spirits, we fear that we might ostracize ourselves by not responding to the expectations not only of our family, friends, neighbors, but all officials we might come in contact with during our personal and professional life. Our role as citizen of a local community as well as citizen of a state and a nation, not to speak of our being citizens of the world, carries more or less well-defined responsibilities. We are still afraid of losing our family and friends meeting an accidental or natural death. We conform to societal and professional norms because we fear that we may lose our job. Increasing pollution and nuclear threats have kindled our fear that our planet is also heading toward destruction. These fears are augmented by the fear of losing our health. Existential needs have, therefore, stayed with us over the millennia.

We are proud of the advancements in the medical field. New biochemical knowledge has, for example, put an end to many epidemic diseases. Vaccinations have successfully reduced the possibilities of being infected by yellow fever or small pox. Treatment of lakes and rivers is preventing the spread of malaria. The fear of epidemics, however, has returned and grows with the emergence of AIDS.

The pollution of our land, rivers, lakes, oceans, and the air increases with each day. With deforestation, strip mining, and other exploitations of our resources, nature is being desecrated at a frightening pace.

In the age of science and technology, securalization has removed us further from the "source" to the point that nuclear discoveries have made the annihilation of our planet possible.

When basic fears have remained and anxieties are still part of our life, these fears and anxieties have to be dealt with. Modern health practitioners are not always equipped to respond to basic fears, neither are representatives of world religions, so the search for holistic solutions continues. The main reason to seek shamans is, indeed, the belief that shamans meet existential challenges and keep fighting battles with life-threatening "demons." Shamans have conquered the fear of death and dying and continue to offer us access to the infinite "source" of all life.

This may be a good time to talk about "spirits." I have to ask the reader to postpone judgment whether spiritual entities exist or not because we have to define first the concept of "spirit," as it is used by shamans.

Shamans continue to mention spiritual threats as well as "helping spirits." The latter may be visualized in the shape of animals by some tribal groups or in the shape of personalities who have lived in the past and still have the wish to be useful to the living as it is believed by Folk Taoists (e.g., among Overseas Chinese in Singapore) or Buddhists in Thailand or the inhabitants of any other region in the world. I resist discussing visions reported in world religions, e.g., of the Virgin Mary at Lourdes (France), Fatima (Portugal), and recently at Medjugorje (Yugoslavia) because I want to stay in the realm where shamans operate.

Lommel ventures the following opinion:

*Many investigators who have concerned themselves with shamanism have avoided the question of how much reality is attached to these spirits.*

*It is, however, perfectly clear and, if we bear in mind the particular conditions of the trance or dreamlike atmosphere, it is entirely understandable that these spirits have only an inner, a psychic reality, that they are simply images or symbols of a transformation of the shaman's psychic structure. This does not mean that the helping spirits have less reality—merely that it is not a reality of the external, material world. By means of his "helping spirits" the shaman influences the people of his group, and this influence is always exercised in a state of trance. The techniques of trance and ecstasy are thus undoubtedly essential character-istics of shamanism (1988:20).*

In other words, spirits may be symbolic representations of what a shaman experiences during trance. These trance expe-riences are real in another dimension and "spirits" are pictographic representations of the ineffable in terms the general public can understand.

I have been asked repeatedly whether I believe in the existence of spirits and my answer always will be:

> *Western scholars are more inclined to respect the power of the Spirit [high god] but hesitate when spiritual powers are given different names in other cultures....with our present scientific tools we can neither prove nor disprove the existence of spirits of whatever nature they may be. However, we can investigate what led up to such beliefs and we can evaluate the results produced in the context of faith (Heinze, 1988:1).*

Let us now turn to a more detailed discussion of the needs fulfilled by contemporary shamans. In Part I, I talked briefly about the three major needs. The need most often expressed in my Asian sample was concern about the clients' health and the health of their family, relatives, and friends.

The concept of illness appears in Asia in a larger context. In the West, illness is seen as entering the body from without; in the East, illness is seen as being caused by loss of personal power which allowed the intrusion. Therefore, the life force of a client has to be re-empowered and restored, for example, by "soul fastening" (Heinze, 1982).

Illness plays also an important role in spiritual growth. In Asia, illness is considered to be "a process that cleanses us of the bad habits we have accumulated by our false attitudes to life" (Kalweit, 1988:76).

In the West, illness comes as a surprise. We treat it like an accident and seldom look for possible reasons, e.g., whether we were under too much stress for a prolonged period of time or overindulged in food, alcohol, cigarettes or drugs. We also do not search further for psychological or other reasons which might have caused an imbalance in our lives. We do not even have a clear concept of what health actually is and seem to speak of it only when it is absent. In the East, people know that their actions, words, and thoughts are constantly either "building" their illnesses or maintaining their physical, emotional, social, mental, and spiritual health.

With the exception of illness caused by accidents and bodily attacks from the outside, illness itself is not the problem but can tell us something about pre-existing problems. Illness may, therefore, be the culmination of months or even years of dis-ease and imbalance.

We realize that the first thing an illness does to us is to disrupt our life style. We have to take time out which leads to investigating who we really are. So illness can become an opportunity to change our self definition.

Illness tests and may interrupt social relationships; on the other hand, some of our relationships may be strengthened through illness. We find out who our real friends are. Superficial acquaintances are not interested in our well-being and we become worthless for those who depend on us. Dependents will have to look elsewhere for somebody they can exploit. However, true friends will reciprocate and offer nourishment and support to us.

Another example for changes in relationships is the following case.

> *An illness sometimes results in a complete change in direction. One woman who developed cancer recalled that she used to say, "This job is killing me." This same woman found that her cancer helped her to cut the apron strings from her two youngest but grown children, something the "healthy" self was having a lot of trouble doing.*

Illness is a great opportunity for introspection.

> *One of the obvious reasons for a serious illness is to rest....Besides healing the body, the enforced rest that an illness can bring also allows us the time to turn our gaze away from the external world and search our inner self. One form imbalance can take is being too active in the world and neglecting the inner self and its equally important needs. Even an illness that is not life-threatening...can awaken our sense of mortality*

*and cause us to re-examine our life priorities and goals....*

There are, however, some negative uses for illnesses which

*can be viewed as punishment for real or imagined sins. They can also be used to manipulate and control others or to elicit sympathy. An illness can serve as an excuse not to do the things we claim we'd like to do and protect us from taking risks that can lead to success or failure....But even these negative uses of illness point to pre-existing problems.*

In the final analysis,

*The body knows how to be healthy and how to heal itself, and listening to its messages can lead us to do the daily healing work that will prevent further illness or other crises. The choice is ours—the mind is the builder (Trowbridge, 1989:4).*

Shamans assist in connecting "the inner self," i.e., the mind, with the body and facilitate the re-examination of priorities and goals.

Health issues were the main reasons in Asia to contact a shaman and, in the majority of cases, individuals ask the shaman for assistance not so much for themselves but to help relatives and friends. This attitude indicates a greater availability of social support systems. In Asia, family and friends involve themselves more readily in the healing process.

It is, therefore, not surprising when we look at the second most frequent reason to consult shamans in Asia. Because social support systems are so important in Asia, this reason concerns problems which might have arisen inside the family (between in-laws, spouses, parents and children). In the West, aggressiveness and self-assertiveness are considered to be virtues. We don't teach how to avoid confrontations. Interpersonal conflicts are less tolerable in Asia and require a quick solution.

I remember a case where a sickly girl was brought to a shaman. When the shaman inquired about the cause of her illness, it turned out that the girl had refused to marry a man her parents had selected for her. The shaman did not talk about her physical illness at all but reminded the girl of her duty toward her parents and the community. I could not find out whether the girl later actually entered the arranged marriage as she had promised the shaman, but she certainly looked different when she left the shaman. She had been reconnected to the source of her being. [As a side-comment, I want to add that I have been told in Asia repeatedly that arranged marriages work out better than so-called love marriages. The general consensus in Asia is that love marriages usually are entered on impulse and without foresight.] The above case is an example that shamans in Asia reinforce the social order. Good social relationships are essential for the well-being of all individual members of a social group. Good relationships are also necessary between social groups to reinforce each other's work. One example for the importance of good social relationships is also the respect with which shamans talk about other shamans.

Third in priority among basic needs in Asia are professional concerns, e.g., career issues, passing an exam, getting a promotion, or expanding one's business. I witnessed at several occasions people asking shamans to bless their business books and this was done openly, in front of a crowd of other clients waiting their turn. In Chiang Mai I met a shaman who has the reputation to be most effective in launching the career of his clients. I was given the name of a professor at Chiang Mai University who had not been promoted for a long time. After consulting this shaman, he became head of the Department of Research within a year. Another official was promoted and became a member of the Thai government in Bangkok. Whatever this shaman did is hard to assess, however, it is obvious that he reinforces the confidence of his clients and empowers them to such an extent that they are able to achieve their goals.

I found three additional needs in Asia which require the services of shamans. People are concerned about fertility, longevity, and wealth, but we have, by far, not exhausted all the reasons to seek the assistance of shamans. Blessings of deities and other spiritual entities are sought throughout the year, e.g., before moving into a new house. In Singapore, shamans are needed to call the gods to bless new houses or altars. In Thailand, shamans perform ceremonies at the opening of new roads and bridges (Heinze, 1988:63-64). In Part II, we learned that David Bray, the Hawaiian *kahuna,* was called to bless new buildings, ships, even a jet fighter plane. (See also, photo 20, where a Chinese shamans blesses new equipment in a factory, in Singapore.)

In the West, we have dispensed with house blessings or the blessings of new roads and new equipment. Only occasionally we find a mascot on the dashboard of a car, a rabbit's foot or a medal. (St.Christopher, for example, has been demoted and is no longer the protector of travelers.)

Shamans are also asked to locate lost persons. Or somebody has lost an object and wants to know whether it has been misplaced or whether it was stolen. Clients want to learn who was the thief and how the stolen goods can be retrieved.

When I was in Pattani, southern Thailand, for example, a young man came to a Muslim shaman asking him to retrieve a stolen motorcycle. He had just bought it and then lent it to a "friend" who had driven off with it. The shaman was an eighty-year-old *haji* (i.e., he had completed his pilgrimage to Mecca). Before the session, he suggested that people should be more careful with their property, then he let the young man look into a glass of water over which he had recited some evocation. The young man tried hard but could not see anything. Attempting to help him, the wife of the shaman suggested to turn the glass. The shaman, in the meantime, used his arms to assure the presence of spirits. He tapped

*from the elbows to the wrists, the left arm with the second and third finger of his right hand and his right arm with the first and third finger of his left hand. He got some vibrations and finally announced the thief was already dead and the motorcycle was being used by insurgents outside of Golok near the Thai border to Malaysia. "They are taking good care of it," he added. The closeness of the border and the need of insurgents*

*for motorcycles were well-known facts. To pronounce
the thief dead, however, seemed to deflect the young
man's anger. One cannot take revenge on a corpse.*

*Although the results of the consultation were incon-
clusive, the young man, who had paid 100 baht
(US$5) before the session, put another 100 baht note
on the table....The theft was a great loss for him. He
was still paying off the installments, but he did not
hesitate to spend even more money on the rather futile
attempt to retrieve the expensive vehicle (Heinze,
1988:251-252).*

In Malaysia, shamans are still called to change the
weather. In contrast to the rain dances of earlier times, they are
now asked to assure good weather for football or cricket
matches. For that purpose, they will "tie" the rain with a knot
in their handkerchief and eye witnesses report that rain fell in
other areas around the football field but not on players and
spectators during the match (Heinze, 1988:126).

I mentioned above that, all over the world, environmental
issues and the spreading of Aids, for example, urgently
require solutions. We recognize, furthermore, that the problems caused by the uneven distribution of wealth are leading
to homelessness, starvation, and despair. Not to speak of the
struggle for power inside countries and the power struggle
between nations in which many individuals get caught and
desperately look for solutions.

Hill tribes, who helped the United States during the
Vietnam War, for example, had to flee their homeland. Some
of them have been relocated in the San Francisco Bay area. My
colleagues and I from the Center for Southeast Asia Studies,
at the University of California, Berkeley, are presently working with Laotian hill tribes who brought their shamans into
suburban, middle-class America. These Laotian shamans
continue to practice their rituals as best as they can. They have
to substitute many substances which are not available in
America but so far they did not change the structure of their
rituals. They call back lost souls when somebody becomes ill

and, if asked to do so, they perform the Flower Bridge Ritual, a fertility ritual for barren women. For this ritual, they literally build a bridge of flowers and shower the woman for whom the ritual is performed with tiny paper embryos. The shaman makes, in this case, the invisible visible, using sympathetic magic, i.e., he suggests that the paper embryos will invite real embryos to cross the Flower Bridge and enter the woman's womb. Folklorists will speak of "like making like possible."

Ancestors have to be contacted to find out their last wishes, sometimes their last will and testament has to be located. Restless spirits may draw attention to themselves and have to be propitiated with offerings. When it is believed that a dead relative still is lingering around a house or an accident victim's soul cannot find the way into the "other" world, the living have to take care of these restless spirits. Especially in Asia, illness in a family is often attributed to a restless spirit making his or her presence known.

I mentioned already that shamans shift the attention of their clients away from their daily mode of thinking but I have to be more specific. Shamans work at least on five different levels. Aside from the physical-biological level, they consider also the emotional-psychological, the social as well as the mental-intellectual-philosophical-moral, and the spiritual levels. Harmony has to be established between all five levels.

That means, a physical problem may have a psychological root (e.g., grief, anger, trauma) which has to be taken care of so that the physical illness can be cured. Or an emotional problem has to be resolved on the physical level (e.g., with breathing exercises, massage, baths, and, if necessary, an exorcism). The resultant emotional release may then also remove circulatory blockages at the same time.

Being alienated from one's environment effects the physical as well as the emotional well-being of an individual and, aside from these social problems, philosophical-moral constraints can upset the balance on the other four levels. Many individuals have difficulties to move out of situations which offend their ethics. Others suffer being ostracized because they made an ethical decision. In the twentieth century we experience the emergence of very profound, new ethical concerns. To name a few, people are concerned about environmental issues, abortion, the freedom to die, nuclear power, and also the recombinant DNA. These issues put a large stress on people, especially those who feel they are powerless and unable to do anything about these issues. In a recent discussion with Marshall Pease (August 1989), we recognized that the "number and severity of unresolved ethical problems" is "unprecedented in human history."

Spiritual crises may indicate an onsetting process of restructuring an individual's life. These crises have to be treated with care which can be offered only by specially trained practitioners.

Sociologists speak of the somatization of conflict. Good examples are the means of conflict resolution available to villagers in India. When the conflict inside a family can neither be resolved by the most respected member of the family nor the village council nor the local courts, the last resource will always be a shaman-like healer or sage who can trigger a catharsis and bring about an emotional release of pent-up feelings.

Shamans are familiar with crises on all levels and can cut the Gordian knot with a ritual dramatizing the process and activating a release. The emotional involvement of the client is reinforced and becomes the driving force in the healing process. Such treatment is obviously more effective than following mechanically the prescriptions of a Western practitioner.

There are, however, now many clinics in the West which use a variety of alternative treatments. I know of a Mental Health Center in Denver, Colorado, which has added a *curandera* (Mexican healer and shaman) to their staff and a hospital in Stanford, California, where a Brazilian healer is called to assist in the treatment of certain patients.

It can only be hoped that holistic treatment will become more widely available in the West. Any discipline carries the tendency toward specialization which led to fragmentation in the past. We witness now many more efforts toward synthesis. Scientists begin to recognize the value of the open-endedness of a shaman's approach which always leaves the door for other possibilities open.

When Maslow discussed psychopathogenesis, he considered neurosis, in its beginning, being

*a deficiency disease...born out of being deprived of certain satisfactions which I called needs in the same sense that water and amino acids and calcium are needs, namely that their absence produces illness. Most neuroses involved, along with other complex determinants, ungratified wishes for safety, for belongingness and identification, for close love relationships and for respect and prestige (1962:19).*

Our human dilemma is that

*Even our best people are not exempted from the basic predicament, of being simultaneously merely-creaturely and godlike, strong and weak, limited and unlimited, merely-animal and animal-transcending, adult and child, fearful and courageous, progressing and regressing, yearning for perfection and yet afraid of it, being a worm and also a hero (Maslow, 1962:164).*

*...the current over-stress on the (supposedly) great gap between self-knowledge and ethical action (and value commitment) may itself be a symptom of the specifically obsessional hiatus between thought and action...the age-old dichotomy among philosophers between "is" and "ought," between fact and norm....clear knowledge generally flows right over into spontaneous action or ethical commitment. That is, when they know what is the right thing to do it, they do it (Maslow, 1962:167).*

Mediating between "old dichotomies," shamans facilitate transcendence and the safe return to the Here and Now so that clients gain a better perspective of their problems. One example for an "unsafe" return would be the incomplete sending away of energies evoked. Or individuals with weak ego boundaries may, after a ritual, stay open toward influences from the outside. Sensitized to and being bombarded by outside stimuli, they have become vulnerable. Past traumata and dissociations may, at that time, rise to the surface and have to be dealt with. Shamans can talk their clients through such crises and can ritually reinforce the weakened ego axis. Western physicians need to be alerted to the importance of working with their patients, i.e., including the patient's cooperation in the healing process.

Shamans are successful in treating not only dissociative disorders (multiple personality/possession), they also reconnect individuals with the universe and, in doing so, counteract the alienation felt by large sections of the population.

In Part III, I talked about different rituals for different purposes, and the seven steps necessary to complete a ritual, i.e., the ritual sequence:

1. *the shaman and all participants decide on the purpose of the ritual,*

2. *the shaman outlines and consecrates the sacred space,*

3. *the shaman purifies him- or herself and all participants before they enter the sacred space,*

4. *the shaman evokes the spirits appropriate to the purpose of the ritual,*

5. *the shaman communicates with the sacred and all participants come into the presence of the "divine,"*

6. *the shaman thanks and sends away the spiritual forces,*

7. *the shaman reintegrates all participants into the daily life of their community.*

This ritual sequence is important and none of the steps can be left out.

The need to come into the presence of the spiritual is

deeply rooted in the human soul. Over thousands of years those seeking a spiritual connection explored different methods and disciplines to come "to know God." In India, some two thousand years ago, Patanjali collected 196 yoga sutras which elaborate on methods and stages of spiritual development. After the first century A.D., Taoist visionaries in China developed complicated systems of evocation to manipulate spiritual energies. The exercises of St. Ignatius of Loyola (1491-1556 A.D.) originated in a Christian setting in medieval Spain. Though St. Ignatius' imagery is culturally determined, if practiced correctly, his exercises will lead to ecstatic experiences similar to that of yogis and Taoists.

Representatives of all religions report that they came into the presence of gods and spirits as the result of intensive prayer, chanting and dancing, and/or asceticism. In the Islamic world, some of the ecstatics call themselves Sufi, in the Jewish world they may be Hasids. In each culture we find spiritual disciplines available for those who look for self-cultivation and peak experiences.

Maslow spoke of the twenty-five aspects of peak experiences which are characterized by

1. *perceiving the universe as an integrated and unified whole which can profoundly change an individual's character (e.g., triggering religious conversion or, to a lesser degree, having therapeutic effects),*

2. *visually perceiving, listening or feeling in the truest and most total kind, non-evaluating, non-comparing, "there is the tendency for things to become equally important rather than to be ranged in a hierarchy...the person is unique...is sacred...everyone is a child of God...";*

3. *perceiving objects, the world and individuals as more detached from human concerns, refraining from projecting human purposes on what is perceived, i.e., seeing and perceiving "in a higher than usual way";*

4. *perceiving in a relatively ego-transcending, self-forgetful, egoless, unselfish way, desireless, detached, not needing or wishing, more object- than ego-centered way;*

5. *perceiving in a self-validating, self-justifying way which gives meaning to life itself;*

6. *recognizing these experiences as end—rather than means—experiences;*

7. *experiencing universality and eternity outside of time and space;*

8. *seeing the world as beautiful, good, desirable, worthwhile.*

In the remaining seventeen criteria, Maslow talks about the "universal understanding" without blame, condemnation, disappointment, a state where only the emotions of pity, charity, kindliness, perhaps sadness and amusement are possible.

The world does not only exist, it is also "sacred." This belief has been anathema to Christian doctrine which, especially in the Middle Ages (Inquisition), maintained that the only reason for being born in this world is that life on this earth prepares the soul for heaven and tests whether the soul is sufficiently cultivated to earn the heavenly bliss. Shamans teach their clients to be more receptive and more humble. We have to be ready to listen so that we can transcend and resolve dichotomies, polarities, and conflicts of life. As individuals we move "toward the perception of unity and integration in the world." We may experience

*a loss, even though transient, of fear, anxiety, inhibition, of defense and control, of perplexity, confusion, conflict, of delay and restraint. The profound fear of disintegration, of insanity, of death, all tend to disappear for the moment. Perhaps this amounts to saying that fear disappears.*

Becoming more loving and more accepting, individuals also are more spontaneous, honest, and innocent.

> *What has been called the "unitive consciousness" is often given in peak-experiences, i.e., a sense of the sacred glimpsed in and through the particular instance of the momentary, the secular, the worldly (Maslow, 1970:59-68).*

My observations tell me that people shy away from the experience of transcendence because they are afraid of "losing" their Self. Everything beyond their comprehension is perceived as being "chaotic" or "void." If they would look closer, they could recognize that the "void" is only void of material objects which are impermanent to begin with. However, they refuse to recognize that there is nothing they can hold on. They need somebody to teach them how to trust the "dynamic flow."

I did not find many individuals who show the inclination and have the time for "spiritual exercises." Everybody seems to look for somebody else who "does the job for them." Those conscious of their needs look for individuals who have developed the ability to access spiritual energies and who can manifest the "Divine" in visible form.

The role of visions and the ways how shamans mediate between the sacred and the profane have been substantiated in the profiles in Part II and in the discussions in Part III.

Shamans have to use myth and rituals and any form of art to convey the ineffable messages. They become story-tellers, musicians, painters, theater directors and act as protectors and custodians of the earth. And, most importantly, shamans look for the "inner causes" and see illness as a way of cleansing body and mind. Shamanic healing is so effective because shamans shift the attention of their clients so that transformational processes can take place.

Andreas Lommel summarized for us the functions of shamans:

> *The shaman is able to influence the psyche of his group, to give it fresh life, to render it creative and*

*restore its healthy, productive equilibrium more effec-*
*tively than any modern psychotherapist, artist or man*
*of the theatre, and also more effectively than any*
*celebrant priest....*

*...we can clearly see the particular form taken by this*
*first "spiritual" man from the primordial epoch of*
*humanity, and the nature of this combination of artis-*
*tic, psychotherapeutic, magical and histrionic abili-*
*ties; thereby we gain an insight into the early mental*
*life of mankind, which reveals an astonishing com-*
*plexity, a complicated psychic structure so modern in*
*appearance that we are reluctant to credit so-called*
*primitives with such minds (1967:140).*

Shamans certainly are not primitives. They have never been.
They stayed close to the primary source and they continue to
do so.

Until we all have become fully "enlightened," there will
be existential needs. Basic fears and anxiety do obscure our
thinking. However, we can find shamans in the twentieth
century who know our fears because they have conquered
these fears themselves. Shamans have been called to become
the mediators between the sacred and the secular and stay in
contact with the "life force" which is infinite and inexhaust-
ible.

To cite two examples documented in this book:
Grotowski, the Polish director/shaman, has come full circle to

*the elimination of the illusion of disconnectedness*
*(with one's body, with human-made and natural*
*rhythms, with others, with the Universe at large)*
*through shamanic performance and communal ritu-*
*als, and back to the specialization of the master*
*performer who uses his//her artistry to wage battle*
*with inner and outer demons to reveal the joys and*
*terrors of the human condition (see his profile in Part*
*II).*

So does Elizabeth Cogburn and her community who

skillfully create and continuously practice around the cycle of the year to

> *maintain their equilibrium, find points of balance for themselves, and maintain the balance. Participants of her ritual dances report that they not only heal old wounds, but they also learn how to live their lives, throughout the year, accepting challenges—which often tend to depress the Spirit—as sources of meaning and causes for celebration (see her profile in Part II).*

During my fieldwork, I found shamans who have been instrumental in formulating new paradigms to guide us on the way. The direction such new paradigms are taking will be discussed in Part V.

# Part V

# New Paradigms

In the previous chapters, we have met shamans of the twentieth century who continue to fulfill vital needs for their community, whether these communities belong to one geographic area or not. We talked about who can be called a shaman and who cannot. We can now expand our perception of shamans and compare a shaman with a spiritual master who stands

> *in the radiance of Life, present within him and infusing his consciousness. And so he stands in the light of a higher insight and in strength that has power to act and transform.*

> *The master is master only in relation to a world that is capable of changing and wants to change...*

> *The master is master only because he is linked to a higher authority, at whose command he acts and to which he is responsible. When he mediates between heaven and earth, he always acts at its bidding. He never claims to be the source himself, but refers to a higher reality...*

> *A master who lacks humility is no master, or is an inverted master—the satanic emanation and embodi-*

*ment of transcendence usurped by the ego.*

*...Life exists only as transition—and the master keeps it alive by making transition a never-ending process (Durkheim, 1989:9).*

Spiritual masters and shamans have access to great knowledge and power. Here we pause already, because we have to be sure what kind of power we are talking about. The difference between the pathological power that comes from the need to control, use, and demean others and the power which actualizes human potential and produces manifestations of the sacred is critical. Power itself is neutral. In its benevolent form, power provides leadership, protection, and security; such power inspires and nourishes creativity. In its malevolent form, power leads to domination and abuse.

Power can safely be measured by its results, but we may not always have the time to wait for the results. We have to find other means to assure ourselves of the quality of a shaman's power before we allow ourselves to be connected with that power. We should, therefore, always inquire whether thoughts, words or actions of a certain shaman are beneficial to us and others? Is his or her power carried by altruistic love and compassion? An affirmative answer may momentarily appease doubts, but we also want to rationalize our findings. We do not only want to exonerate shamans but also want to assure ourselves that their work is intimately related and instrumental to solving vital problems.

The main difficulty appears to be that shamans have to speak our "language." A shaman's almost impossible task is to translate the sacred into words of the profane. "Moreover, he often masters a complex vocabulary of terms outnumbering those customarily used in many literate cultures" (Rogers, 1982:8). The Yakut shaman of Siberia, for example, commands a poetic language of at least 12,000 words (Fürst, 1977), compared to 3,000 words or less used by an average speaker of any language.

Furthermore, many prophets have been misunderstood by their contemporaries and it took sometimes centuries to decipher sacred messages. Shamans, working with pragmatic problems on the mundane level, are hard pressed to find a language which is understood by their contemporary clients. Being result oriented, they use rituals and symbolic actions to leave an immediate impression. A shaman's assets are personal charisma, strength of character, and reputation. These assets qualify shamans to serve as model when we are looking for new paradigms to restructure our lives.

Confronted with the task to perceive ourselves in a new light, we recognize where our difficulties started.

*The shift from a mythological interpretation of reality to a purely rational one is considered to be the main achievement of the Greek intellectual heritage. As early as the fifth century B.C., Ionian philosophers distinguished between knowledge and belief...." No man has ever had, or ever will have sure knowledge about Gods; even if he should chance to hit on the exact truth, he cannot know that he has done so, though we can all have our opinions" ....The philosopher Parmenides cautioned "not to trust the senses," but instead to "judge by reason" (Wautischer, 1989:36).*

Over two thousand years ago, logos entered the scene and began to overrule mythos. The relevancy of communication with the divine decreased as human beings

*became more independent from their gods. However, divinatory perception does not necessarily have to be interpreted as communication with the gods. Rather, it can be seen as a meticulously refined perception made possible through the complexity of the human nervous system, in combination with a volitional effort. Furthermore, it has been argued that such perception could allow the individual to perceive energetic frequencies of reality (Bohm 1981), as opposed to ordinary physical objects that are regularly perceived through the five senses (Wautischer, 1989:36).*

The foundations of science and reason are build upon objectivization while mystics experience reality as unity of which man is an integral part. The mystic approach is, by nature, subjective and defies objectivity. It is very hard for us to understand that everyone of us is unique as an individual and that we all are intimately connected at the same time. Scientists as well as theologians have tried to solve this dilemma since science and religion split.

Furthermore, Judeo-Christian beliefs assert that God is separate from man and will stay separate forever. We are told that we can look to God for salvation but we cannot become God. Qabalistic scholars, like the Hasidic Jews, probably come the closest to subjectivity when they say that the most man can attain is the sephiroth Chokmah, i.e., man coming face to face with God. The reader is reminded of Patanjali's yoga sutras which were collected to show individuals the way how they could come "to know God."

Now quantum mechanics pick up at the point where logos started to discredit perceptual knowledge. Shamans never mistrusted their contact with the sacred and skillfully survived in an increasingly skeptic world.

The main problem is that logicians never felt and expressed the limitations of intellectual conclusions. Increase in knowledge was celebrated without mentioning the wide areas of the unknown which overshadowed the limited amounts of knowledge presented. Were we unaware (and nobody warned us) that the small candles of insight did not light the vastness of the universe?

The limitations of human thoughts have been widely discussed elsewhere. However, a pluralistic methodology has not yet been established because contemporary scientists are just beginning to learn how to combine conceptualization, reason, and metaphysics.

Another turning point in the past was certainly the time when the Church or other religious authorities who had been the keepers of sacred knowledge began to take routes different from secular sciences. Sacred knowledge froze and became dogma which had to resist change to defend its superiority. Other sacred knowledge was suppressed by theocratic authorities and stayed accessible only to the elite. On the other side, the sciences themselves became caught in their own rules to such an extent that the bridges between the sacred and profane were literally burned. We have now to enlist individuals with shamanic faculties to rebuild these bridges. We have to look for mediators between the sacred and secular and have to learn how to integrate shamanic knowledge into our world view.

The translation of shamanic terms into modern Western languages will also ease the phobia against so far unexplained phenomena and prepare the ground for collaboration, among others, with Western health officials.

In contrasting traditional and contemporary forms of healing, Kleinman describes two radically different healing functions. Contemporary forms of healing are concerned with "controlling the sickness," traditional forms with "providing meaning for the individual's experience of it" (1973:159). He calls

> disease any primary malfunctioning in biological and psychological processes....And...illness the secondary psychosocial and cultural responses to disease, e.g., how the patient, his family, and social network react to his disease (1979:7-26).

In his study on *Patients and Healers in the Context of Culture*, Kleinman explains that

> The ingrained ethnocentrism and scientism that dominates the modern medical and psychiatric professions (both in developed and in developing societies) follows the paradigm of biomedical science to emphasize in research only those variables compatible with biological reductionism and technological solutions, even if the problems are social ones. This disastrous bias has diminished the significance of all social science inputs into medicine and psychiatry.... Cultural and sociopolitical analysis of the determinants of health care delivery, for example, have not been considered appropriate venues for medical research, and the description and analysis of the total environmental context that ethnography provides has not

*yet been accepted as an appropriate scientific approach (1980:32).*

Kleinman asks us to analyze the core functions of an illness. Each culture constructs concepts of illness so that illness itself becomes a "psychosocial experience." It is, therefore, important to establish "general criteria to guide the health care seeking process and to evaluate treatment approaches that exist prior to and independent of individual episodes of sickness." In other words, we have to be aware of the difference in concepts of health and illness between cultures.

Working with Laotian immigrants in the Bay area, I found that hill tribes, who never saw a hospital from the inside, were terrified to death by modern equipment which, they thought, was designed to torture them. Their fears could only be appeased when a Laotian speaking translator was found. But even among people who speak the same language, illness episodes have to be managed "through communicative operations such as labeling and explaining" (Kleinman, 1980:71-72).

The quality of communication between healer and patient does, indeed, determine the outcome. Health practitioners have to be cautioned not to use, for example, "negative programming." I heard Western health practitioner describe the expected course of an illness in great detail and it sounded almost like a hypnotic induction which the patients had no choice but to follow.

Despite more and more clinics offering holistic approaches, physicians, in general, hesitate to include other alternative approaches which may contribute to the cure. They fail to enlist the cooperation of their patients and hide behind a highly professional jargon. Kleinman talks about Horton's work in Nigeria, where

*explanations given by biomedical practitioners are usually delivered in an impersonal, objective, scientific idiom; they provide technical information but lack personal and social significance....the cognitive and communicative structure of modern professional*

*health care are not comparable with those of folk and*
*popular health care (1980:100).*

Healing activities can include all types of therapeutic intervention, "from drugs and surgery to psychotherapy, supportive care, and healing rituals." The last two approaches are high on the priority list of shamans who will call in the social support available from family, friends, and neighbors and work in a ritual context.

Health practitioners should be concerned with the management of "therapeutic outcomes, including cure, treatment failure, recurrence, chronic illness, impairment, and death." They should study how shamans prepare themselves to handle crises situations and how they ritualize the healing as well as the dying processes. Shamans do not hesitate to tell when their clients have to face fate but ritualize the transition and transform it into a period of inner growth.

I fully agree with Kleinman who has worked with Western health practitioners as well as folk healers.

*Healing rituals move through three separate stages.*
*The sickness is labeled with an appropriate and sanc-*
*tioned cultural category. The label is ritually manipu-*
*lated (culturally transformed). Finally a new label*
*(cured, well) is applied and sanctioned as a meaning-*
*ful symbolic form that may be independent of behav-*
*ioral or social change (1980:372).*

These stages correspond to the sequence of shamanic healing rituals.

Achterberg, another expert working on new approaches, discusses interventions which have been classified by Western physicians as "medically worthless." She reminds us of another important factor. Clients all over the world

*are administered placebos of one kind and another.*
*Often they show decreases in pain, nausea, anxiety,*
*and even in tumor cells. It is not just their attitude that*
*changes; their biochemistry has also undergone a*
*transformation (1985:4).*

Achterberg refers to reports that placebo treatment has been successful in

> *from 30% to 70% of all drug and surgical interventions. Even repair of injured tissues has been encouraged.... It no doubt accounts for healing when inappropriate treatments are prescribed, and even for some of the positive effects of appropriate treatment. Placebos, like imagery, hypnosis, and biofeedback, surely must have a direct effect on the immune system....The wise doctor within each of us knows how to make pain disappear, and tumors melt. It knows whether to call forth T-cells or histamines or endorphins—all in the proper order and combination (Achterberg, 1985:85).*

Although the biochemistry of the human body has not fully been explored, during the last decade, researchers reported, for example,

> *that electrical stimulation of the periaqueductal gray area in the brain produces an analgesia that can be reversed by an analgesia-blocking agent, naloxone.... reports came in of opiate receptors in the central nervous system. Why would the brain have such a specific binding site unless opiates were actually produced? (Achterberg, 1985:137).*

Achterberg saw the endorphins

> *in high concentration in the limbic system, the thalamus, the periaqueductal gray mater, the substantia gelatinoso of the spinal cord—all areas know to be involved in pain transmission. They are also found in areas of the brain that regulate respiration, motor activity, endocrine control and mood....This information on the relationship between endorphins and the immune system, and endorphins and the imagination, puts them in the position of being likely candidates for the healing chemicals of hope (1985:138-139).*

Readers are also referred to Jilek's review of previous research on the endogenous opioid agents enkephalin and beta-endorphin, and other neuroendocrine peptides such as neurotensin and bradykinin (1982:339). Chemical processes in the human body can be triggered by what Achterberg calls "preverbal" imagery,

> ...the imagination acts upon one's own physical being. Images communicate with tissues and organs, even cells, to effect a change. The communication can be deliberate or not. It is preverbal in the sense that it probably evolved much earlier than language, and uses different neural pathways for the transmission of information. The second type of healing imagery is transpersonal, embodying the assumption that information can be transmitted from the consciousness of one person to the physical substrata of others.... Shamanism is and has been the most widely practiced type of medicine on the planet, particularly for serious illness. The shamans are the ones who are said to understand, in a spiritual sense, the nexus of the mind, the body, and the soul. Their chief task has always been to heal their people of the ills of humanity— whatever form those maladies might assume (1985:5-6).

Malaysia is among those countries which suffer from a shortage of trained physicians. The Malaysian government has, therefore, begun to license folk practitioners. After a brief crash course in sanitation, the *bomohs* (shamans) are permitted to work. The only warning they have to follow is that they send "serious" cases to the hospital. They would do this anyway because shamans are very much concerned about their reputation.

From my own observations, I can report that shamans all over the world are careful not to accept cases they cannot solve. I heard in Singapore, for example, shamans tell clients that they will try to intervene but when an individual's time is up they could not change the fate which may be predetermined by an individual's *karma* or by a decision of the gods.

A businessman in Singapore told me about a shaman's warning that it was too late for shamanic intervention. His brain tumor was too advanced to be removed spiritually. In unmistakable terms, the spirit (through the medium) told the client that he needed surgery fast if he wanted to survive. The spirit (a deified general from the Three Kingdoms, appr. 200 A.D.), however, promised the terrified client that he would come to the operation room and guide the hand of the surgeon. If he would be of pure heart, he would even see the spirit. The hospital personnel were surprised about the sudden calmness of their patient. The operation turned out to be comparatively easy, the tumor was removed successfully, and the patient also recuperated unusually fast (Heinze, 1988:64).

The Malaysian solution was a full success, because the folk practitioners relieved the overworked physicians from a large amount of their case load (Heinze, 1988:132-133). Similar efforts have been made in Thailand. The reader is also reminded of the barefoot doctors in China. Although most of them don't qualify to be called shamans, the cooperation of so-called folk practitioners with medical authorities is possible if prejudices are overcome. In Western societies, we meet still reluctance. I know only of two exceptions: a clinic in Denver, Colorado, which has built a Mexican shaman into the therapeutic process and a hospital in Stanford, California, which calls a Brazilian shaman to assist in the healing process of certain patients (personal communication, 1988).

Shamans can, furthermore, teach social and behavioral scientists ways how individuals as well as societies can "regulate" their well-being.

Most of all, shamans can teach psychotherapists the importance of shifting attention. In the Colorado case, the Mexican shaman was able to talk also in terms of the *DSM-III-R*, but shamans rarely consult textbooks for their diagnosis. A Malay shaman showed me, in 1979, a small book into which he had written down his observations, mainly the herbs he used for certain illnesses and he had added at what time of the day they should be administered. Similar prescriptions about time of the day and the interrelationship of the different organs in the body has been cultivated by acupuncturists over the millenia. Shamans developed a psychology of their own similar to that of Maslow who saw psychology in part as

> a branch of biology, in part a branch of sociology. But it is not only that. It has its own unique jurisdiction as well, that portion of the psyche which is not a reflection of the outer world or a molding to it. There could be such a thing as a psychological psychology (1962:174).

We find, indeed, today transpersonal psychologists who use spiritual approaches which are very similar to methods used by shamans. These attempts have opened new ways which require further study. Maslow found, for example, that

> The balance between spontaneity and control varies...as the health of the psyche and the health of the world vary. Pure spontaneity is not longer possible because we live in a world which runs by its own, non-psychic laws....Pure control is not permanently possible, for then the psyche dies. Education must be directed then both toward cultivation of controls and cultivation of spontaneity and expression. In our culture and at this point in history, it is necessary to redress the balance in favor of spontaneity, the ability to be expressive, passive, unwilled, trusting in processes other than will and control, unpremeditated, creative, etc. But it must be recognized that there have been and will be other cultures and other areas in which the balance was or will be in the other direction (1962:185).

> This development toward the concept of a healthy consciousness and of a healthy irrationality, sharpens our awareness of the limitations of purely abstract thinking, of verbal thinking and of analytic thinking. If our hope is to describe the world fully, a place is necessary for pre-verbal, ineffable, metaphorical, primary process, concrete experience, intuitive and esthetic types of cognition, for there are certain as-

*pects of reality which can be recognized in no other way. Even in science this is true, now that we know (1) that creativity has its roots in the non-rational, (2) that language is and must always be inadequate to describe total reality, (3) that any abstract concept leaves out much of reality, and (4) that what we call "knowledge" (which is usually highly abstract and verbal and sharply defined) often serves to blind us to those portions of reality not covered by the abstraction (1962:194).*

Shamans can prove to clients, in one session, that change is possible and clients can, with this certainty in mind, remember the event when the shaman triggered their self-healing powers. For most people, it is difficult to understand that we have the capability to heal ourselves. The approach is simple. Healing occurs from the inside out. However, many of us are still looking for outside help, e.g., somebody else who comes and fixes the problem, somebody else who sets the healing mechanism in motion.

The usage of mental imagery to stimulate well-being can be taught already in primary schools. Children can learn, at a very young age, how to balance energies for themselves and others. Research will soon produce "repeatable data" to legitimize therapeutic touch (see Krieger, 1979, *et al*) which can also be used in mainstream health care, especially in preventive medicine, but also to ease pain and alleviate stress in terminal cases, and to assist in the process of aging (e.g., in hospices, convalescent and old age homes).

The topic of holistic education came up in the 1960s

*with the realization that the human being is wholly and innately connected to the unfolding of the universe.... schooling in modern societies...has neglected this organic and vital connection between ourselves and nature. Modern learning...has forgotten that true learning involves not just academic discipline but also wonder, and awe, spontaneity and joy. This is a minority view, however, and holistic educators have always been found on the romantic and mystical fringes of Western industrial civilization.... Materialism presumes that the human being is innately passive and aimless, without spontaneous curiosity or sociability....The child is seen as an undisciplined threat to the carefully constructed social order, and adult-directed education as a necessary means of protecting it....According to Montessori, education is not instruction but "a natural process which develops spontaneously in the human being" (Miller, 1989:65).*

When we begin to talk about the "reconstruction of experience," self-knowledge, self-cultivation and transformation play an important role in the educational process;

*strategies other than those associated with mastering objective data and content must be explored, experimented with, and developed at all stages of educational development....If education participates in and is reflective of life and living, then it needs to be grounded in the transpersonal ultimate reality.... Consequently all forms of human understanding and reflection are understood as relative and tentative.... An education rooted in an experienced context of meaning is one characterized less by informing and answering and more by acknowledging (bringing to conscious attention) and apprehending (integrating meaning, significance, and implication). ...Learning, then, is not simply a search for explanation and future fulfillment; it is also a process of self-transformation and responsible living grounded in the transpersonal reality. Acknowledging that we are our own greatest mystery, appropriate education cultivates, stimulates, and critically assesses the "truth" and meaning of experiences and understandings that encompass us a whole person. "Know thyself, and thou wilt know the universe and the gods." In like manner, know the universe and the gods, and thou wilt know thyself (Massanari, 1989:27-30).*

Centuries ago, Sufi, among others, distinguished already

between the observable reality and the world that is unseen. If we stay attracted to the world of multiple images, we miss life's essential purpose. "Know that the outward form passes away, but the world of meaning remains forever" (Rumi). We can asked shamans to teach us alternative life styles or, at least, facilitate cathartic release in appropriate rituals.

Paradigms have been called constellations of concepts, perceptions, values, and practices. It is important that especially values and practices are shared by a "community." Each community needs to base its social organization on such paradigmatic visions of reality. When we invite shamans to assist in the formulation of new paradigms in science and technology, we are entering new territory.

Physicists and mystics have met in the past. In the way they view the world, they are moving closer together again in our century. The theoretical physicist Stephen W. Hawking showed at his lecture series on the University of California, Berkeley Campus, in 1988 that "according to Einstein's theory of general relativity, within each black hole there must also be a singularity, a place where space, time and matter are crushed to a single point—virtual 'rips in space-time'." Black holes have been explained as areas in space which are "so dense with matter that gravity traps even light, preventing it from escaping to any outside observer, they are believed to form when stars collapse" (Lipkin, 1988:54). Hawking recently also suggested that the universe we experience may have "budded off" from another, older universe through an infinitely complex system. He proposed that the fluctuations of the so-called zero-point energy of free space may occasionally produce a point at which the energy is so high that it collapses into the above-mentioned black hole. When it becomes self-sustaining, it blows out into a new universe. The connection remains but has a diameter far smaller than an atom or subatomic particle. Without discussing the usefulness of this theory, it illustrates, at least, how strange the world of physicists has become from a layman's perspective.

Although the existence of singularities has so far been proven only by mathematicians, the reader will find that historians of religion and philosophers have, for thousands of years, been talking about areas where space and time do not exist. (Shamans have always worked on a level beyond space and time.) Now we see this concept brought up again by theoretical physicists and mathematicians, e.g., Elizabeth Rauscher who discusses in her essay, "A Set of Generalized Heisenberg Relations and a New Form of Quantization." Attempts are being made to "geometrize" space-time concepts.

Bohm's holographic model proposes that every element is connected with everything else in the universe. This implies a multi-dimensionality. The Christian church as well as some Indian belief systems maintain that there is a fundamental difference between spirit and matter. The explicate level is that of the ordinary, material domain and most individuals operating on this level are not aware of the implicate order. When our thinking shifts to the implicate level, we do not find any separation. In theology, panentheism states most clearly that god is in everything and everything is god. While mystics have contemplated for centuries on the whole in everything, shamans went one step further and effected the dynamics of the life processes in the explicate order. We are living in the twilight zone of unfolding reality which is facilitated by shamans in a most creative way.

In biophysics, the living state is viewed to be analogous to a tunable laser, resonating to particular frequencies imposed by the environment. When we begin to study the universal process of coherent excitation ranging from ELF (Extremely Low Frequency), we can develop a guide to tune lifeforms which govern healing processes.

When we begin to realize how much we have become caught in superseded scientific patterns, we can again allow our creative capacity to be stimulated far beyond the limitations we have imposed on our own being.

*The holomovement represents a new order that has its beginning not in energy fields or elementary particles, but rather in an undivided totality of reality (Bohm, 1981:149).*

In the past, we have learned to accept the fact that the earth is not the center of the universe. We have learned to fly and our planes are carrying sometimes over four hundred passengers into heights which had been reserved for shamans in the past. Man has landed on the moon and plans to land on distant stars in the future. When we allow our body to travel to such heights, we have to allow our thoughts and our soul to travel even further. On the other hand, we also have to learn that all solutions can be found in the Here and Now.

Stevens assures us of

> *the continual abundance of everything in nature. Shamans believe that the invisible web of power is infinite in its potential. From the world of spirit all physical forms are supported and infused with life energy. From this infinite source of power there is no limitation....only two things cause scarcity and imbalance. The first is the limitations within a person's own imagination. If you believe there is limitation there is. The second cause of scarcity is a person's own greed and selfishness generated by feat (lack of power). When people act from these imbalanced perspectives, they perpetrate acts of violence toward their environment and support systems. This upsets the natural balance maintained by the dynamic tension between the ordinary world (tonal) and the spirit world (nagual)....People especially suffer because they have cut off the flow of power that comes from the spirit world into the ordinary world (1988:124-125).*

In a paper, presented at the Fifth International Conference on the Study of Shamanism and Alternate Modes of Healing, Klimo spoke about his new book, *The Imagining of God: A Study of How We Create Our Own Reality* (1990). What he says confirms the thoughts developed in this book. He postulates that All is One and that One is not physical. He continues to say that the universe is a multiple personality. While we are subpersonalities of and within It, we may wonder who is the lover and who is the beloved. We have to explore the state dependent relationship between a subpersonality and the nature of reality it is capable of experiencing. Each of us can self-modulate our own subpersonality system, however, dissociation of subpersonalities from their causal origins become problematic. He suggested the study of vibratory fields.

According to Bell, components are quantum-mechanically linked to a system of common origin and seem to function correlatedly in "non-local" ways. Physicists, having apparently joined the ranks of shamans, are now offering us possibilities and are making practical suggestions to transcend known processes of causality and connectedness.

Fritjof Capra, the author of the *Tao of Physics,* talked in an interview of *New Directions* (March 1989), about an "ecological" paradigm. He prefers to call it

> *ecological rather than holistic. The terms are similar in that they emphasize the whole rather than the parts. However, ecological implies an embeddedness in larger systems—an awareness of individuals and societies being embedded in nature and ultimately being embedded in the cosmos....The central difference is that the world is no longer seen as a collection of separate objects composed of basic building blocks but rather as a network of relationships that is fundamentally interconnected (1989:1).*

Capra refers to the ecological movements of the 1960s and 1970s, the peace movements, and various spiritual movements which seem to have flown together in the 1980s.

> *The proverbial man and woman on the street often know more about new-paradigm thinking than academics or political leaders. It is something that intuitively makes sense—to do things on a more human scale, to be in communion with nature rather than trying to dominate it. There is great latent knowledge present....I think the key issue is the role of experience (1989:3).*

Religious experiences have become comparable to scientific experiences. So experiences will

> *allow people to communicate across cultures and*

*among religions....there is no objective world out there being represented in the process of knowing.... we create the world together, through language and through consciousness—a term which means "knowing together"...it's a collective effort. If we change our outlook on the world—and a paradigm shift is such a collective change of our outlook on the world—then we create a different reality (Capra, 1989:3).*

We have come full circle. Shamans emerged in prehistoric times to fulfill the needs of their contemporaries and they are offering the same services today.

*Shamanism seems to be a concentration of concepts and psychic techniques which, in the course of time, have been worked out by a particular group of hunting people and have spread over every continent.*

*At a time when man inevitably felt inferior to his environment he sought to assert himself and influence his environment by increasing his psychic force. In the course of his development this attempt and this activity was transferred to particular people.*

*...The question of whether artistic creation under primitive conditions always arises out of such a psychic process must remain unanswered here. In any case, however, it is by giving shape and form to the traditional ideas and images that the shaman overcomes his original condition of psychic weakness... and attains his function (Lommel, 1988:19-21).*

In this book, the reader has been presented with evidence how shamans of the twentieth century continue to respond to the needs of their contemporaries.

No claim is made that all aspects of shamanism have been covered. This book has been written in an attempt to raise interest in the work of contemporary shamans. The main purpose was to support theories with actual field data. The book has also been written to heighten our awareness of what still remains to be done.

# References

Aberle, David F. "'Arctic Hysteria' and Latah in Mongolia," *Transactions of the New York Academy of Science,* Series 2, 14:7 (1952):291-297.

Achterberg, Jeanne. *Imagery in Healing: Shamanism and Modern Medicine.* Boston, MA: Shambhala, 1985.

Ackerknecht, E.H. *Medicine and Ethnology, Selected Essays.* Baltimore, MD: The John Hopkins Press, 1971.

Allison, Ralph B. *Minds in Many Pieces.* New York: Rawson, Wade, 1980.

*American Psychiatric Association. Diagnostic and Statistical Manual. DSM-III-R.* Washington, D.C.: American Psychiatric Association, 3d ed., 1980.

Amoss, Pamela. *Coast Salish Spirit Dancing: The Survival of an Ancestral Religion.* Seattle: University of Washington Press, 1978.

Anderson, Michelle. "Authentic Voodoo is Synthetic," *The Drama Review,* 26:2 (Summer 1984): 89-110.

Arbman, E. *Ecstasy or Religious Trance,* vol. 1-3. Stockholm, Sweden: Scandinavian University Books, 1963-1970.

Avedon, John F. *In Exile from the Land of Snows.* New York: Alfred A. Knopf, 1984.

Baeckman, L. and å. Hultkrantz. *Studies in Lapp Shamanism.* Stockholm: Almqvist-Wiksell, 1978.

Baer, Gerhard. "Social Aspects of the South American Shaman," paper delivered at the 44th Congress of Americanists, Manchester, 1982.

Balazs, Janos. "A magyar saman revulete" [The Ecstasy of the Hungarian Shaman], *Ethnographica,* LXV:3-4 (1954):416-440.

Bancroft-Hunt, Norman. *The Indians of the Great Plains.* London: Orbis, 1981.

Barnett, L. *The Universe and Dr. Einstein.* New York: Morrow, 1966.

Basilov, V.N. "Shamanism in Central Asia," *The Realm of Extra-Human Agents and Audiences,* ed. A. Bharati. The Hague/Paris: Mouton, 1976, pp. 149-157.

Bean, Lowell John. "California Indian Shamanism and Folk Curing," *American Folk Medicine: A Symposium,* ed. Wayland D. Hand. Berkeley/Los Angeles/London: University of California Press, 1976, pp. 109-123.

Bekker, Sarah M. "Talent for Trance: Dancing for the Spirits in Burma," paper presented at the workshop on "Folk Religions," Association for Asian Studies Conference, Washington, D.C., March 1980.

Belo, Jane. *Trance in Bali*. New York: Columbia University Press, 1960.

Benedict, Ruth F. "Anthropology and the Abnormal," *Journal of General Psychology*, 10 (1934).

_____.*The Concept of the Guardian Spirit in North America*. Menasha, WI: Memoirs of the American Anthropological Association, No. 29, 1923.

Berger, Peter L. *The Sacred Canopy, Elements of a Sociological Theory of Religion*. Garden City, NY: Doubleday & Company, Inc., 1969.

Berreman, Gerald D. "Brahmins and Shamans in Pahari Religion," *Religion in South Asia,* ed. Edward B. Harper. Seattle, WA: University of Washington Press, 1964, pp. 53-69.

Besmer, Fremont E. *Horses, Musicians and Gods: The Hausa Cult of Possession-Trance*. Nigeria: Ahmadu Bello University Press, 1983.

Blacker, Carmen. *The Catalpa Bow: A Study of Shamanistic Practices in Japan*. London: George Allen and Unwin, 1975.

Boas, Franz. "The Central Eskimo," *Annual Report of the Bureau of American Ethnology,* 6 (1988);593-599.

_____."Ethnology of the Kwakiutl," *Annual Report of the Bureau of American Ethnology,* 35 (1921):43-794.

Bode, Derk. "Myths of Ancient China," *Mythologies of the Ancient World,* ed. Samuel N. Kramer. Garden City, NY: Doubleday, 1961.

Bogoras, Waldemar G. "K psichologii samanstva u naradov Severovostocnoj Azii [Zur Psychologie des Schamanentums bei den Völkern Nordostasiens]," *Etnograficeskoe Obozrenie* [Ethnographische Rundschau], 1-2 (Moscow, 1910).

_____.*The Chukchee*. New York: American Museum of Natural History Memoirs XI, Jessup North Pacific Expedition VII. New York: G.E. Stechert & Co., 1909.

Bohm, David. *Wholeness and the Implicate Order*. London: Routledge & Kegan, 1981.

Bohr, Niels. "Discussion with Einstein on epistemological problems in atomic physics," *Albert Einstein: Philosopher-scientist,* ed. P.A. Schilpp. New York: Harper, 1959.

Boshier, A. and D. Costello. *Witchdoctor*. Johannesburg, South Africa: Museum of Man and Science, 1975.74.

Bourguignon, Erika, ed. *Religion, Altered States of Consciousness, and Social Change*. Columbus, OH: Ohio State University Press, 1973.

_____."World distribution and patterns of possession states," *Trance and Possession States,* ed. Raymond Prince. Montreal, Canada: R.M. Bucke Memorial Society, 1968, pp.3-34.

Bouteiller, Marcelle. *Chamanism et guerison magique*. Paris: Presses Universitaires de France, 1950.

Boyer, L. Bryce. "Shamans: to set the record straight," *American Anthropologist,* 71 (1969):307-309.

# References

_____."Further Remarks Concerning Shamans and Shamanism," *The Israel Annals of Psychiatry and Related Disciplines*, 2:3 (October 1964):235-257.

_____."Remarks on the Personality of Shamans, With Special Reference to the Apache of the Mescalero Indian Reservation," *The Psychoanalytical Study of Society*, 2, (1962):233-254.

_____.B. Klopfer, F.B. Brawer, and H. Kawai. "Comparisons of the shamans and pseudoshamans of the Apaches of the Mescalero Indian reservation: A Rorschach study," *Journal of Projective Techniques*, 28 (1964):173-180.

Brame, G.A. "Religious functionaries in African traditional religion," *Journal for Religion and Psychical Research.* 7 (1984:231-241).

Bray, David K. *Lessons for a Kahuna.* Pasadena, CA: David K. Bray, 1967.

_____.with Douglas Low. *The Kahuna Religion of Hawai'i.* Vista: Borderland Sciences Research Foundation, 1959.

Brodsky, Anne Trueblood *et al,* eds. *Stones, bones and skin. Ritual and shamanic art.* Toronto: Artscanada, 1977.

Cannon, Walter B. "Voodoo death," *American Anthropologist,* 44 (1942):169-181.

Capra, Fritjof. "Interview," *New Directions,* II:2 (March 1989):1, 3.

_____. "The New Vision of Reality," *The World & I,* (May 1986):599-606.

_____. *The Tao of Physics. An Exploration of the Parallels Between Modern Physics and Eastern Mysticism.* Boulder, CO: Shambhala, 1975.

Cardeña, Etzel. "The Phenomenology of Possession: An Ambiguous Flight," *Proceedings of the Fifth International Conference on the Study of Shamanism and Alternate Modes of Healing, 1988,* ed. Ruth-Inge Heinze. Berkeley: Independent Scholars of Asia, Inc., 1989.

Chang, K.C. *The Archaeology of Ancient China.* New Haven, CN: Yale University Press, 4th ed., 1986.

_____. *Art, Myth, and Ritual: The Path to Political Authority in Ancient China.* Cambridge, MA: Harvard University Press, 1983.

Cleghorn, Robert A. "Morphine-Like Peptides of Brain and Their Relation to Hormonal Neurotransmitters," *Psychiatric Journal of the University of Ottawa,* 2 (1977):133-137.

Closs, Alois. "Die Ekstase des Schamanen," *Ethnos* (1969):1-4.

_____. "Der Schamanismus bei den Indoeuropäern," *Studien zur Sprachwissenschaft und Kulturkunde, Innsbrucker Beiträge zur Kulturwissenschaft,* vol.14. Innsbruck, Austria: Rauchdruck, 1968.

_____."Das Religiöse im Schamanismus," *Kairos* (1960):20-38.

Coe, Ralph T. *Sacred Circles: Two Thousand Years of North American Indian Art.* London: Arts Council of Great Britain, 1976.

Colson, Elizabeth. "Spirit Possession among the Tonga of Zambia," *Spirit Mediumship and Society in Africa,* ed. John Beattie and John Middleton. New York: Africana, 1969.

Cosentino, Donald. "Who is the fellow in the many-colored cap? Transformations of Eshu in old and new world mythologies," *Journal of American Folklore,* 200 (1987):263-275.

Cousins, Norman. *Anatomy of an Illness as Perceived by the Patient: Reflections on Healing and Regeneration.* New York: Norton, 1979.

Crabtree, A. *Multiple Man: Exploration in Possession and Multiple Personalty*. New York: Praeger, 1985.

Czaplicka, M.A. *Aboriginal Siberia: A Study in Social Anthropology*. Oxford: Clarendon Press, 1914.

Davidson, J. and R. Davidson, eds. *The Psychobiology of Consciousness*. New York: Plenum, 1980.

De Groot, J.J.M. *The Religious System of China*. Leiden, Netherlands: Brill, 1892-1910.

Deikman, A.J. *The Observing Self: Mysticism and Psychotherapy*. Boston: Beacon Press, 1982.

Devereux, George. *Essai d' Ethnopsychiatrie Generale*. Paris: Gallimard, 1970.

_____."Shamans as neurotics," *American Anthropologist*, 63 (1961):1008-1090.

_____."Normal and Abnormal, The Key Problem of Psychiatric Anthropology," *Some Uses of Anthropology: Theoretical and Applied*, eds Joseph B. Casagrande and Thomas Gladwin. Washington, D.C.: The Anthropological Society of Washington, 1956, pp. 23-48.

Diószegi, Vilmos. *Tracing Shamans in Siberia*, transl. Anita Rajkay Bubo. Oosterhout, Netherlands: Anthropological Publications, 1968.

_____."Tuva Shamanism: Intraethnic Differences and Interethnic Analogies," *Acta Etnographica*, 11 (1962):143-190.

_____.and M. Hoppál, eds. *Shamanism in Siberia*. Budapest: Akademiai Kiado, 1978.

Dow, James. *The Shaman's Touch: Otomi Indian Symbolic Healing*. Salt Lake City, UT: University of Utah Press, 1986.

Drucker, Philip. *Cultures of the North Pacific Coast*. San Francisco, CA: Chandler Publishing Co., 1965.

Dürckheim, Karlfried Graf. "The Call for the Master," *Parabola*, XIV:1 (1989):4-13.

Durkheim, Emile. *The Elementary Forms of the Religious Life*, transl. Joseph Ward Swain. New York: The Free Press, 1965 (1915).

Dusenberg, Verne. *The Montana Cress: A Study in Religious Persistence*. Stockholm: Almqvist & Wiksell, 1962.

Eaton, E. *The Shaman and the Medicine Wheel*. Wheaton, IL: Theosophical Publication House, 1962.

Edsman, Carl-Martin, ed. *Studies in Shamanism*, based on papers read at the Symposium on Shamanism held at åbo from September 6-8, 1962. Stockholm: Almquist & Wiksell, Scripta Instituti Donneriani Aboensis I, 1967

Eliade, Mircea. *Shamanism, Archaic Techniques of Ecstasy*, transl. Willard R. Trask. Princeton, NJ: Princeton University Press, Bollingen Series LXXVI, 2d printing, 1974 (1951).

_____.*Rites and Symbols of Initiation, The Mysteries of Birth and Rebirth*. New York: Harper Torchbook, 1958a.

_____.*Patterns in Comparative Religion*. New York: Sheed & Ward, 1958b.

_____.*The Sacred and the Profane, The Nature of Religion: The Significance of Religious Myth, Symbolism, and Ritual Within Life and Culture*. New York: Harper and Row, 1957.

# References

Elliott, Alan J.A. *Chinese Spirit Medium Cults in Singapore.* London: London School of Economics and Political Science, 1955.

Festinger, Leon. *A Theory of Cognitive Dissonance.* Stanford, CA: Stanford University Press 1957.

Findeisen, Hans. *Schamanentum, dargestellt am Beispiel der Besessensheits-priester nordeurasiatischer Völker.* Zürich/Wien: Europaverlag, 1957.

Frank, J.D. *Persuasion and Healing.* New York: Schocken, rev.ed., 1974.

Frankl, Victor. *From Death Camp to Existentialism.* New York: Washington Square, 1963.

Freesoul, John Redtail and Riverwoman Freesoul. *Breath-Made Visible: The Pipe as Spirit, Object and Art.* Santa Fe, NM: Freesoul Art Studio, 1984.

Frigerio, Alejandro. "Levels of Possession and Awareness in Afro-Brazilian Religions," paper presented at the 5th Annual Conference of the Association for the Anthropological Study of Consciousness, Pacific Palisades, CA, March 1-5, 1989.

_____."The Politics of Spirit Possession in Afro-Brazilian Religions in Argentina," paper presented at the 87th Annual Meeting, American Anthropological Association, Phoenix, AZ, November 16-20, 1988.

Fuerer-Haimendorf, Christoph S., ed. *Contributions to the Anthropology of Nepal,* Proceedings of a Symposium, School of Oriental and African Studies, University of London, 1973. Warminster, England: Aris & Phillip, 1974.

Fürst, Peter T. "The roots and continuities of shamanism," *Stones, bones and skin,* eds. Anne Trueblood Brodsky *et al.* Toronto: Artscanada, 1977, pp. 1-28.

_____.*The Flesh of the Gods: The Ritual Use of Hallucinogens.* New York: Doubleday, 1972.

Gardner, H. and E. Gardner, eds. *Five Great Healers Speak Here.* Wheaton, IL: Quest, 1982.

Garter Snake. *The Seven Visions of Bull Lodge,* ed. George Horse Capture. Ann Arbor, MI: Bear Claw Press, 1980.

Geertz, Clifford. "Religion as a Cultural System," *Anthropological Approaches to the Study of Religion.* London: Tavistock Publications, 1966.

Gendlin, E. *Experiencing and the Creation of Meaning: A Philosophical and Psychological Approach to the Subjective.* New York: Glencoe Free Press, 1982.

Gilberg, R. "How to recognize a shaman among other religious specialists?" *Shamanism in Eurasia,* ed. Mihaly Hoppál. Göttingen, FRG: Edition Herodot, 1984, pp. 21-27.

Glasser, Penelope. "An Interview with Marilyn Johnson, Ojibwa Soul Traveller," *Shaman's Drum* (Mid-Winter, 1989):41-45.

Goodman, Felicitas D. *Ecstasy, Ritual, and Alternate Reality.* Bloomington, IN: Indiana University Press, 1988a.

_____.*How About Demons? Possession and Exorcism in the Modern World.* Bloomington, IN: Indiana University Press, 1988b.

_____."Visions," *The New Encyclopedia of Religion,* ed. Mircea Eliade, 15 (1987):282-288.

_____."Body Posture and the Religious Altered State of Consciousness: An Experimental Investigation, *Journal of Humanistic Psychology,* 26:3 (1986):81-118.

_____.*The Exorcism of Anneliese Michel.* New York: Doubleday & Co., Inc., 1981.

_____.*Speaking in Tongues.* Chicago, IL: The University of Chicago Press, 1972.

_____.Jeannette H. Henney and Esther J. Pressell. *Trance, Healing, and Hallucination: Three Field Studies in Religious Experience.* New York: John Wiley and Sons, 1974.

Grotowski, Jerzy. "Tue es le fils de quelqu'un [You are somebody's son], *The Drama Review,* 31:3 (Fall 1987):30-41.

_____.*Grotowski and His Laboratory,* ed. Zbigniew Osi'nski, transl. & abridged by Lillian Vallee and Robert Findlay. New York: Performance Journal Publications, 1986.

Hahn, L. "A Zulu voice: Fighting apartheid from within," *New Leader* (1982):8-9.

Halifax, Joan. *Shaman, the Wounded Healer.* New York: Crossroad, 1982.

_____. *Shamanic Voices: A Survey of Visionary Narratives.* New York: E.P. Dutton, 1979.

Handelman, D. "The Development of a Washo Shaman," *Ethnology,* 6 (1967):444-464.

Handy, E.S. "Craighill: Polynesian religion," *Bayard Dominick Expedition Publication,* 12. Honolulu: Bernice P. Bishop Museum, 1927, pp. 53, 237-245.

Hanna, Judith L. *Performer-Audience Connection.* Austin, TX: University of Texas Press, 1983.

Harner, Michael. *The Way of the Shaman, A Guide to Power and Healing.* New York: Harper and Row, 1980.

_____.*The Jivaro: People of the Sacred Waterfalls.* Garden City: Doubleday/ Natural History

_____.ed. *Hallucinogens and Shamanism.* New York: Oxford University Press, 1973.

Harwood, Alan. "Puerto Rican Spiritism," *Culture, Medicine, and Psychiatry,* 1 (1976/77):69-95 and 135-153.

Hatto, A.T. *Shamanism and Epic Poetry in Northern Asia.* London: University of London, 1970.

Heery, Myrtle. The Meaning of Inner Voice Experiences: Theory and Discussion of Thirty Cases. Dissertation presented to the California Institute of Integral Studies, San Francisco, May 1987.

Heinze, Ruth-Inge. *Trance and Healing in Southeast Asia Today.* Bangkok/Berkeley: White Lotus/Independent Scholars of Asia, Inc., 1988.

_____."The Multiplicity of Being, An Investigation of the Relationship of Multiple Personality and Possession," *Proceedings of the Fourth International Conference on the Study of Shamanism and Alternate Modes of Healing, 1987,* ed. Ruth-Inge Heinze. Berkeley, CA: Independent Scholars of Asia, Inc., 1988, pp.2-18.

_____.*Tham Khwan, How to Contain the Essence of Life, A Socio-Psychological Comparison of a Thai Custom.* Singapore: Singapore University Press, 1982.

# References

_____."Shamanism or Mediumship: Toward a Definition of Different States of Consciousness," *Phoenix, Journal of Transpersonal Anthropology*, VI:1-2, (1982):25-44.

_____.ed. *Proceedings of the Fifth International Conference on the Study of Shamanism and Alternate Modes of Healing, 1988.* Berkeley, CA: Independent Scholars of Asia, Inc., 1989.

_____.ed. *Proceedings of the Fourth International Conference on the Study of Shamanism and Alternate Modes of Healing, 1987.* Berkeley, CA: Independent Scholars of Asia, Inc., 1988.

_____.ed. *Proceedings of the Third International Conference on the Study of Shamanism and Alternate Modes of Healing, 1986.* Berkeley, CA: Independent Scholars of Asia, Inc., 1987.

_____.ed. *Proceedings of the Second International Conference on the Study of Shamanism, 1985.* Berkeley, CA: Independent Scholars of Asia, Inc., 1985.

_____.ed. *Proceedings of the International Conference on Shamanism,* 1984.Berkeley, CA: Independent Scholars of Asia, Inc., 1984.

Heisenberg, Werner. *Physics and Philosophy.* New York: Harper, 1958.

Heissig, Walter. *The Religion of Mongolia.* London: Routledge and Kegan Paul, 1980.

Herskovits, Melville J. *Man and His Works: The Science of Cultural Anthropology.* New York: Alfred A. Knopf, 1949.

Hilgard, E.R. *Divided Consciousness: Multiple Controls in Human Thought and Action.* New York: Wiley, 1978.

Hilgard, Josephine R. *Personality and Hypnosis: A Study of Imaginative Involvement.* Chicago, IL: University of Chicago Press, 2nd ed., 1979.

Hitchcock, John T. "A Nepali shaman's performance as theater," *Stones, bones and skin,* eds. Anne Trueblood Brodsky *et al.* Toronto: Artscanada, 1977, pp. 42-48.

_____.and Rex L. Jones, eds. *Spirit Possession in the Nepal Himalayas.* Warminster, England: Aris and Phillips Ltd., 1976.

Höfer, Andreas. "Is the bombo an ecstatic? Some ritual techniques of Tamang shamanism," *Contributions to the Anthropology of Nepal,* ed. C. von Fuerer-Haimendorf. Warminster, England: Aris and Phillips, pp. 168-182.

Hoppál, Mihaly. "Shamanism: An Archaic and/or Recent System of Beliefs," paper delivered at the XIth International Congress of Anthropological and Ethnological Sciences, Symposium on Shamanism, Vancouver, B.C., 1983.

_____.ed. *Shamanism in Eurasia.* Part I and II. Göttingen, FRG: Edition Herodot, 1984.

Howitt, A.W. *The native tribes of South-East Australia.* London: Macmillan and Co., Ltd., 1904.

Hultkrantz, Å "The Shaman and the Medicine-Man," paper delivered at the XIth International Congress of Anthropological and Ethnological Sciences, Symposium on Shamanism, Vancouver, B.C., 1983.

_____."North American Indian Religions in a Circumpolar Perspective," *North American Indian Studies,* ed. Pieter Hovens. Göttingen, FRC: Edition Herodot, 1981, pp. 11-28.

_____.*The Religions of the American Indian,* transl. Monica Setterwall. Berkeley/ Los Angeles, CA: University of California Press, 1979a.

_____."Ritual in Native North American Religions," *Native Religious Traditions,* ed. Earle H. Waugh and K. Dad Prithipaul. Waterloo, Ont.: Wilfried Laurier Press, 1979.

_____."Ecological and phenomenological aspects of shamanism," *Shamanism in Siberia,* eds. V. Diószegi and M. Hoppál. Budapest: Akademiai Kiado, 1978, pp. 27-58.

_____."A Definition of Shamanism," *Temenos,* 9 (1973):25-37.

_____.*Conceptions of the Soul Among North American Indians, A Study in Religious Ethnology.* Stockholm: Statens Etnografiska Museet, 1953.

Huxley, A. *The Doors of Perception* and *Heaven and Hell.* New York: Harper & Row, 1963.

Jahn, R.G. and B. Dunne. *On the Quantum Mechanics of Consciousness, with application to anomalous phenomena.* Princeton, NJ: Princeton University, Princeton Engineering Anomalies Research Laboratory, Research Report PEAR 83005.1, 1984.

James, William. *The Varieties of Religious Experience.* New York: Collier, 1901/ 1972.

Jilek, Wolfgang. *Indian Healing—Shamanic Ceremonialism in the Pacific Northwest Today.* Surrey, B.C., Canada: Hancock House, 1982.

_____."Altered States of Consciousness in North American Indian Ceremonials," *Ethos,* 10:4 (Winter 1982b):326-343.

_____."The Psychiatrist and his Shaman Colleague: Cross-Cultural Collaboration with Traditional Amerindian Therapists," *Journal of Operational Psychiatry,* IX:2 (1978):32-39.

Jochelson, Waldemar. "Religion and Myths of the Koryak," *Jessup North Pacific Expedition, 6. Memoirs of the American Museum of Natural History,* 10. Leiden: J. Brill; New York: G.E. Stechert, 1905.

Kahn, Martin C. Djuka, *The Bush Negroes of Dutch Guinea.* New York: Viking Press, 1931.

Kakar, Sudhir. *Shamans, Mystics and Doctors, A Psychological Inquiry into India and Its Healing Traditions.* Boston, MA: Beacon Press, 1982.

Kalweit, Holger. *Dreamtime and Inner Space, The World of the Shaman.* Boston/ London: Shambhala, 1988.

Kardiner, Abram. *The Psychological Frontiers of Society.* New York: Columbia University Press, 1963.

Katz, R. *Boiling Energy: Community Healing Among the Kalahari Kung.* Cambridge, MA: Harvard University Press, 1982.

_____."The Painful Ecstasy of Healing," *Psychology Today* (December 1976):81- 86.

Keightley, David N. "Shamanism in *Guo Yu?* A Tale of *Xi* and *Wu,*" paper presented at the Center for Chinese Studies Regional Seminar, University of California, Berkeley, April 7-8, 1989.

Kendall, Laurel. *The Life and Hard Times of a Korean Shaman: Of Tales and the Telling of Tales.* Honolulu, HI: University of Hawaii Press, 1988a.

# References

_____."The Shaman's Journey, Real and Ideal in a Living Folk Tradition," unpublished paper, 1988b.

_____.*Shamans, Housewives, and Other Restless Spirits, Women in Korean Ritual Life*. Honolulu, HI: University of Hawaii Press, 1985.

_____."Supernatural Traffic: East Asian Shamanism," *Culture, Medicine, and Psychiatry*, 5 (1981):171-191.

Kiev, Ari, ed. *Magic, Faith, and Healing*. New York: Macmillan, 1964.

Kihlstrom, John F. "The Cognitive Unconscious," *Science*, 237 (September 1987):1445-1452.

King, C.D. "The Meaning of Normal," *Yale Journal of Biology and Medicine*, XVII (1945):493-501.

Kleinman, Arthur. *Patients and Healers in the Context of Culture, An Exploration of the Borderland between Anthropology, Medicine, and Psychiatry*. Berkeley/Los Angeles/London: University of California Press, 1980.

_____."Some Issues for a Comparative Study of Medical Healing," *International Journal of Social Psychiatry*, 19:159 (1973):159.

_____.and L.H. Sung. "Why Do Indigenous Practitioners Successfully Heal?" *Social Sciences and Medicine*, 13B (1979):7-26.

_____.Peter Kunstadter, E. Russell Alexander, James L. Gale, eds. *Culture and Healing in Asian Societies, Anthropological, Psychiatric and Public Health Studies*. Cambridge, MA: Schenkman Publishing Co., 1978.

Klimo, Jon. *Channeling, Investigations On Receiving Information From Paranormal Sources*. Los Angeles, CA: Jeremy P. Tarcher, Inc., 1987.

Knight, J.W. "A physician's use of healing energies," *Dimensions in Wholistic Healing*, eds. H.A. Otto and J.W. Knight. Chicago, IL: Nelson-Hall, 1979.

Krieger, Doris. *The Therapeutic Touch: How to Use Your Hands to Help or Heal*. Englewood Cliffs, NJ: Prentice-Hall, 1979.

Krippner, Stanley. *Healing States, A Journey Into the World of Spiritual Healing and Shamanism*. New York: Simon & Schuster, Inc., 1987.

Kuhn, T.S. *The Structure of Scientific Revolution*. Chicago, IL: University of Chicago Press, 2nd ed., 1970.

La Barre, Weston. "Shamanic Origins of Religion and Medicine," *Journal of Psychedelic Drugs*, II:1-2 (1979):7-11.

_____.*The Ghost Dance, The Origins of Religion*. New York: Dell Publications, 1978, 3rd printing.

_____.*The Peyote Cult*. New York: Schocken Books, 1975. 4th ed.

Lamb, F.B. *Wizard of the Upper Amazon*. Boston, MA: Houghton Mifflin, 1975.

Lambek, Michael. *Human Spirits: A Cultural Account of Trance in Mayotte*. Cambridge, MA: Cambridge University Press, 1981.

Lame Deer, John (Fire) and Richard Erdoes. *Lame Deer: Seeker of Visions*. New York: Simon and Schuster, 1972.

Larsen, S. *The Shaman's Doorway*. New York: Harper & Row, 1976.

Laufer, B. "The Origin of the Word Shaman," *American Anthropologist*, 19 (1917):195ff.

Lebra, William P. "Shaman and Client in Okinawa," *Mental Health Research in Asia and the Pacific* (1969):216-222.

Lee, Jung Young. *Korean Shamanistic Rituals*. Leiden: Mouton Publications, 1981.

LeShan, L. *The Medium, the Mystic, and the Physicist*. New York: Ballantine, 1975.

Lessa, William A. and Evon Z. Vogt, eds. *Reader in Comparative Religion: An Anthropological Approach*, 3d ed. New York: Harper and Row, 1972.

Lévi-Strauss, Claude."The Sorcerer and His Magic," *Structural Anthropology*. New York: Basic Books, 1967.

_____."The Structural Study of Myth," *Journal of American Folklore*, 47 (1955):428-222; reprinted in, *Reader in Comparative Religion: An Anthropological Approach*, eds. William A. Lessa and Evon Z. Vogt, 2d edition. New York: Harper and Row, 1965, pp. 289-302.

Lévy-Bruhl, Lucien. *How Natives Think*. New York: Academic Press, 1966.

_____.*Primitives and the Supernatural*. New York: E.P. Dutton & Co., Inc., 1935.

Lewis, I.M. *Ecstatic Religion, An Anthropological Study of Spirit Possession and Shamanism*. Harmondworth, Middlesex: Penguin Books, Ltd., 1975 (1971).

Lex, Barbara W. "The Neurobiology of Ritual Trance," *The Spectrum of Ritual: A Biogenetic Structural Analysis*, ed. Eugene d'Aquili. New York: Columbia University Press, 1979, pp. 117-151.

Lindberg, T. "Homegrown plan offers hope," *Insight* (November 23, 1987):64.

Lipkin, Richard. "Black Holes Figured Back in Time," *Insight* (June 6, 1988):54-55.

Locke, Ralph G. and Edward F. Kelly. "A Preliminary Model for the Cross-Cultural Analysis of Altered States of Consciousness," *Ethos*, 13:1 (1985):3-56.

Lommel, Andreas. "Shamanism in Australia," paper presented at the XIITH International Congress for Anthropological and Ethnological Sciences, Zagreb, July 24-31, 1988.

_____.*Shamanism: The Beginnings of Art*, transl. Michael Bullock. New York/Toronto: McGraw Hill Book Co., 1967.

Ludwig, Arnold M. "Altered States of Consciousness," *Arch.Gen. Psychiatry*, 16 (1966):225-234; also in *Trance and Possession States*, ed. Raymond Prince. Montreal: R.M. Bucke Memorial Society, 1968.

Lumholtz, Carl. *A Nation of Shamans, The Huichols of the Sierra Madre*. Oakland, CA: The Shamanic Library, 1988.

Lynn, S.J. and J.W. Rhue. "The fantasy-prone personality: Hypnosis, imagination, and creativity," *Journal of Personality and Social Psychology*, 51 (1986):404-408.

MacKenzie, Donald A. *The Migration of Symbols and their Relation to Beliefs and Customs*. New York: Alfred A. Knopf, 1926.

Maddox, John Lee. *The Medicine Man: A Sociological Study of the Character and Evolution of Shamanism*. New York: The Macmillan Co., 1923.

Mahler, H. "The Staff of Aesculapius," *World Health* (November 1977):2-2.

Malinowski, Bronislaw. *Magic, Science and Religion*. New York: Doubleday Anchor Books, 1954.

Maslow, Abraham H. *The Farther Reaches of Human Nature*. New York: Penguin, 1980.

# References

_____.*Religions, Values, and Peak-Experiences.* New York: Viking Press, 1970.

_____.*Toward a Psychology of Being.* New York: D. Van Nostrand, 1962.

Massanari, Ronald L. "Re-visioning Education," *ReVision,* 11:2 (Fall 1988):27-30.

Metraux, Alfred. "Religion and Shamanism," *Handbook of South American Indians, V. The Comparative Ethnology of South American Indians.* Washington, D.C., 1959a, pp. 559-599.

_____.*Voodoo in Haiti.* London: Andre Deutsch, 1959b.

_____."Dramatic Elements in Ritual Possession," *Diogenes,* 11 (1955):18-36.

Michael, H.N. *Studies in Siberian Shamanism,* transl. from Russian sources. Toronto: The Arctic Institute of North America, 4, 1963.

Michaels, Eric. "Constraints on Knowledge in an Economy of Oral Information," *Current Anthropology,* 26:4 (August-October, 1985):505-510.

Mikhailowskii, V.M. "Shamanism in Siberia and European Russia," *Journal of the Royal Anthropological Institute of Great Britain and Ireland,* 24 (1894):62-100, 126-158.

Miller, Ron. "Educating the Whole Child," *New Age* (January/February 1989):65, 68.

Mischel, Walter and Frances Mischel. "Psychological Aspects of Spirit Possession," *American Anthropologist,* 60 (1958):249-260.

Murphy, Jane M. "Psychiatric Labeling in Cross-Cultural Perspective," *Science,* 191:4231 (March 12, 1976):1019-1028.

Mutwa, V.C. *Indaba my children.* London: Kahn and Averill, 1985 (1965).

Myerhoff, Barbara G. "Shamanic Equilibrium: Balance and Mediation in Known and Unknown Worlds," *American Folk Medicine: A Symposium,* ed. Wayland D. Hand. Berkeley: University of California Press, 1976, pp. 99-108.

Nadel, S.F. "A study of shamanism in the Nuba mountains," *Journal of the Royal Anthropological Institute of Great Britian and Ireland,* 76:1 (1946): 25-37.

Needleman, Jacob and George Baker, eds. *Understanding the New Religions.* New York: Seabury Press, 1978.

Neher, Andrew A. "A Physiological Explanation of Unusual Behavior in Ceremonies Involving Drums," *Human Biology,* 34 (1962):151-160.

Neihardt, John G. *Black Elk Speaks.* Lincoln, NB: University of Nebraska Press, 1961.

Nicholson, Shirley, ed. *Shamanism, An Expanded View of Reality.* Wheaton, IL: The Theosophical Publishing House, 1987.

Nioradze, George. *Der Schamanismus bei den sibirischen Völkern.* Stuttgart, Germany: 1925.

Noll, Richard. "What has really been learned about shamanism?" *Journal of Psychoactive Drugs,* 21:1 (1989).

_____."Mental imagery cultivation as a cultural phenomenon: The role of visions in shamanism," *Current Anthropology,* 26:5 (1985):443-452.

_____."Shamanism and schizophrenia: A state-specific approach to the schizophrenia metaphor of shamanic states," *American Ethnologist,* 10 (1983):443-459.

Norbeck, Edward. *Religion in Primitive Society.* New York: Harper & Brothers, 1961.

# Shamans of the Twentieth Century

Nowak, Margaret and Stephen Durrant. *The Tale of the Nisan Shamaness: A Manchu Folk Epic.* Seattle, WA: University of Washington Press, 1977.

Oesterreich, Traugott K. *Possession and Exorcism,* transl. D. Ibberson. New York: Causeway, 1974.

Ohlmarks, A. *Studien zum Problem des Schamanismus.* Lund, Sweden: Gleerup, 1939.

O'Keefe, D.L. *Stolen Lightning: The Social Theory of Magic.* New York: Vintage Books, 1982.

Ornstein, Robert. *The Psychology of Consciousness.* San Francisco, CA: W.H. Freeman, 1972.

Osumi, Ikuko and Malcolm Ritchie. *The Shamanic Healer, The Healing World of Ikuko Osumi and the Traditional Art of Seiki-Jutsu.* Rochester, VT: Healing Arts Press, 1988.

Oswalt, W.H. *Alaskan Eskimos.* San Francisco, CA: Chandler, 1967.

Otto, Rudolf. *The Idea of the Holy.* London: Oxford University Press, 1958.

Paper, Jordan. *Offering Smoke, The Sacred Pipe and Native American Religion.* Moscow, ID: The University of Idaho Press, 1988.

Park, Willard Z. *Shamanism in Western North America: A Study in Cultural Relationships.* Chicago, IL: Northwestern University Press, 1938; New York: Cooper Square, 1975.

_____."Paviotso Shamanism," *American Anthropologist,* 36 (1934):98-113.

Paulson, Ivar. "Zur Phänomenologie des Schamanismus," *Zeitschrift für Religions- und Geistesgeschichte,* XVI:2 (1964):121-139.

Peters, Larry G. "A Phenomenological Overview of Trance," *Transcultural Psychiatric Review,* 20 (1983):5-39.

_____.*Ecstasy and Healing in Nepal: An Ethnopsychiatric Study of Tamang Shamanism.* Malibu, CA: Undena Publications, 1981.

_____.and Douglas Price-Williams. "Towards an experiential analysis of shamanism," *American Ethnologist,* 7 (1980):397-418.

_____."A phenomenological overview of trance," *Transcultural Psychiatric Research Review,* 20:1 (1983):5-39.

Popov, A.A. "How Sereptie Djaruoskin of the Nganasans (Tavgi Samoyeds) Became a Shaman," *Popular Beliefs and Folklore Tradition in Siberia,* ed. V. Diószegi. Bloomington, IN: Indiana University; and The Hague: Mouton, 1968.

_____.*Materialy dlja bibliografii russkoj literatury po izuceniju samanstva Severo-Aziatskich narodov.* Leningrad: Academic Nauk, 1932 (650 studies).

Powers, Stephen. "Tribes of California," *Contributions to North American Ethnology,* 3 (1877).

Powers, William. *Yuwipi.* Lincoln, NB: University of Nebraska Press, 1982.

Pribam, Karl. "The Holographic Hypothesis of Brain Function: A Meeting of Minds," *The World & I* (March 1986a):591—598.

_____."The cognitive revolution and mind/brain issues," *American Psychologist,* 41:5 (1986b):507-520.

Prince, Raymond. "Shamans and Endorphins: Hypotheses for a Synthesis," *Ethos,* 10:4 (1982):409-423.

# References

_____.ed. *Trance and Possession States*. Montreal: Proceedings of the Second Annual Conference, R.M. Bucke Memorial Society, 4-6 March 1966, publ. 1968.

Rank, Gustav. "Shamanism as a research subject: some methodological viewpoints," *Studies in Shamanism*, ed. Carl-Martin Edsman. Stockholm: Almqvist and Wiksell, 1967, pp.15-22.

Rasmussen, Knud. "The Netsilik Eskimos: Social Life and Spiritual Culture," transl. W.E. Calvert, *Report of the Vth Thule Expedition, 1921-24*, vol. 8. Copenhagen: Gyldendal, 1931.

*Rituale Romanum* (The Rites of the Catholic Church as Revised by the Second Vatican Ecumenical Council). New York: Pueblo, 1976 (1st published 1614).

Rogers, S.L. *The Shaman: His Symbols and His Healing Power*. Springfield, IL: Charles Thomas, 1982.

Rouget, G. *Music and Trance: A Theory of the Relations between Music and Possession*. Chicago, IL: University of Chicago Press, 1985.

Sandner, Donald. *Navajo Symbols Healing*. New York/London: Harvest/HBJ Book, 1979.

Sapir, Edward. "Symbolism," *Encyclopedia of the Social Sciences* (1967):493.

Schieffelin, Edward L. "The Unseen Influence: Trance Mediums as Historical Innovators," *Journal de la Societé des Oceanistes*, 33 (September-December 1977):170-178.

Schmidt, Wilhelm. *The Origin and Growth of Religion: Facts and Theories*. New York: Lincoln MacVeagh, 1931.

Schröder, Dominik. "Zur Struktur des Schamanismus," *Anthropos*, 50 (1955):848-881.

Sharon, Douglas. *Wizard of the Four Winds: A Shaman's Story*. New York: The Free Press, 1978.

Shirokogoroff, Sergei M. "Versuch einer Erforschung der Grundlagen des Schamanismus bei den Tungusen," *Baessler-Archiv*, 18:2 (Berlin, 1935a):55ff.

_____.*Psychomental Complex of the Tungus*. London: Routledge, 1935b.

_____."General Theory of Shamanism among the Tungus," *Journal of the Royal Asiatic Society, North-China Branch*, LIV (Shanghai, 1923):246-249.

Shweder, Richard. "Aspects of Cognition in Zinacanteco Shamans: Experimental Results," *Reader in Comparative Religion*, eds W.A. Lessa and E.Z. Vogt. New York: Harper and Row, 1979, pp. 327-331.

Siikala, A. *The Rite Technique of the Siberian Shaman*. Helsinki: Soumalainen Tiedeskaremia Academia, Folklore Fellows Communication No. 220, 1978.

Silverman, Julian. "Shamans and acute schizophrenia," *American Anthropologist*, 69 (1967):21-31.

Sivin, Nathan. "Taoism and Science," paper presented for the Third International Conference on Taoist Studies, Unteraegeri, Switzerland, September 3-9, 1979.

Skeat, Walter William. *Malay magic: Being an Introduction to the Folklore and Popular Religion of the Malay Peninsula* (reprint of the 1900 edition). New York: Benjamin Blom, Inc., 1972.

Spiro, Melford E. "Religious Symbolism and Social Behavior," *Proceedings of the American Philosophical Society,* 113:5 (October 1969):341-349.

_____.*Burmese Supernaturalism, A Study in the Explanation and Reduction of Suffering.* Englewood Cliffs, NJ: Prentice-Hall, 1967.

_____."Religion: Problems of Definition and Explanation," *Anthropological Approaches to the Study of Religion,* ed. Michael Banton. London: Tavistock, 1966, pp. 85-126.

_____."Religious Systems as Cultural Constituted Defense Mechanism," *Context and Meaning in Cultural Anthropology,* ed. Melford E. Spiro. New York: The Free Press of Glencoe, Inc., 1965.

Stevens, Jose and Lena S. Stevens. *Secrets of Shamanism, Tapping the Spirit Power Within You.* New York: Avon Books, 1988.

Stewart, Kenneth M. "Spirit Possession in Native America," *Southwestern Journal of Anthropology,* 2 (1946):323-339.

Stiglmayr, E. "Schamanismus, eine spiritistische Religion ?" *Ethnos,* 27:1-2 (1962):40-48.

Tambiah, Stanley J. *Buddhism and the Spirit Cults in Northeast Thailand.* Cambridge, England: Cambridge University Press, 1970.

_____."The Magical Power of Words," *Journal of the Royal Asiatic Institute,* III:2 (1968).

Tart, Charles T. *Waking Up, Overcoming the Obstacles to Human Potential.* Boston, MA: New Science Library, Shambhala, 1986.

_____.ed. *Altered States of Consciousness.* New York: Dutton, 1972; Wiley, 1969.

Torrey, E.F. *Witchdoctors and Psychiatrists: The Common Roots of Psychotherapy and Its Future.* New York: Harper and Row, 1986.

_____."What Western Psychotherapists Can Learn From Witchdoctors," *American Journal of Orthopsychiatry,* 42:1 (1972):69-76.

Trowbridge, Bob. "Transformation Through Illness," *A.R.E.* (1989):4.

Turner, Victor. *From Ritual to Theater: The Human Seriousness of Play.* New York: Performance Journal Publications, 1982.

_____.*The Forest of Symbols. Aspects of Ndembu Ritual.* Ithaca, NY: Cornell University Press, 1974 (1967).

_____.*The Ritual Process, Structure and Anti-Structure.* Chicago, IL: Aldine Publishing Co., 1966.

Van Gennep, Arnold. The *Rites of Passage,* transl. M.B. Vizedom and G.L. Caffee. London: Routledge & Kegan Paul, 1960.

Vastokas, Joan M. "The Shamanic Tree of Life," *Stones, bones and skin,* eds Anne Trueblood Brodsky *et al.* Toronto: Artscanada, 1977, pp. 93-117.

Voget, Fred W. *The Shoshoni-Crow Sun Dance.* Norma, OK: University of Oklahoma Press, 1984.

Walker, James. *Lakota Belief and Ritual,* eds Raymond J.DeMallie and Elaine A. Jahner. Lincoln, NB: University of Nebraska Press, 1980.

Walker, Sheila S. *Ceremonial Spirit Possession in Africa and Afro-America.* Leiden, Netherlands: E.J. Brill, 1972.

Wallace, Anthony F. *Religion, An Anthropological View.* New York: Random House, 1966.

# References

Wallace Black Elk and William S. Lyon. *Black Elk, The Sacred Ways of a Lakota*. San Francisco, CA: Harper & Row, 1990.

Walsh, Roger. "Mapping States of Consciousness: Comparing Shamanic, Schizophrenic, Insight Meditation, and Yogic States," *Proceedings of the Fifth International Conference on the Study of Shamanism and Alternate Modes of Healing, 1988*. ed. Ruth-Inge Heinze. Berkeley, CA: Independent Scholars of Asia, Inc., 1989.

Walter, V.J. and W Grey Walter. "The Central Effects of Rhythmic Sensory Stimulation," *EEG and Clinical Neurophysiology*, 1 (1949):57-86.

Wasson, R.G. *Divine Mushroom of Immortality. Ethno-Mycological Studies*, No. 1. New York: Harcourt, Brace, Jovanovich, 1968.

Waters, Frank. *Book of the Hopi*. New York: Viking Press, 1963.

Wautischer, Helmut. "A Philosophical Inquiry to Include Trance in Epistemology," *Journal of Psychoactive Drugs*, 21:1 (January-March 1989):35-46.

Weber, Renée. "The Physicist and the Mystic—Is a Dialogue Between Them Possible? A Conversation with David Bohm," ed. Emily Sellon. *The World & I* (May 1986):569-590.

Webster, Hutton. *Primitive Secret Societies: A Study in Early Politics and Religion*, 2nd ed. New York: The Macmillan Co., 1932.

Wilber, K., ed. *The Holographic Paradigm and Other Paradoxes*. Boston/London: New Science Library, 1982.

_____. *The Atman Project*. Wheaton, IL: Quest, 1980.

Wildschut, William. *Crow Indian Medicine Bundles*. New York: Museum of the American Indian, 1975.

Wilson, S.C. and T.X. Barber. "The fantasy-prone personality: Implications for understanding imagery, hypnosis, and parapsychological phenomena," *Imagery: Current Theory, Research, and Application*, ed. A.A. Sheik. New York: John Wiley and Sons, 1983, pp.340-387.

Winkelman, Michael. "Trance States: A Theoretical Model and Cross-Cultural Analysis," *Ethos* (Summer 1986):174-203.

_____."A Cross-Cultural Study of Magico-Religious Practitioners," *Proceedings of the International Conference on Shamanism*, ed. Ruth-Inge Heinze. Berkeley, CA: Independent Scholars of Asia, Inc., 1984, pp. 27-38.

Worrall, A.A. and O.N. Worrall. *The Gift of Healing*. New York: Harper & Row, 1965.

Yardley, Laura Kealoha. *The Congruence of the Huna Code to Current Practices of the Hawaiian Kahunas*. Cape Girardea: Huna Research, 1982.

Youngsook, Kim Harvey. *Six Korean Women, The Socialization of Shamans*. New York: West Publishing Company, 1979.

Zaretsky, Irving. *Bibliography on Spirit Possession and Spirit Mediumship*. Evanston, IL: Northwestern University Press, 1966.

Zühlsdorff, Volkmar. "The Witch Doctors of Chiangmai," *Zeitschrift für Kultur und Geschichte Ost- und Südostasiens*, 112 (1972):79-87.

# Index

Index